THE AUTHOR

ALISON ALEXANDER was born and educated in Hobart. She is a well-known Tasmanian historian, having written many histories of Tasmanian institutions as well as several biographies. Her book *The Ambitions of Jane Franklin* won the National Biography Award in 2014.

BOOKS BY ALISON ALEXANDER

Fiction

Cold Water Killer. A Tasmanian winter solstice mystery [with Jude Alexander] (2025)

Death at a Festival. An Australian Hippie Murder Mystery [with Jude Alexander] (2024)

Biographies and general

Corruption and Skullduggery: Edward Lord, Maria Riseley and Hobart's tempestuous beginnings (2015; second edition 2024)

Tasmania v. British Empire: the battle to end convict transportation (2022)

A salute to Max Angus, Tasmanian painter (2021)

The waking dream of art: Patricia Giles, painter (2019)

'Duck and green peas!' Finding utopia in Tasmania (2018)

The ambitions of Jane Franklin: Victorian lady adventurer (2014)

Tasmania's convicts: how felons built a free society (2010)

The companion to Tasmanian history (editor) (2005)

A mortal flame: the life of Marie Bjelke-Petersen (1995)

Governors' ladies: the wives and mistresses of Van Diemen's Land's governors (1987)

Commissioned histories

The O'Connors of Connorville: a great Australian story (2017)

Beneath the Mountain: a history of South Hobart (2015)

The Southern Midlands: a history (2012)

Jane Franklin Hall (2010)

From tiny acorns mighty oaks grow: the history of Oak Tasmania (2010)

Yours very truly: Dobson Mitchell & Allport 1834–2009 (2009)

Mary Ogilvy: the evolution of a grand lady, 1946–2006 (2006)

Brighton and surrounds (2006)

Hobart City Council (with Stefan Petrow, 2006)

The Eastern Shore: a history of Clarence (2003)

A wealth of women: the extraordinary experiences of ordinary Australian women from 1788 to today (2001)

Putting people first: Island State Credit Union, 1970–2000 (2000)

Students first! Tasmania University Union 1899–1999 (2000)

Charles Davis: 150 years (1998)

Glenorchy 1964–1998 (1998)

The history of the Clarence District Football Club, 1884–1996 (1996)

Blue, black and white: the history of the Launceston Church Grammar School, 1946–1996 (1996)

The history of the Australian Maritime College (1994)

Journal

Tasmanian Historical Research Association *Papers and Proceedings* (editor since 2014)

LAND OF ROGUES AND SCOUNDRELS

Starting from Scratch in
Van Diemen's Land

Alison Alexander

EER
Edward Everett Root Publishers 2025

EER

Edward Everett Root Publishers Co. Ltd.
Third Floor, 15 West Street,
Brighton, Sussex, BN1 2RL, UK.
www.eerpublishing.com
LAND OF ROGUES AND SCOUNDRELS
Starting from Scratch in Van Diemen's Land

© Alison Alexander 2025
This edition
© Edward Everett Root Publishers
Co. Ltd., 2025
Design: preparetopublish.com

Hardback ISBN 978191511593
Paperback ISBN 978191511409
All rights reserved. This book is copyright.

The moral rights of the author have been asserted.

The events in this book took place on land that the British invaders took from the Aboriginal people. We acknowledge and pay respect to the Tasmanian Aboriginal people as the traditional and original owners of this land and pay respects to their continuing culture here.

The people who made Tasmania: an ordinary family on their small farm at Richmond. Detail from *Richmond, Van Diemen's Land* by T.E. Chapman, 1843
(TA ALMFA AUTAS001124066796w800)

CONTENTS

MAP viii

INTRODUCTION 1

PART 1. 1804 TO 1819

1   THE NEWCOMERS 6

2   MAKING AN HONEST LIVING 12

3   MAKING A DISHONEST LIVING: CONVICTS 26

4   MAKING A DISHONEST LIVING: OFFICIALS 41

FLIGHT OF FANCY: GOVERNOR DAVEY LEAVES ENGLAND 51

5   THE NADIR: GOVERNOR DAVEY 53

FLIGHT OF FANCY: GETTING A LAND GRANT 63

6   SLIGHT IMPROVEMENT: GOVERNOR SORELL 64

7   ABORIGINAL TASMANIANS 73

FLIGHT OF FANCY: BIGGE MEETS SORELL 79

8   THE BIGGE REPORT: VAN DIEMEN'S LAND IN 1820 81

PART 2. DAILY LIFE

9   FOOD, CLOTHING AND HOMES 100

10   JALOP AND TRAGACANTH: HEALING ILLNESS 112

11   EDUCATION AND CULTURE 129

12   SPORT AND RECREATION 144

13   COMMUNITY LIFE 157

14   A SMALL MINORITY: WOMEN 166

PART 3. TOWARDS A MODEL COLONY, 1820 TO 1831

15   FREE SETTLERS ARRIVE 184

FLIGHT OF FANCY: ADVICE ON A VOYAGE 207

16   THE LAND COMMISSIONERS: FARMING IN 1826–1827 209

FLIGHT OF FANCY: ISABELLA LEWIS TRIES TO HIDE THE PAST 219

17   CHURCHES BRING NEW OPPORTUNITIES 221

18   GOVERNOR ARTHUR 228

FLIGHT OF FANCY: AN EVENING AT GOVERNMENT HOUSE 244

19   THE BLACK WAR WITH THE ABORIGINAL PEOPLE 246

CONCLUSION 255

ACKNOWLEDGEMENTS 257

ENDNOTES 258

MAJOR CHARACTERS 278

BIBLIOGRAPHY 282

INDEX 285

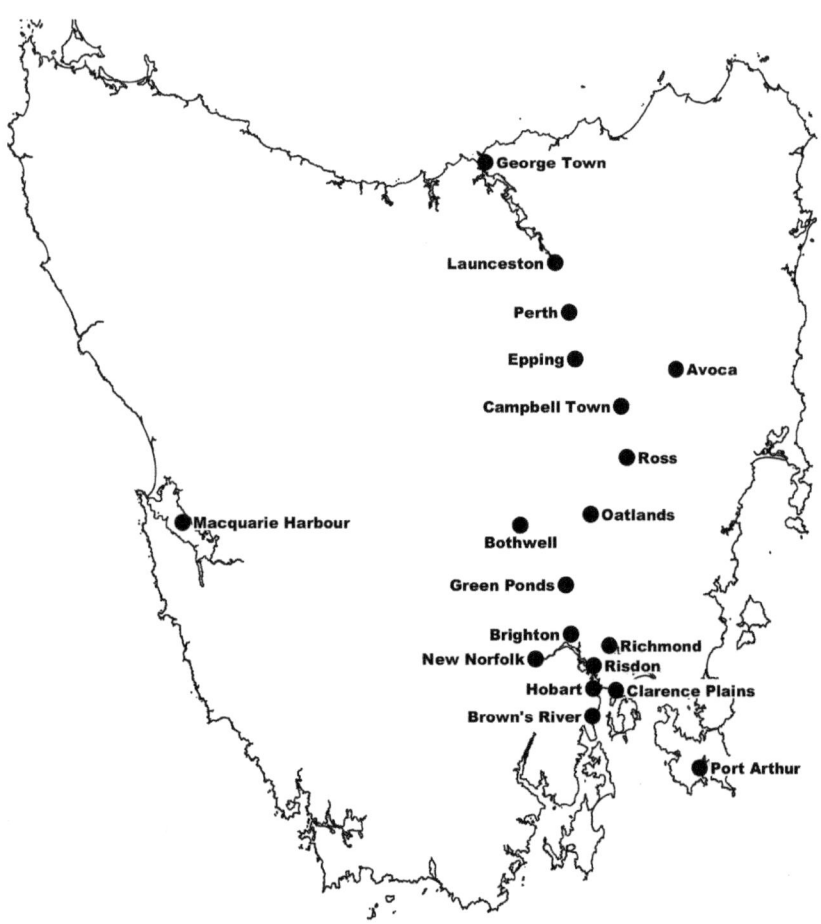

Van Diemen's Land, 1803–1831 (Eddy Steenbergen)

INTRODUCTION

It's 1820, and Agnes Williamson is about to receive a letter from her brother William. She's a spinster, perhaps in her twenties, living in genteel poverty in the town of Lancaster, England. I picture her, gloomily eying her meagre luncheon, as her aunt enters with the letter. 'From William', she says. They roll their eyes. 'My dearest Agnes', it begins. The women grimace.

> I do not know how to disclose the fatal secret – O Agnes I have by my infamous connections robbed you of all you possess Do not ask me how I have done it but if a life of penitence and devoting my talents and industry will atone for my villainous conduct it shall be done ... You would not hang me Agnes ...

'No?' surely crosses her mind. 'Your most affectionate & penitent brother' has himself only £15 in the world, but his training as a lawyer will let him earn enough to repay her.

That letter was written as 23-year-old William was about to leave England, escaping charges of embezzlement. His next comes from Hobart Town, far from English police, creditors, courts and cheated relations. William reports an excellent journey of only three months during which 'I was only sick about half an hour and suffered no inconvenience further than just throwing up'. Van Diemen's Land's climate and scenery are beautiful in the extreme, but

> The people here are all the biggest rogues and scoundrels in the world ... every body running down the other – every one in fear of the other – either of bodily harm or property ... in short the inhabitants are like a set of vultures preying upon each other with the greatest rapacity guilty of every crime and defacing one of the finest Countries in the whole world.

Here, he continues with sublime self-assurance, ignoring any irony, 'my crime is unknown'. He is determined to 'do my duty to all as a truly honest man. I certainly have since I came here (in order to obtain a larger grant of land) given in a fictitious Capital'. (His brackets – and his version of being honest!)

William apologises again and again for 'leaving an only sister and Aunt in a most wretched state of misery penury and wretchedness', and promises over and over to repay them. He himself is fine, for he can live 'with the respect which my profession will command'. He concludes, 'With the utmost contrition for my baseness I remain yours most sorrowfully, W Williamson'.[1]

Words are cheap, as Agnes and her aunt must have reminded each other. It is doubtful if they ever saw a penny. Despite telling Agnes that free people scorned to marry children of convicts, William did just that. He married Rebecca Walford – a shotgun wedding, perhaps in reality, with tough ex-convict publican Bernard Walford at the other end of the gun. The first child was born 24 days after the wedding. More children followed.

After an initial flurry of advertisements on behalf of clients, William's legal career languished. He moved his family north to Launceston to try afresh, but there he died aged only 37.[2] Such early deaths often indicated alcoholism.

William's story sums up early Van Diemen's Land. A land of rogues, wrote a free settler, himself as much a rogue as any convict. A land where you could not believe a word anyone says. A land where new arrivals could hide their dubious pasts – but had none of the support they might have had back in Britain, no networks of relatives and friends, no established businesses and farms to take over. Success was hard to come by, as William found out. It was a land where you had to do anything you could, any way you could, in order to make a living. How did such a feral place turn into the settled Tasmanian community of only a decade later?

This book is not about the Aboriginal inhabitants – there are excellent books on that topic – but is concerned with the earliest years of the white colony, ending in 1831, a watershed. Land grants stopped: usable country was already divided into farms, the basis of a stable yeomanry. The wool industry was just starting to bring good profits, the basis of a sound economy. A settled, prosperous community was in the making. The Aboriginal population had either died or been moved to Flinders Island, perhaps the only such complete ethnic cleansing in world history. The white invaders had a free hand to develop the colony. Because of the efforts of some early settlers – despite Williamson and his ilk – as well as newcomers, churches and Governor Arthur, the community had turned itself round and was admired as an amazingly almost-model British colony.

The biggest rogue and scoundrel of them all was arguably Lieutenant Edward Lord of His Majesty's Marines. I wrote about him and his convict wife Maria in *Corruption and Skulduggery: Edward Lord, Maria Riseley, and Hobart's tempestuous beginnings*. This present book is a companion volume, answering questions that book threw up. Was everyone a scoundrel? With all this roguery going on, how did a functioning community build up? What made the difference? (Edward Lord left, for a start.) As an interlude, I also grapple with the question a friend put to me: 'How did they live then? What was it like?'

Although the settlement was tiny, remote and unimportant, Van Diemen's Land's early white enclave has been depicted in many different ways. Firstly, as a place of barbarism, where the original inhabitants were forced off their land and all but exterminated. Then, also barbaric, as the land of convicts and gothic horror, a place of chains, lashes, fetters and general brutality, ferocious bushrangers and desperate cannibals – and a home of crime, ranging from widespread petty theft to large-scale embezzlement of British government funds. Yet at the same time it was a place of hope, where outcasts from Britain could forge new and happier lives. The land itself was, to the British, a weird upside-down place, with summer instead of winter and peculiar animals like the kangaroo and platypus. And, according to historian John West, it was a quirky place, home of amusing stories.

All these narratives are intertwined in the story of how a land of rogues and scoundrels turned into an almost-normal British community.

Nomenclature and measurements

I refer to the island as both its official name of Van Diemen's Land and as Tasmania, the local name coming into widespread use from the 1820s. This was the name of the future, not tainted by convict chains and whips. Similarly, the largest settlement was officially Hobart Town but Hobart was widely used.

Land was measured in acres. To give each metric equivalent throughout the book would be cumbersome, and trying for the reader. As a rule of thumb, two acres are roughly one hectare: 100 acres = about 40 hectares. A kilometre is slightly more than half a mile: 1 km = 0.6 miles, 5 miles = 8 km.

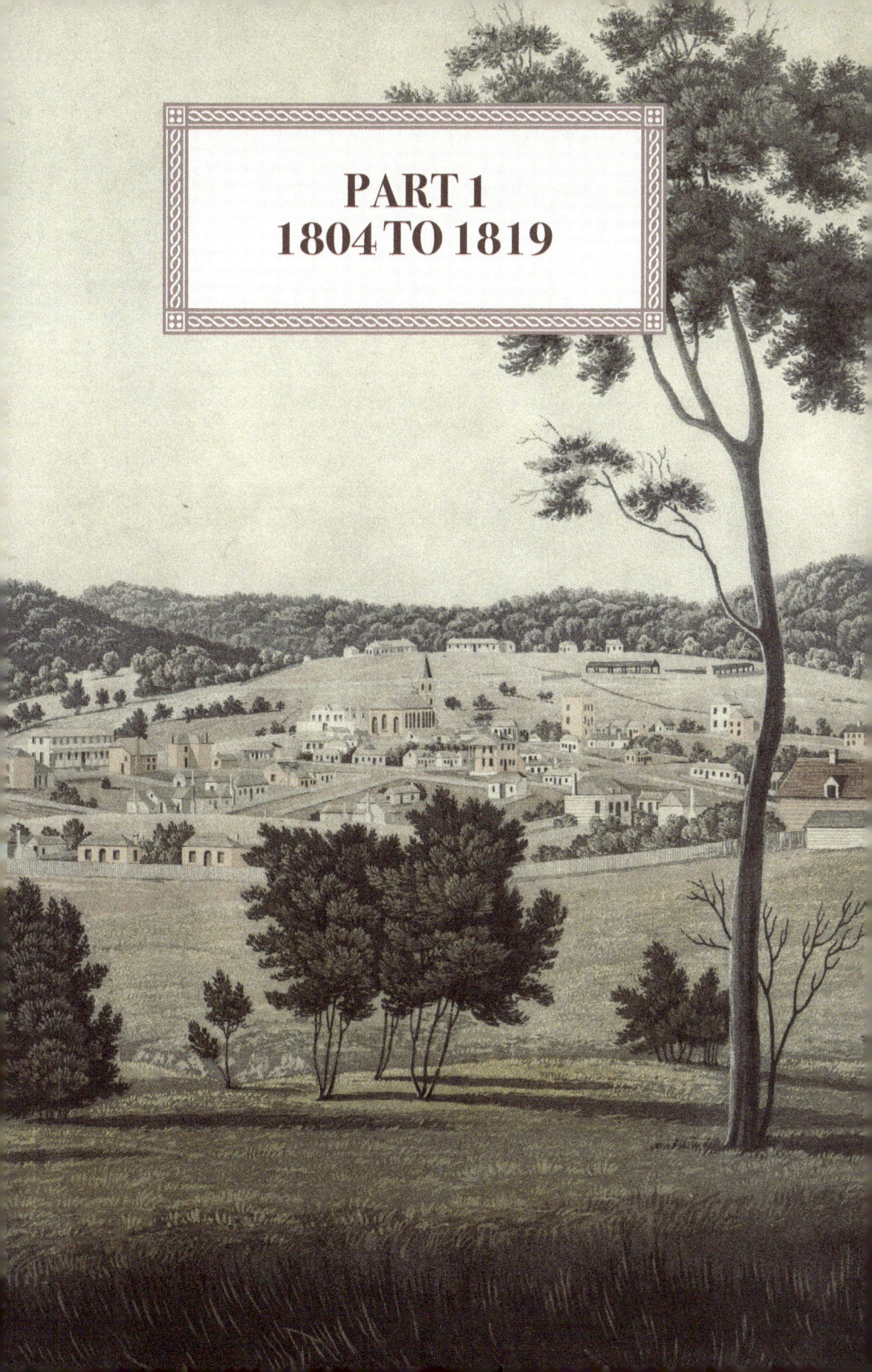

PART 1
1804 TO 1819

1. THE NEWCOMERS

Why did William Williamson flee from his crime to a tiny colony at the end of the world?

Until 1803 the island to the south of the Australian mainland was the home of Aboriginal people. They were hunter-gatherers, eating animals or seafood and the scanty vegetable products of the bush. Nomadic life has inherent problems – storing food and accumulating possessions, challenges for the old and sick. The population probably never exceeded five to ten thousand, but the Aboriginal people established a viable way of life, and inhabited their island for tens of thousands of years.

An unlikely sequence of events led the British to establish settlements in the island in 1803-04. A belief that crime was hereditary and therefore getting rid of criminals would eliminate crime, led the government to exile criminals to its American colonies from 1615. Settlers took these men off the government's hands: a cheap and easy solution to crime (though it continued in Britain unabated). But in 1776 the American colonies announced their independence and refused to receive convicts. Unable to think of any alternative except a new colony, the British formed one in New South Wales. Convicts, guards, officials and a handful of free settlers arrived at what became Sydney in 1788.

In 1799 the British realised that Van Diemen's Land was separate from New South Wales – and the French started nosing around. This was alarming. The French were the enemy. What if they claimed the island? Desperately, in 1803 Sydney sent a small, temporary group to the River Derwent in the island's south. The next year saw two permanent settlements, in the north at Port Dalrymple (Launceston, eventually) and in the south at Hobart Town on the Derwent.

British settlers aimed to recreate the British way of life, partly because they knew no other, and partly because they assumed it was best. Hadn't it resulted in the wonderful British Empire? No one actually announced this, however, which was just as well as they could hardly have started with less promising ingredients.

The two settlements, north and south, housed between them 570 people:

	Men	Women	Children
Convicts	333	18	
Convicts' wives & children		18	10
Officials, civil & military	18		
Officials' wives & children		4	8
Marines & Soldiers	96		
Military wives & children		10	4
Settlers	21	7	17
Servants	6		

Or, more simply
Men & boys	493 or 86%
Women & Girls	77 or 14%

A normal society has about half each, women and men. This was not a normal society.[1] Furthermore, there were few children, only 39, 7 per cent of the population.

It's difficult to obtain figures for the elderly (or define what 'elderly' meant – anyone over fifty?), but they were even fewer than children. Few convicts were over forty: the oldest was William Lewis, a 55-year-old yeoman from Wales who had stolen a sheep. Most were in their twenties. Officials, the military and free settlers were young or at most middle-aged.[2] Again, a skewed society.

The British Empire was ruled by a small elite of wealthy, well-educated, 'well-born' gentlemen and their families. In Van Diemen's Land the elite consisted of 30 individuals, 5 per cent of the population. This was one of the few ways the community resembled British society back Home.

There were other abnormal aspects. The 351 convicts were convicted criminals – 61 per cent of the population. I can't find a similar statistic for Britain at the time, but surely the number of criminals was nowhere near 61 per cent. And many of the rest of the population, such as later arrival William Williamson, had committed worse crimes than most convicts.

This situation remained until 1820. More convicts arrived, nearly all male; so did a few free settlers, but they were not encouraged by London. The largest 'free' influx was about 600 settlers from Norfolk Island, forced to move south between 1808 and 1813 when that settlement was

George Harris, surveyor, was a talented artist. Here is his painting Speckled Manikins (Pardelotes) at Hobart Town in 1806. There are signs of progress: a new fence, trees cut down, a house, buildings on Hunter Island, and the Union Jack flying over this tiny outpost of Empire.
(State Library NSW FL3259727)

abandoned. They were mostly ex-convicts, some married with children, and since many had come to New South Wales with the First Fleet they were generally middle-aged. They did bring more females into the community, with marriageable daughters especially appreciated. Other free arrivals were mostly those who came by chance, the flotsam floating round the fringes of the empire. By 1820 the European population was still only 5468, with four men to each woman.[3]

Few people actually wanted to go across the world to a new settlement in the wilds of Australia. Most were ordered there (convicts, the military) and most civil officials were driven by debt, poverty, scandal or the need for a career. Governor David Collins desperately wanted a job; Lieutenant Edward Lord was the poor relation of a baronet; surveyor George Harris needed money; Leonard Fosbrook the commissary joined at the last minute for a reason no one has been able to discover, which sounds suspicious.

With free settlers, the bar was even lower. Brothers Henry and Thomas Hayes, long-standing London thieves in and out of the Old Bailey for years, emigrated because Henry's wife had been transported to Sydney, taking their daughter. While the British government would doubtless have preferred honest, industrious settlers, they had to take what they could get and accepted these highly unlikely farmers. Jane Hobbs, widow of a naval officer, had nothing but a small pension to support five children. She too was unlikely to farm, but at least the family improved the gender ratio – though the government's aim in allowing her to come was probably more to help a fellow member of the elite.

Everyone's dream was to gain a fortune and return to Britain. As George Harris wrote, he aimed to make money and gain 'the unspeakable felicity of again beholding all my dear friends in England'.[4] There were opportunities. Matthew Power was transported for fourteen years for uttering a forged banknote. His wife Hannah, acquitted of the same crime, accompanied him. Before the ship even left England, she had caught Collins' eye, and became his mistress. There were no complaints from Matthew. The pair gained excellent pickings, until Hannah was supplanted by a younger model. In 1808 she and Matthew returned to England with their loot, early achievers of the contemporary dream.

What sort of society formed from this collection of criminals, men on the make and chance comers? To outward appearances it recreated British life, more or less: little towns, farms, pubs and shops, church services. But the overwhelming majority of colonists did not come from Jane Austen's England, respectable and well-behaved. They came instead from the working class, labourers and vagrants, struggling to make a living in any way possible including theft. This was the only life they knew – and the one they would recreate.

In England, strong influences urged people to embrace upright behaviour. Churches preached moral living, but the first clergyman in Van Diemen's Land, Robert Knopwood, was 'not much of a parson', though kindly and well-liked.[5] He conducted church services as required, but did nothing to improve morality or encourage Christianity, and was on excellent terms with men living in adultery, such as governors Collins and Sorell. He himself was rumoured to have mistresses, with Governor

Macquarie in Sydney deploring his 'very loose morals'.[6] There was no clergyman in the north until John Youl arrived in 1818. An upright man, he was driven to despair by the moral laxity in Launceston, but ill-health lessened his effectiveness.[7] So the Church of England had little influence, and there were no other ministers at all.

In British society, women were generally held to be upholders of moral behaviour, 'angels of the hearth', but as we have seen they were a tiny minority – and even those who appeared respectable could fall short of the ideal. Jane Hobbs' four daughters were gentry, 'young ladies', but on the voyage Rebecca became pregnant to John Ingle, a free settler – appallingly immoral – though she later married him. Ingle set up as a merchant and made a fortune by corruption. The family returned to live in luxury in England, the 'wages of sin' proving excellent.

Aged sixteen, Rebecca's younger sister Ann Jane married thirty-year-old surveyor George Harris. Though young, Ann Jane understood domestic management, George assured his mother, adding tactfully, 'my sweet little Girl ... often reminds me [of] my D[ear]r Mother when I see her so busily employed about Household affairs'. But George died in 1810, leaving Ann Jane, 22, a widow with a toddler and a baby on the way. She moved in with a prosperous settler – shockingly immoral! – then married him, reared another family and died aged 74 (the wages of sin proving good again).[8]

Also weak in influence were the police. In the absence of anyone else, constables were mostly ex-convicts or even serving convicts, open to bribery and intimidation. Their superiors were little better and the police as a whole were ineffective. In Britain, education could be an uplifting influence but Van Diemen's Land had few schools, often run by ex-convicts. In any case they influenced only children, mostly still young in 1831, so had little effect on the general population.

Peer pressure and a sense of community can be effective in encouraging people to live upright lives, but in a society where well over two-thirds of the inhabitants were convicted criminals, peer pressure was unlikely to have a beneficial effect – indeed, it might encourage people to break the law.

A strong leader can influence people to obey the law, but there were no strong leaders in Van Diemen's Land until 1824. Those there were actually led people into unrespectable behaviour such as drinking,

George Harris's painting of the first settlement in the north, at York Town: a cleared area with a collection of small houses, a small boat sailing, and two men watching from the opposite shore
(State Library NSW FL1151945)

embezzling and general incompetence. It was ironic that these settlers, supposedly exemplars of British civilisation to ignorant savages, behaved in a manner which was uncivilised in the extreme.

But amid all this crime and anti-social activity were forces encouraging some community activity. Most people arrived alone, as convicts or soldiers, but a minority had families and others married in the colony. Families could provide stability, a stake in the community, something to work for. Other people had enough in common to form networks. The long voyage from Britain with nothing to do but chat produced friendships (and enmities). People from the same areas in Britain, farmers sharing tips on how to deal with the new environment, drinkers in the same pub, convicts from the same ship – all could forge friendships. There was even cohesiveness in crime, a feeling of unity in networks supporting bushrangers, and the sheep-stealing fraternity, as we'll see. Growing up was a small cohort born in the colony and intensely proud of it. In the background of this odd assortment of people thrown together, the green shoots of community were visible.

2. MAKING AN HONEST LIVING

Dumped down in the bush of a new country, how were these British outcasts going to support themselves?

They brought food with them, supposedly enough to last until they could produce food themselves. They would do this by farming (both growing crops and grazing animals), an essential part of the British government's plan for its Australian colonies.

Agriculture brought major advantages. Firstly, providing food. The staple English diet was meat and bread. Meat was easy enough to hunt but bread needed wheat, which had to be grown. Secondly, farmers employed convicts, giving them something useful to do and, even more important for the government, paying for their food, clothing and accommodation. Thirdly, a network of farms would recreate the Mother Country, setting up a sturdy yeomanry, the backbone of Britain. A yeomanry supported towns and villages with their churches, shops and households: a community, a new Britain in the antipodes. A big ask of this ragbag collection of forced migrants.

To encourage farming, the government gave free land to anyone who applied for it and looked as if he, or even she, could wield a hoe. At first there were few free settlers and only a handful of officials. Lesser military, privates and NCOs, were not allowed to farm since it would interfere with their duties (this did not, of course, apply to the officials). As a result, there were not many prospective farmers, and the government had to turn to ex-convicts. Almost anyone would do. If he or on a few occasions she failed, it was no skin off the government's nose, for it could give the land to someone else to have a go.

Experience was largely ignored – good to have, perhaps, but not necessary. For tens of thousands of years, most men had been farmers. The Industrial Revolution with its radical change had only just started, and rulers assumed that the default career for men remained farming. (For women it was domestic duties.) So men were given land on condition that they live on it, cultivate it and not sell it for five years[1] – though governors had no way of enforcing this rule, and in this period did not even try.

Detail from Joseph Lycett's 1825 painting, *View from the Top of Mount Nelson*, showing small farms dotted along the river south of Hobart (State Library of Victoria 9939650932707636)

Even some serving convicts and convicts' wives were given grants. Sixteen intrepid – or desperate, or ambitious – wives of convicts accompanied felon husbands to the southern colony. Some were too busy having affairs with officials to bother about farming, but the more virtuous ones were given land grants and had their husbands assigned to them as labourers. Ann Peters and their baby accompanied her husband Thomas, an illiterate labourer transported for theft. Collins granted Ann 40 acres beside the creek in what is now Lenah Valley. There she and Thomas built a house, and the 1808 muster showed them growing wheat and barley and grazing fifteen cows and a pig. (The baby grew up to become mistress of the huge Como estate in Victoria – a meteoric rise.) Though serving convicts were not meant to receive grants, two did. Matthew Power, husband of the governor's mistress, received an excellent grant in central Hobart. John Fawkner, merely an industrious convict, received his at distant Claremont.

Who gained free land grants? In 1804 there were 473 adult males in the two little colonies. An astonishing 197, or 42 per cent – almost half – received land grants:

	Number	Gained grants	Percentage with grants
Officials	23	21	91%
Settlers	17	14	82%
Convicts	331	125	38%
Military	100	35	35%
Unknown	2	2	

Eight women also received grants: seven were spouses of convicts (28 percent of these spouses) and three were womenfolk of officials.

So nearly all officials and most settlers obtained grants; and over a third of the convicts and military (marines in the south and soldiers in the north, many of whom returned to Sydney or Britain). Officials and settlers obtained their land almost immediately; most military and convicts had to wait till they finished their terms of service or gained their freedom. (These figures are rubbery, given the scrappy records, and should be taken as approximate rather than exact.)

The Australian convict colonies were unique: no other country exiled their criminals in this way, and certainly no other country gave criminals free land. Australia's convicts were not the worst British criminals (they were executed there) but the next rung down: predominantly thieves, sometimes violent. Most came from the poor working class and few had any agricultural experience. But when their sentences ended, they could apply for land grants.

Collins gave 97 of his 281 ex-convicts free land.[2] Which ones? There were no rules, no minimum qualifications: governors could grant as they liked. In fact, Collins had little option. A good half of his ex-convicts were not able to receive a grant, for one reason or another. As far as can be ascertained from scanty and sometimes conflicting records, this is the picture:

Collins' convicts

Not able to be given grants		
Died under sentence	39	
Left the colony	88	
Committed more crimes	19	
Total	146	52%
Farmed or held grants		
Received grants	97	
Bought or rented land	5	
Held grazing licences	3	
Claimed they had grants	3	
Total	108	38%
Unknown	2	
No grant	25	9%

The eleven men who seemed to farm but had no official grant perhaps did not apply, or preferred to rent better land, or just farmed, claiming a grant which never appeared officially. Of the other 25, some had other jobs and perhaps did not relish the hard work of farming: Edward Guest ran a blacksmithing business, Thomas Williams was a stockkeeper. Others were in poor health. None looks like an aspiring farmer who missed out. It seems that Collins gave land to virtually anyone who applied for it.

No relevant documents survive about how grants were given before 1824 – if they existed in the first place. The one description shows a very casual process. Probably a deserter from a ship, Thomas Keston (or Kenton) arrived in Hobart in 1808 as a labourer, employed by Norfolk Island settler John Foley. Keston later jotted down some memoirs. Foley tried to farm a grant in South Hobart, he wrote, but it was poor soil and nothing would grow. Foley sold it and returned to his trade of bricklaying. 'The poor honest old man' could make a comfortable living in this way. (Foley was 59.)

So Keston lost his job, and friends advised him to ask Collins for a farm. There was no special time people could speak to the governor. 'If you wanted any business with him you must catch him in the St[reet] after the Guard had mounted,' Keston wrote. 'You must take great notice how he took his Snuff for if you see him put it up his nostrils by handfulls, it was the best way to leave him for that day.' Waiting in the street to waylay Collins, Keston hesitated, but his friends urged him on, saying, 'Go now, he will soon be off, go now you fool you, he will soon be housed & you will not see him to-day any more'. Collins was shovelling snuff up his nostrils in handfuls but, unaware of the significance, Keston caught him up.

> As he was going up the steps of his House I said, I would be glad to speak to his Honor, he turned round & look'd on me with all the disdain imaginable & said what do you want Sir, I told him I would thank him to allow me a Farm.

Collins asked who he was: Foley's servant. Assuming he was a convict, Collins asked when his sentence expired. Keston said he was never a prisoner. Collins replied, 'O I must inquire into that & slap'd the Door in my face'. Keston heard nothing and went to the Foleys for help. They asked Collins for a farm for him, giving him a good character reference. This was enough and Collins authorised the grant.[3]

Though literate, Keston (or Kenton) was poor, working class, and in Britain could never have dreamed of owning land. How unbelievable must the document have been: 'Unto Thomas Kenton his Heirs and Assigns to have and to hold for ever Fifty Acres of Land'.[4]

If people are given free land and cheap labour, they'll succeed as farmers, won't they? Many writers have assumed this: people given land grants had it easy. It's accepted in biographies of successful families – the Stanfields, Archers, Gibsons, Bisdees, Lords and so on – and is also a common theme in family history. Because far more men were transported than women (a ratio of 6:1), women could pick and choose their husbands. They favoured, naturally, good providers, and so people researching family histories tend to find they are descended from the more successful colonists. These two trends skew the general perception of life in the colony. It's seen as successful, the home of prosperous families.

The authorities also thought people who were given free land

A map showing Thomas Keston/Kenton's land grant, on Brown's River (TA AF396/1/19)

should succeed. In 1813 the marines who had served in the south since 1804 were disbanded and given the choice of returning to Britain or remaining as settlers. They would receive land, double the usual convict grant; they would be clothed and fed from the stores for eighteen months, and given seed grain, tools, a convict labourer for a year, and a cow on hire purchase. 'With these indulgences, it is hoped they will soon become wealthy and useful Settlers', opined the lords of the Admiralty in London.[5] What more could such people need?

However, when I was writing the biography of settler Roderic O'Connor, I read his extremely frank journals as a land commissioner in 1826–28, reporting on the colony's farmers. I was struck by how many failed. Farm after farm was abandoned, unoccupied or unsuccessful, with farmer after farmer drunk, lazy, incompetent, accident-prone or dead. O'Connor was a natural exaggerator: how accurate was his description? What were the chances of people developing land grants into viable farms?

People might well have had a rosy idea of farming, as in Britain: snug farms, cultivated for centuries, the result of generations of labour, each learning from the one before. It was different in Van Diemen's Land, with its virgin soil where no one had ever farmed. Farming was challenging: hard manual labour, dawn to dusk.

On the surveyor's advice, Thomas Keston took his land at Brown's

River (Kingston), south of Hobart, 'but I did not know the disadvantages of the place' he wrote gloomily. The land was thickly timbered, very hard to clear: 'I have been two days felling one tree with an axe'. Keston had no 'indulgence' from government, no tools or convict labourer. He could get rations, but 'there was nothing but a few lbs of stinking Kangaroo to serve out half the time' (in the days before refrigeration). He built a small hut and cleared four acres by felling trees, though he could not move the fallen logs and had to sow his wheat around them. He also planted potatoes and turnips. With no income, he lived on animals he caught – kangaroo rats, bandicoots, native cats and devils – and stinging nettles and turnip tops. He reaped the crop (by hand, using a sickle or scythe) and took it to sell in Hobart, but there was no road and hiring a boat took a third of his profit. With the rest of the money, he paid a man to help him cut up the tree trunks so he could pile them up and burn them.[6]

The Fawkner family – father John, mother Hannah and children John Pascoe and Elizabeth – found farming almost as arduous. In 1803, John junior wrote delicately, 'circumstances led to the family leaving England' – these being his father's arrest for receiving stolen goods. John senior was a middle-class convict, a London metal refiner. In 1806 the family moved to his grant at Claremont. Fourteen-year-old John junior cared for the animals: sheep, goats and cows. 'Oh the trouble, the time, the kicks and tossings, experienced to obtain milk from these very small, but singularly turbulent cattle!' The family was so poor that when they killed a sheep they had to sell the meat and themselves ate only the offal. Then bushrangers stole their clothes and food.

Like Keston's land, the Fawkners' was thickly timbered, and clearing it and burning the logs was 'a heavy drawback'. John senior 'managed to have broken up and chipped and finally sown with wheat two acres of land'. The authorities provided seed but it was tainted. 'We knowing little of farming sowed [the seed] as it was without preparation of any sort and suffered accordingly.' Then smut, a fungal disease, attacked the crop and a hoped-for harvest of 60 bushels brought in only half that amount. However, the Fawkners learned from experience and by 1809 had a better crop, 150 bushels from five acres, double the yield.[7]

George Harris, a favoured official, had an easier but not more successful farming career. He could afford to employ convict workmen on his 100-acre grant near Hobart. In 1805 they reaped an acre of wheat, 'which considering is doing wonders'. Harris and two fellow officials bought farm animals 'and the governor allows us an old man to take them out to graze'. But in 1807 the crops failed, and Harris gave no more news of his farm. It sounds as if it was too hard – and as a surveyor, he had his profession to fall back on.

How did Keston (probably a sailor), Fawkner (metal refiner) and Harris (surveyor, but trained as a lawyer) know how to farm? They didn't. In 1805 Hobart was visited by Joseph Holt, an Irish gentleman farmer exiled to New South Wales for his role in the 1798 rebellion against British rule. Collins asked this expert to look at the wheat crop. Holt was appalled to find it ruined by smut, which farmers and even the superintendent of crops did not recognise – but the superintendent had been a London shoemaker, so what could be expected? His counterpart with the animals had been a tailor. Collins offered Holt both superintendents' jobs and as much land as he wanted, for 'I might as well have two old women as the present [men]'. Holt declined.[8] His story shows Collins desperate for someone with experience to show his colonists how to farm.

Not that the sixteen convicts who did have experience as farmers, farm labourers or sawyers were any more successful. Only five gained land grants, with four establishing farms. The others presumably did not apply. They died, absconded, became bushrangers or had jobs: as shepherds, a gardener, a ferryman.[9]

Norfolk Islanders arrived from 1808, after the government closed that settlement. Most islanders had lived and usually farmed on their beautiful island since the early 1790s, so were experienced. It was a balmy place where farming was easy, but starting afresh in harsher, colder, less fertile Van Diemen's Land was a challenge. 'Years after, they spoke of the change with regret and sadness.'[10] Nearly two-thirds of grantees were originally convicts, the other adults mostly sailors or soldiers, and a fifth were children, given grants when they were old enough.

Norfolk Islanders had a poor reputation among the middle class: 'hopeless and dissipated', doing little farming but drawing their rations and bartering away their land: 'it was no idle boast, that a keg of rum was then worth more than a common farm'. John Pascoe Fawkner, son of a convict, was more sympathetic:

> This accession to our numbers gave us a great accession of the skill required in opening up a new country, the finest of Axe men to cut down our timber, the best of workmen to fall, burn off and also to split our timber ... Men accustomed to work hard and skillfully – men that were used to the hoe.[11]

Certainly some Norfolk Islanders established flourishing farms, and children of Norfolk Islanders, young and vigorous, were notably successful.

My own Norfolk Islander ancestors were typical of those who survived on the land. James Pillinger had a large family and small farm at Clarence Plains and probably just struggled along, especially after his wife died aged only 39 – such deaths could be disasters for families. His son James junior started working in his teens as an overseer, then gained a spectacularly barren and remote land grant at Kitty's Corners, way out east of Oatlands. He tried farming but it was hopeless, so he sold the grant and bought land at Tunbridge, where by hard work he built up a flourishing grazing property. James senior sold his grant and joined his son. So both tried farming, though without much success on the actual grants.

With farmers learning by experience, and the arrival of the Norfolk Islanders, agriculture increased. Those not doing so well, or hating the hard manual work, often moved on – the Peters family ran a pub in Hobart, the Fawkners a shop, and George Harris died. Neighbours bought their land to increase their own holdings. Farmers now understood the southern seasons, oxen made ploughing less arduous, and careful farmers could grow good crops. Wheat acreage expanded around Hobart and Port Dalrymple, with large amounts exported to Sydney from 1816. Writers praised local fertility: a farmer at Pittwater claimed the extraordinary achievement of growing 135 stems of wheat from one grain![12]

Farmers also raised animals: cattle, sheep and pigs for meat, with a few dairy cows and hens and the occasional goat. Meat could be sold to the commissariat, which at first had to feed almost everyone in the colony. But capitalists who could afford bribes dominated: men like Edward Lord who ran huge herds of cattle in the backblocks, illegally on crown land. No one had the power to stop them: more of that later. Most farmers, like James Pillinger senior, had small grants. For them it was subsistence farming, scratching a living as best they could. If other, less law-abiding ways of making a living appeared, many seized them gratefully. More of that later, as well.

There were as yet no big estates with gracious two-storey houses. Writing in 1823, Edward Curr warned immigrants that farms in Van Diemen's Land were the opposite of neat, comfortable English establishments. Houses were built of sods, logs or mud, thatched with straw. Round them lay disgusting piles of wool, bones, sheepskins and manure, dotted with ploughs, carts, firewood and watercasks. Quarters of mutton or kangaroo hung from trees, and tribes of 'dogs and idlers' lounged about. 'Everything betokens waste and disorder', the inhabitants lost to 'idleness and profligacy.'[13]

Gentlemen like Curr had servants to make sure everything was neat and clean, and had no idea of the hard manual labour involved in farming. Why should these farmers be neat? Where else would they hang their meat and put their ploughs? Curr might think their farms showed waste and disorder, but they were managing to make a living from them.

More convicts arrived, in dribs and drabs. After the initial 281 on the *Calcutta* in 1804, another shipload arrived in 1812: the *Indefatigable* with 199 men. By 1817, when men from the *Indefatigable* started to become eligible for grants, there were more farms and less pressure on the authorities to find farmers; yet 22 per cent of these men gained grants.

More convicts arrived via New South Wales, sent down in small batches to provide labour. Approximately 4461 arrived and 223 received grants, 5 per cent – a low figure, but it took time to establish a reputation, get to be known by people willing to give a reference, build up a little cash or stock. A few brought letters from the authorities recommending a grant. Usually no reason was given, but James Frost's wife had 'nursed' (possibly wet-nursed) Governor Macquarie's baby son, and so James was recommended for a grant.[14] Emigrant Samuel Guy, writing home from Hobart in 1825, was surely voicing general opinion by saying that 'before emigration was on so large a scale' – before 1820 – 'every encouragement was given to the convicts that was in the least Industrious'.[15]

Governors did not seem so worried about free settlers' industriousness. The most unlikely people were given grants, such as visiting ship's captains who obviously had no intention of farming. Jonathan Taylor, chief mate on a whaling ship, visited in 1808 and scored 100 acres which he might never have even seen. He soon left and presumably sold the grant. Did bribes change hands, in these days of rampant corruption?

Governor Macquarie in Sydney, who was meant to authorise all grants, became so exasperated that in 1816 he proclaimed that no governor of Van Diemen's Land had any power to make grants, and all to date were to be deemed null and void.[16] It seemed to have no effect, especially on Governor Davey who was used to taking no notice of his boss Macquarie. He was certainly not going to turf people off their grants, and none appeared to have been nullified by Macquarie's ruling.

In the sixteen years from 1804 to 1819, 1073 land grants were given. Most went to men who seemed likely to farm them, but others went because of someone's job (ex-soldiers received grants automatically); social position, with officials' families receiving grants even if they were toddlers; or as a reward for service, such as catching bushrangers or even, as noted above, nursing the governor's son. Women (mostly Norfolk Islanders who had inherited land there from fathers or husbands and had to be recompensed in Van Diemen's Land, but also some womenfolk of officials) gained 53 grants. The average grant size

Small farms along the Derwent at Claremont, by Joseph Lycett (SLV, ID50628998)

was 304 acres, quite small. Nearly three-quarters, 70 per cent, were in the south, with the rest in the north.

The convict group – ex-convicts (55 percent) and their relations, mostly their children but sometimes wives (11 per cent) – made up two-thirds of grantees. Free arrivals, a mix of soldiers, sailors and chance arrivals, and a handful of emigrants from Britain wanting a new life, made up the rest.

How successful were grantees? I have divided them into three groups: those who did nothing discernible to their land; those who did something (sold meat or wheat, advertised for workers, were called 'farmers' on children's birth registrations) but then left; and those who remained on their farms.

	Ex-Convicts	Convict Relations	Always free
Number	330	50	205
Percentage	56	9	35
Did nothing	24%	14%	27%
Did something	48%	44%	46%
Remained	28%	42%	27%
Died in colony	71%	70%	65%
Average grant	123a	325a	712a
Married	22%	12%	18%
Married, children	45%	68%	59%
Single, no children	33%	20%	23%

Least successful in establishing a farm were free people; convicts were more so, and their children were the most successful group. (Though many people who gave up farms were successful in other areas such as running a business.) The question of what brought success is discussed in chapter 15 but having children was a factor, as seen above. Most grantees of all types remained in the colony, dying there (and these are minimal figures, people whose deaths can be traced) – though roughly a quarter seem to have left, for one reason or another.

But the grim fact staring out from these statistics is that about three-quarters of grantees were unsuccessful in establishing a long-term farm. They might not have wanted to – who knows how many gained grants only aiming to sell them and pocket the proceeds – but for those who did there were many possible problems. Ill health, accidents, death of a spouse, bad seasons, drought, a low price for produce – any of these could mean disaster.

Finance was a major problem. Peter Harrisson, who arrived in 1822, was determined at all costs to 'keep clear of the gulph that swallows up the means of many settlers': running out of money in establishing their farm and having to borrow from merchants to keep afloat. Once merchants had you in their grip it was next to impossible to get clear of them, and people ended up dependent on them or having to sell their farms. If the crop failed, or they drank away the loan, the merchants could repossess the farm.[17] This could show merchants' rapacity but also farmers' drunkenness or business incompetence. Many an advertisement for a sheriff's sale has a sad story behind it, of someone trying to succeed at farming but being overcome by problems.

After all, how could an urban vagrant who had never had much farming or financial experience cope with running a business? Some hard-working people did well, but for the three-quarters who did not manage to establish a farm, it was a dog-eat-dog environment where all too often only the strong – which can be translated as dishonest, cheating and brutal – survived. Harrisson commented that farmers and others not used to trade were easily imposed on by merchants, but he was scornful of one fellow passenger who lacked 'a persevering spirit to fight through difficulties'. The man was in despair, talking of giving up and returning to Britain.[18] But not everyone has the strength of mind or physical energy to overcome problems by perseverance.

For some people, like James Pillinger senior, subsistence living was enough of an achievement, far more than he could have hoped for as a street urchin in Bristol. However, for those wanting to establish a larger farm, income was essential. A few might grow wheat, the only really profitable farming activity, but otherwise it was extremely difficult. In 1820 Commissioner Bigge conducted an investigation into the colony's economy (see chapter 8) which revealed a grim picture for farmers. Sheep and cattle could be sold to the government for meat, but a few individuals dominated this market and ordinary people could not always get their meat accepted. Wool was thrown away as there was no market for it. Some potatoes were exported to Sydney; a little barley was grown; a few people made butter, but nothing really brought in much cash.

There were other ways of making an honest living. Whaling was in its infancy and the one whaling ship employed only 26 men; sealing in the Bass Strait islands was dying out due to over-exploitation. But people could work as labourers, or set up a business, running a pub or using their skill as a tradesman – though here, too, there were problems. With no bank, finances were difficult. Businessmen wrote promissory notes – 'I promise to pay the bearer sixpence' – which were used for currency, but they could be lost, torn or destroyed. It was hard to get debts repaid and many a businessman went broke. Meanwhile, employees could be sacked at the whim of their employer. There were no unfair dismissal laws, no trade unions, no minimum wage and no social security. Making a living honestly in Van Diemen's Land before 1820 was a tough call.

3. MAKING A DISHONEST LIVING: CONVICTS

Crime was rampant in early European Van Diemen's Land. Why? Let's start with the other side of the coin: why do people *not* commit crimes?

- They're afraid of getting caught
- They're afraid of public shame
- They're brought up to obey the law
- They have principles
- They realise that if everyone does whatever they like, the country will go to the dogs

Many factors enforce these reasons. Strong law and order; an efficient police force; churches, schools and parents instilling principles: – all these encourage us to be honest, to keep the rules. Jane Austen's novels of upper-class England, written at the time Van Diemen's Land was colonised, describe people who were in the main not worried by crime.

The poor in Britain – people Jane Austen did not write about – felt few of these restraints. Few went to church or school or had law-abiding parents to instruct and set an example. Few feared the inadequate police force. In a hard world with little outside help, they got by as best they could.

For them, stealing was part of life, one way to get along if earning failed. It's easy to justify stealing. He has so much, he won't miss one pheasant. Life is unfair and I'm just evening it up. Why not? 'The door was open', said one girl, justifying herself at the Old Bailey against a charge of theft.[1] If someone's silly enough to leave things lying around … Writing to his wife from Spithead, about to leave England, convict James Batt merely mourned being 'unforagenate' (unfortunate), a typical attitude.[2] Unfortunate to be caught, but not feeling morally guilty.

Convicts transported to Van Diemen's Land brought their attitudes with them, and found themselves in a haven for criminals. What did the British government think would happen, sending a population of thieves to form a new colony? There was no attempt to reform them while they served out their sentences, or train them in any way. When they were set free, how were they going to earn a living? Some gained a grant but, as we've seen, it was hard work establishing a farm, and it was entirely foreign to many of the ex-convicts, who were often urban thieves. They could find a job, but a large percentage were not used to working all day. Instead, they were used to stealing.

The result was that crime, particularly theft, was rampant. Robbing, selling sly grog, abetting bushrangers – anything that could make a hard life that bit easier. Just the thought of a hefty bribe to keep quiet, as in the sly grog enterprise (see below), must have been very appealing.

'**No one can have any idea of the infamy** of the people of the colony (the prisoners I mean) who has not witnessed it: nothing but flogging and stealing', Adolarius Humphrey wrote to his parents from Hobart.[3] He had not lived among the poor in Britain, so a culture of theft was a shock. The excuse often used for theft in Britain was that people were starving or had to feed starving families, but in the colony for the most part food was plentiful. However, people

Convicts enjoying an evening by the fire, by John Glover (the central figure). This is one of the few portrayals of convicts as ordinary people, enjoying themselves (NLA 618820)

need more than food: clothes, housing, pleasures – in particular, in the colony, rum.

It's likely that some convicts, brought up in hard environments and treated brutally by authorities and, often enough, their families, suffered from anti-social personality disorder: an enduring pattern of disregard for the rights of others, often caused by neglect or abuse as a child.[4]

Thieving was easy. Constables were mainly convicts or ex-convicts, inclined to intimidation and bribery, as well as sympathy with criminals. There were not enough of them in any case, and not enough military either. The island was sparsely settled and thieves could find plenty of hideaways in the bush. Many, probably most, thieves were not caught. To make matters more difficult for the authorities, while Van Diemen's Land's magistrates tried people for minor offences, there was no court for major crimes. Serious criminals had to be sent to Sydney to be tried. For plaintiffs, this meant up to six months away from work and an uncertain outcome, 'a step which [settlers] consider tantamount to certain ruin'.[5] In any case, many people tried in Sydney were acquitted 'for want of evidence'. The result was that few people pressed charges. According to contemporaries, this was a major inducement to crime.

The authorities' weapons against crime were few. With an ineffective police force, governors found it impossible to compel obedience. On dark nights convicts could commit thefts with ease, and they had the sympathy of many ex-convict settlers. All the authorities could do was inflict severe punishments on those unlucky enough to get caught, and offer rewards for information. This could be quite successful but was hard to organise on a large scale.

The result was that every diary, letter and newspaper is full of reports of theft. The clergyman, Robert Knopwood, wrote not so much about prayer but about gardening, dining and theft. Men robbed the government stores, thieved from their masters, stole cabbages from gardens, stole sheep, killed a cow: 'continual robberies which were daily committed in the camp by the convicts and the servants, all of which I was subject to'. The only topic of conversation was 'the daily account of Robberies during the night', wrote George Harris. Thieves could be daring: one night George and his new wife Ann Jane were in bed and perhaps not paying attention while someone cut the lining of their tent and stole a large cask of spirits.[6]

There are no paintings of crimes. Instead, here are convicts at work with spade and pick, while a surveyor shows plans to the foreman. 'PB' on their clothes means 'Prisoners' Barrack'. Detail from George Evans, *Hobart Town Van Diemen's Land* (National Library of Australia 135297750)

Punishments were horrifyingly harsh. Knopwood's servant, convict John Earl, committed a 'very daring robbery', breaking into a closet. Knopwood searched him and found brandy and picklock keys. The magistrate – Knopwood himself or a colleague – sentenced Earl to the appalling punishment of 500 lashes.[7] This was severe even by Hobart standards. Most thieves received 'only' 200 or 300.

Some crimes seem minor. Knopwood asked convict Daniel McAllenan to repair his fence: 'he put his hands in to his pocket, lookd at me and laughd, and said he could not do it'. Shocked, Knopwood had him arrested, and told Collins he could not overlook such an insult. Collins asked him to pardon McAllenan who, he said, 'was getting forward now, better than he has for some time'. Knopwood insisted on 25 lashes. The outcome is not clear – but what is clear is that these gentlemen demanded deference. Officials George Harris and Lieutenant Hopley had two men arrested for laughing at them.[8]

Crimes continued. Once the *Hobart Town Gazette* began in 1816, every issue reported theft of one sort or another. A constable – supposedly catching thieves – stole from a garden; an ex-convict stole the palings around a grave. Someone grabbed clothes from a cart standing outside the pub at Kangaroo Point; a prisoner collecting her rations seized six pounds of mutton, over two kilos. No wonder she was caught, as this would have been hard to hide. And so on. One *Gazette* issue alone reported thefts from four shops, one by making a hole in the cellar door, one by removing weatherboard at the back.[9]

Many crimes were ingenious. One night shopkeeper William Jemott was woken by a groan. Grabbing his pistols he went downstairs – to find a thief had escaped, after having picked the lock of Jemott's gate, bored a hole in the wall of his shop and inserted a tin tube into a cask of rum. The rum was flowing into another cask outside. Shops seemed regarded as fair game. Thieves dug up the pavement outside Mr Read's shop, dug a hole into the cellar and made off with a load of goods. The *Gazette* warned householders to beware of thieves trying to enter houses through walls. Brick houses were particularly vulnerable as they were easy to take apart: 'in the brick-work alone there is neither safety nor dependence'. Residents should strengthen their defences.[10] Tougher bricks and better mortar sound like a good start, but presumably were not available.

A few thefts were serious enough for people to go through the arduous process of sending prisoners to Sydney for trial. In 1806 Governor Paterson at Port Dalrymple sent three soldiers and a cooper, James Keating, to be tried in Sydney for robbing the stores. Witnesses reported seeing Keating and accomplices stealing 35 pounds (16 kg) of pork with the connivance of a sentinel. Found guilty of this 'heinous and inexcusable offence', as the judge put it, the men were sentenced to death. Two were merely transported for fourteen years, but Keating was sent to Hobart for execution. This was made a spectacle everyone was forced to watch, administrators, military and convicts, to see the result of committing such a crime – or of being caught.[11]

Sheep and cattle stealing were treated more seriously than the general run of petty theft. As soon as people started keeping stock, others started stealing it. It was simple. No one had fences, shepherds and stockmen could be bribed or intimidated, the animals were easy enough to move, there were plenty of secluded valleys where sheep could be hidden, and they were easy to sell or eat. John Fawkner claimed that sheep-stealing began as a system in 1811, with 'stolen sheep hidden amongst the interminable hills and sheltered by the thick underwood'. From 1816 the *Gazette* often reported thefts of large flocks of sheep, up to seven hundred at once.[12]

Governor Sorell tried to clamp down on sheep-stealers, and in 1817 sent three members of the Crahan family to Sydney for 'stealing sheep to an enormous amount', he told Macquarie:

> The System of Cattle Stealing in this Settlement, which is both a cause and an effect of Bushranging, had arrived at such a pitch, and had assumed so much of an organised system that it is most difficult to check it.

'A large portion of the Community' was involved. Sorell felt he must act, and who better to charge than 'one of the worst and most notorious plunderers in the Colony, Crahan, who, with his Sons, has carried on for years … a system of Sheep-Stealing to the extent of Hundreds in a Year'.[13]

The Crahan family – ex-convict Thomas, his wife Mary and five children – were Norfolk Islanders, and their small land grants at New Norfolk proved ideal bases for sheep-stealing (and selling meat to the government). In Sydney, Thomas and his son Thomas junior were sentenced to execution, commuted to banishment for life to the penal station at Newcastle. Meanwhile, Mary ran the farm and sold meat to the government – the stolen sheep? A surprise came when her husband returned unexpectedly: at Newcastle he helped save a stolen ship and was given a passage home. He kept out of trouble, but his son James was in and out of court, accused of arson (twice), stealing pigs and beating up an old man.[14]

Farmers were advised to be vigilant, to count sheep more regularly, to make stockmen more attentive to their duty – but nothing worked and sheep-stealing continued. John Hudsepth at Jericho took it for granted. 'Sheep stealing is going on to a great extent, one settler has had 300 taken away, but this is thought nothing of in Van Diemen's Land.'[15]

In 1827, settler Henry Widowson described ex-convicts' small grants as the home of idle inmates whose main activities were selling sly grog, sheep-stealing and receiving stolen property. He saw the property of a notorious sheep-stealer being searched. Nothing incriminating could be found until the searchers came to the pigsty, where under loose slabs was a large barrel of mutton, but no evidence such as marked fleeces to show which sheep it was from. 'These fellows are very good at not being detected.'[16]

One morning young George Lloyd was having breakfast with his uncle on their property of Frogmore at Sorell:

> "George," remarked my poor broken-spirited uncle one day, whilst discussing our early repast, "I have not seen our favourite, Hong Kong Bess, this morning; have you?"
>
> "No sir," was my reply; "I presume she was marched to the Woolly Hut stubble in company with the other pigs."
>
> But poor fat Bess, the costly China sow, as was afterwards revealed, long ere that early hour had been so skilfully carved, and shaped into chumps of prime mess pork as to baffle all attempts at recognition.
>
> Fat cattle and sheep, ewes, wethers, and lambs, were regularly abstracted from the herds and flocks of every stockholder in the district, and driven into unfrequented dells known only to crime and misdeeds. From these gloomy recesses the prey was duly apportioned amongst the numerous accomplices ... ticket-of-leave farmers, living without let or hindrance upon their wealthier neighbours, the free emigrant settlers.[17]

Told from the opposite point of view was the story of a settler on a land grant, a former 'unwilling servant of the government'. Seeing a stockkeeper pass with a mob of fine young beasts, the ex-convict asked him in for a bite of dinner and plied him with liquor. As the sun went down, the stockkeeper agreed to stay the night, leaving his cattle in the yard.

Slipping out to the kitchen, the settler whispered to his wife, 'Now, Molly, the irons, old gal'. Molly put the irons to heat on the fire and, while the two men were drinking rum and singing, she rebranded the cattle. In the morning, the settler claimed the cattle as his. There was nothing the stockkeeper could do.[18]

Heavy drinking was the norm in Britain at this time – just think of those paintings by Hogarth of drunken people lying about the streets of London, 'drunk for a penny, dead drunk for twopence'. Drunkenness was at least as bad in Van Diemen's Land, where too many people had no other solace – no family, no friends unless they'd managed to make some, no cosy home. The only comfort was rum or beer, and the only warm, welcoming place was the pub.

John Fawkner, who did have a warm and welcoming home and family, was horrified. Aged fifteen, he witnessed in 1807 the arrival of a shipload of rum after the colony had run completely dry:

> Then was seen that most disgraceful of all sights, men drunk, all over the camp, sitting, lying or rolling about: the rum was poured into tubs and buckets and bailed out in tin pannicans, in front of almost every tent and house in the settlement; officers marines and all joined in this drunken revelry.[19]

Drunkenness raged throughout Van Diemen's Land for the whole convict period and beyond. At one time or another in their sentences, a majority of convicts were punished for drunkenness (mostly fairly leniently). As with theft, from when the *Gazette* began in 1816, hardly an issue appeared without a mention of someone drunk: 'drunkenness last Night'; 'drunk in the streets of Hobart'; 'drunkenness on the Sabbath day'.[20] Alcohol was used as currency and was very much part of life. Employers used it as an incentive to work; Mr Kennedy offered a reward of a gallon of rum for finding a small kangaroo that had strayed from his house, perhaps a children's pet. When David Jones gave evidence against a man for sly grog selling (see below), he said that, feeling indisposed, he ordered half a pint of rum – half a pint, 300 ml! Hardly a remedy for indisposition, unless it was the hair of the dog. But everyone drank. The same amount, half a pint, was given to the troops for celebrations such as the King's Birthday. Looking back on the period, observers saw it as a time when 'open profligacy and drunkenness pervaded all ranks'.[21]

Drunkenness, however, was criticised far more in convicts than in the upper classes. When Commissioner Bigge enquired into the colony in 1820, many witnesses complained of drunkenness among convicts. No one admitted there were alcoholics among officials – that, for example, Governor Davey drank as much as any convict.

People died of drink. In 1818 evidence at an inquest found that the deceased had called on an acquaintance and asked permission to lie down, 'being quite intoxicated'. After two hours, his host asked if he wanted to go home, and found he was dead. 'The deceased was immoderately given to drinking of spirits, which no doubt hastened his end.' Fawkner told of a storekeeper opening a cask of rum '33 over proof'. A marine asked for some; the storekeeper gave him half a pint and told him to add water, but the marine drank it and more: and dropped dead.[22] Such tales were all too familiar.

Fighting was endemic in the heavily masculine, heavy drinking society of early European Van Diemen's Land, the instinctive reaction to a grievance. As with other crimes, once the *Hobart Town Gazette* newspaper appeared in 1816, stories of fighting were frequent – in the street, in pubs, in homes.

Fighting could end in murder. In 1816 William Clarke was charged with the wilful murder of William Price at a pub in Hobart. Evidence showed Price made an unprovoked attack on Clarke who, 'actuated by a sudden impulse of passion', returned the blow 'which immediately proved fatal'. However, his conduct (apologetic? grovelling?) earned him 'the kindest consideration of the court', and he was acquitted. Three years later a judge told the *Gazette* that hostile, abusive and provoking words and gestures could be considered as excusing, even justifying, assault.[23]

Selling alcohol could involve two major offences. The most notorious was smuggling, but that was mainly organised by the upper classes. Working men were more likely to be involved with making and/or selling alcohol illegally, 'sly grog'. 'It is well known that more liquor and beer are vended in what are elegantly called "Sly Grog-shops," than in all the Licensed Houses', wrote the editor of the *Hobart Town Gazette* in 1825.[24]

Once independent newspapers were established (the *Gazette* was a government publication), letters to the editor raged about 'the many sly grog shops in Hobart Town', 'sewers for vice and immorality', 'a disgrace to society'. One man claimed he had walked up Hobart's main street and counted thirteen (so they must have been obvious, not much attempt at secrecy). Launceston was just as bad. 'Gambling, drinking, fighting, indeed, scenes which would appal any parent, are hourly practised.' The police knew about sly grog shops but gave the weak excuse that they could not force a way into a private house unless a complaint had been made. Bushrangers and sheep-stealers ran sly grog shops in the interior, encouraging shepherds and stockmen who paid in stolen sheep.[25]

Only a few sly grog sellers were caught. In 1827 one at Constitution Hill was fined and his stock was poured into the ground in front of a large crowd. 'The faces of the group when the precious cordials were moistening the thirsty earth was a scene for a painter.'[26]

Hobart and to a lesser extent Launceston were port towns, with ships coming and going, and some convicts dreamed of stowing away. In 1805 Collins was told that a group planned to escape in the ship *Myrtle*. A party of marines searched it but two men managed to evade them. However, the captain found them and put them ashore at Sydney, for return to Hobart. There are other mentions of stowaways being caught, such as four prisoners found hidden on a ship in 1818. They were sentenced to work for six months in irons.[27]

However, men did escape. This does not sound hard – captains were often short of crew, what with death, accident and desertion, and were often only too eager to find more men. Since ships were searched before leaving port that was chancy, but it was easy enough to pick them up at a secluded beach down the river.

Some convicts planned to steal boats. In 1805 Collins was told that nine planned to steal a whaleboat and sail to New Zealand. They were caught and examined by magistrates. 'Although the information was true that we received', wrote magistrate Knopwood, 'yet [we] could not get anything from them to convict them.'[28] They were freed. This seems surprisingly lenient compared with hundreds of lashes for minor theft, perhaps indicating how precious their own belongings were to those in charge.

Combining the themes of smuggling, bribery, escaped convicts and general roguery was the saga of the *Argo*. In 1814 it arrived in Hobart with 3500 gallons of arrack. James Gordon, naval officer, whose job it was to catch smugglers, did all he could to stop the arrack being landed. *Argo*'s Captain Dixon assaulted him, and seventeen casks were smuggled ashore to ex-convict Andrew Whitehead's pub at New Town. Citizens who saw them were bribed to keep quiet with the equivalent of half the naval officer's annual pay; but the authorities found out, confiscated the spirits and forfeited the *Argo*.

Dixon, his crew and twelve absconding convicts overpowered the guard placed on the ship and made their escape. Whitehead, who was well connected (his wife having been the mistress of Governor Bowen), was sent to Sydney for trial but was acquitted owing to lack of evidence. Governor Macquarie, who had not a shadow of doubt of Whitehead's guilt, was appalled. He had the last laugh, however, for *Argo* was never heard of again, with everyone on it assumed perished.[29]

All the above crimes – theft, drinking, fighting, selling grog illegally, escaping imprisonment – also went on in Britain. Perhaps to a lesser extent, but they were part of working-class life, and so were naturally replicated in the colony. However, Van Diemen's Land (and New South Wales) saw several novel crimes, which earned the colonies notoriety in Britain as places of horror.

Bushrangers were a new menace. At first sight, escape into the Tasmanian bush seemed pointless as there was little to eat there, and men could not catch animals with their bare hands. But in 1805, before crops came to fruition, the colony was short of food, and the authorities sent out men with guns and dogs to shoot kangaroo. Those wanting freedom realised they could steal dogs and guns and shoot kangaroo themselves, supporting themselves as 'bushrangers'. In 1806 Knopwood sent his men to catch kangaroo, but they reported that while they were asleep Fossett (Fawcett or Falsett), a bushranger, had stolen his bitch, Miss, as well as their pork and a kettle. (This sounds suspicious – how did they know it was Fossett if they were asleep?) Knopwood sent the men to search for Miss, but only after he offered a reward did a settler bring Miss to him. 'She came to him while he was at dinner', he said innocently.

If caught, bushrangers were severely punished. Two days after Miss was returned, Knopwood tried four men for absenting themselves and dog-stealing: 100 lashes.[30] But there is no other mention of Fossett, Fawcett or Falsett, or what he was doing in the colony in the first place, an example of the difficulty of researching with scanty records.

In 1807, the colony was terrorised by bushrangers Richard Lemon and John Brown. Convicts in Port Dalrymple who absconded, they brutally murdered three soldiers, possibly for revenge. Forcing a convict, John Morey, to go with them, they walked to the east coast where they met up with a party of eight runaways from Hobart. Hearing of the murders from Morey, the runaways tied up Lemon and Brown, stole a schooner and escaped, taking Morey.

Lemon and Brown freed themselves from their bonds and walked south, living on shellfish, birds' eggs and anything else they could find. From kangaroo hunters near Hobart they obtained weapons and supplies, and made for the safety of the midlands where no Europeans lived – except one other bushranger. Lemon shot him dead. They terrorised Aboriginal people, shooting, torturing and wounding them with 'every species of cruelty'.

Venturing south for supplies, they robbed two settlers and kept one, Michael Mansfield, as a guide. He escaped by promising to bring supplies, but instead brought two men, hoping to gain the reward offered for the bushrangers' capture. In a violent struggle, Mansfield shot Lemon dead. The men cut off his head and forced Brown to carry it in a bag to Hobart. Brown was tried and executed.[31]

The authorities tried persuading bushrangers to give themselves up, and several times a date was given: if bushrangers surrendered before it, they would be pardoned, but if not they would be considered outlaws and, said Macquarie, 'extirpated by force of arms as a last alternative'.[32] No threats worked because, once in the bush, bushrangers were almost impregnable. They could steal from householders, or kill kangaroo; the meat was no longer necessary in the settlement but they could swap the skins and the proceeds of their thefts with supporters for necessities of life. Living in the bush must have had its moments, particularly in winter, but at least they were free, away from the bosses with their whips and chains.

When incompetent Davey took over as governor, the number of bushrangers increased alarmingly. In mid-1814 Macquarie proclaimed that those who surrendered by 1 December would be pardoned. This was a mistake: the bushrangers openly boasted that they had no fear of punishment for six months.

There were two versions of the bushranging story. One, told by Fawkner, saw them as heroes. He claimed that the threat of flogging made men become bushrangers. 'I heard one Bushranger tell the government officer when on the drop, with the halter round his neck, It was you Sir that drove me to the Bush, you flogged me cruelly for a crime I never committed ... you murdered me!!!' Thirty years later, historian James Bonwick agreed, claiming that the prisoners class sympathised with bushrangers, seeing each 'as a sort of martyr to convictism'. Victims of oppression, Robin Hoods among convicts, they fought against tyranny.[33]

The other version saw bushrangers as brutal villains, preying on their fellows. In 1814 Corporal Feutrill and a party of soldiers were walking from Port Dalrymple to Hobart. At Epping they saw five suspicious-looking men and managed to catch one. Taking him with them, at York Plains they met Edward Lord's overseer, in charge of his cattle. Feutrill told him they would spend the night at Jericho. Once there, at midnight the party was woken by bushrangers aiming muskets at them, exclaiming, 'Lay still you buggers!' They freed the captured bushranger and tied up the soldiers, but took one, Craig, back to Lord's tents, where Lord's men had breakfast ready.

The bushrangers' leader, the feared Mike Howe, told Craig they were going to steal a ship and he was to navigate it. But first they were going to take the soldiers' kangaroo rugs and clothes, and flog Feutrill with the sinews of a kangaroo tail. There were eighteen bushrangers, said Craig, and they had no intention of handing themselves in on 1 December; they 'had not done half mischief enough'. Craig managed to escape. Hearing his news, the soldiers left for Hobart, off the beaten road. This story alarmed the authorities: bushrangers defeating soldiers, making them scurry off for safety, and in cahoots with the servants of leading colonist and ex-officer Edward Lord.[34]

Similarly alarming was a story of bushrangers robbing the McCarty house at New Norfolk, with implications of assistance by the servants. Mary McCarty was chatting to a visitor, William Holsgrove, when an armed man with a charcoal-blackened face burst in and aimed a musket at William, telling him to lie down or he would blow his brains out. Eight more bushrangers appeared, some in cloth jackets and trousers, some in 'complete kangaroo dress'. They tied William up, but he defended Mary verbally when the men tried to rape her and managed to stop them.

The bushrangers had a list of Mary's property and ransacked the house for it. She asked them to return a small box, having heard there was honour among thieves. Not thieves, they rebuked her – they were bushrangers and freebooters (as they stripped her house, keeping the

The Macquarie Harbour settlement by Thomas Lempriere (TA PH30-1-376)

small box). So they saw themselves as Fawkner did, as heroes. They too rejoiced in the amnesty; 'the old gentleman' (Davey) had given them a fine chance to do just as they liked.³⁵

It's easy to see why people were terrified of bushrangers: the danger of being shot, losing so many hard-won possessions, the lack of respect for the law, for ordinary inhabitants, the terrifying prospect of a man wearing kangaroo skins, his face and hands blacked with charcoal, pointing a musket at you, perhaps raping you. It's also easy to see why some people supported them, out of fear, sympathy or the possibility of gain.

The story that more than anything else depicted Van Diemen's Land as a place of extreme barbarism was that of Alexander Pearce, cannibal. An Irish convict, Pearce arrived in 1820. He committed offence after offence, was punished again and again, absconded multiple times and in 1822 was sent to the penal settlement at

Macquarie Harbour. Wet, cold, storm-ridden and isolated, 'hell on earth', this aimed to break recalcitrant convicts by cruelty.

Pearce and seven others absconded and started to walk eastwards, through the almost impenetrable, wet, cold, mountainous bush. They could find no food. Starving, they killed one of the gang and ate him. Two men, appalled, slipped away and struggled back to Macquarie Harbour, where they confessed all before dying of exposure. That left five men in the bush.

The only food they found was in an Aboriginal camp, where they brutally bashed the people to scare them away, seized the meat they were cooking, destroyed their spears, and went on. But this food ran out, and a pattern emerged: struggling through the bush, starving, they would kill one of their number, eat him, and struggle on until, starving again ... Finally only two were left, Pearce and Greenhill, each eyeing the other warily. Pearce managed to kill Greenhill while he was asleep, and ate him.

Pearce finally reached the settled districts and joined two bushrangers, but they were caught. Sent back to Macquarie Harbour, Pearce escaped again with a young boy, whom he killed and ate. Exhausted, he gave himself up. He was tried and executed.[36]

Pearce's story of brutal cannibalism was fully reported in the press both in Australia and Britain, to the utter horror of readers. No more cannibalism was publicised, but once was enough to give the island a terrible reputation. (Even more so from 1874, when Marcus Clarke made it a highlight of his convict novel, *For the Term of his Natural Life*.)

4. MAKING A DISHONEST LIVING: OFFICIALS

Convicts could be expected to steal, drink, fight and so on, but their rulers, the gentlemen in charge of the colony, were not. As gentlemen, they should be upright, sober and hard-working, running the colony to the best of their ability and setting a good example to the lower classes. These men were the officials, military officers and senior public servants. They felt entitled to rule, with the lower classes relegated to doing what they were told.

This did not work out in practice. All too many of the gentlemen could drink and carouse as much as any convict, as well as committing even more serious crimes – mainly embezzlement from the British Government. They gained their positions either through being army officers on the spot (lesser jobs) or through patronage in Britain (well-paying ones). Such jobs were never advertised. A competent, honest, industrious man capable of doing a job might apply – but without the vital, much more important qualification of being a gentleman, he would fail. Gentlemen ruled the empire and did not want to share power. In their view it was better to have a drunken, half-witted gentleman in a senior position than a non-gentleman, no matter how well he could do the job.

How much crime is there in today's public service? I asked two retired senior public servants this question. Some areas have more opportunity than others, they thought, and when there is opportunity, some people will take it – fired by greed rather than need. It can be a slippery slope, starting with small gifts from concerned businesses or individuals – tickets to the grand final, a box of prawns at Christmas, a holiday in the Maldives ...

If this happens today, with stricter government regulations and enforcement, and more ways of detecting such crime, how about the early nineteenth century, with no cameras, no recording or electronic devices, no code of ethics or strong tradition of public service? When a royal prince, the Duke of York, and his mistress were in trouble for selling army commissions? Being royal, he could not be punished, only told not to do it again. If the king's son does it ... and has a mistress ... And while Van Diemen's Land officials might not gain as much protection as the king's son, they were still looked after: perhaps dismissed or made to pay back a few debts, but never with the imprisonment, chains and flogging, let alone execution, a working-class man would have received. The authorities did not want scandal, did not want to have incompetent members of the ruling class shown up.

Van Diemen's Land and other colonies were used as dumping grounds, to provide jobs for gentlemen who could not succeed at home but knew the right people. They were all too often incompetent, lazy, unintelligent or drunk – sometimes all four. Many were only too keen to make money on the side. It was easy. The colony was four months' voyage from head office in London, which had little control over money spent there. If a bill was countersigned by the governor, Treasury had to pay. The Sydney governor-in-chief had to approve large amounts but even he had little control; again, if the right signatures were there, he had to approve. Furious letters could eventually arrive from London and Sydney, but in reality the man in charge of Van Diemen's Land had complete control – until they sacked him. Given that governors did little to rein in subordinates, they too could do what they wished.

Working-class settler Thomas Keston felt bitterly that too many officials were not up to the job. Competent men could find work in Britain, with no need to come to a colony to make their fortunes 'in the depraved & scandalous manner as our selfcreated Gentn have done'. Unfortunately, 'Offices & Professions are often necessaryly entrusted to persons in no way qualified to fill them'. We think rulers of other nations are savages but:

> Oh Englishmen! when you come to hear all the Tyranny of English Officers when invested with a small Share of authority over their fellow creatures & then committing by far worse Crimes than it is in the Power of the low order of People to commit, give them but Power & the Life of a poor Man is no more in their Hands than a Fly for they will be lashing them by candlelight there not being day light enough for their savage Practices, & there are Men set over us that is a mockery to the Laws of God & Man & they are more fit to be in Bedlam than to hold an office under our gracious Sovereign[1]

Note that 'selfcreated'; not gentleman-born but poorer men making money and assuming this status. Why did Keston condemn that? It's hard to understand when you're not born into the attitudes of the time, but did Keston, like the men concerned, accept that gentlemen-born were entitled to do what they wanted? Some certainly acted as if they were. The officials all needed money and promotion, the reason they came to Van Diemen's Land. In the colony, away from prying eyes, with little chance of anyone likely or brave enough to rebuke them, they felt they could do what they liked. 'Wealth & Power the Gentn of this Country think a Sanction for every Species of Villainy' (Keston again).[2]

The few upright men were appalled. 'They call it the end of the world', wrote James Grove, an educated convict, 'and for vice it is truly so, as here wickedness flourishes almost unchecked ... words are considered but wind, and strict regard for truth is generally unknown'. 'I cannot at present say all I know but I believe the Colony going fast to ruin', George Harris told his mother. 'Many serious Complaints are going home.'[3]

But no complaints are extant: the government was experienced at keeping embarrassing details hidden. 'It would be imprudent to mention any thing that makes me disgusted with this place', George wrote to his brother – did he fear his letters were read? – 'but Mr. Henderson if you see him will give you an account of transactions here which will astonish you. He is sent home under an Arrest by the Govr.' Lieutenant Henderson was arrested for ungentlemanlike conduct, which could mean anything – including criticising the governor. London saw no case against him; but Collins had got rid of him.[4]

Why were Keston, Harris, Grove and Henderson appalled? One reason was immorality, officials taking mistresses, as they did in Sydney. Often they lived faithfully with these women in long-term partnerships, but the morality of the day saw this as wrong. These men were ignoring moral conventions, acting as if rules did not apply to them, setting a bad example. Governors Collins, Lord and Sorell lived with women unmarried, as did many of their subordinates.

Keston and co were also appalled by corruption and hypocrisy. Collins himself was honest – he died owning only two shillings and eightpence – but he ignored dishonesty in others and favoured his officers and marines. Knopwood even criticised him, once, in his diary.

Fraternisation between convicts and free men was forbidden: two sinners received a hundred lashes for drinking together – and Collins 'that same morn breakfasted with a convict and his wife by the name of Mathew Powers – she always lives at the Col. [Collins'] table'.[5] One rule for the rich ...

Keston praised the next governor, Edward Lord, for not condemning people without a trial and for stopping the marines patrolling the streets with loaded pistols, confining people in the guard house at will, as they had under Collins.[6] But despite this, Lord was a major offender: his enduring and appalling dishonesty is described in the companion volume to this book, *Corruption and Skulduggery*.

In charge of government stores, a string of commissaries had many chances to defraud both the government and other people. Many took them. The initial commissary, Fosbrook, had two clerks, Francis Shipman and John Boothman. Transported for embezzling from their employers, they had form – but no one else was literate enough for the job. Rumours about Fosbrook circulated, but no action was taken until Shipman was dismissed. He returned to England and in hope of reward spilled the beans.

Shipman's story was electrifying – not necessarily entirely true, but he did give it on oath. As early as 1806, he said, a captain arrived with a cargo of damaged rice and bribed Fosbrook with the equivalent of his annual salary to buy it. Later it was condemned and destroyed. The commissariat accepted all kangaroo meat that hunters brought in, often far more than was needed – again, for a bribe? If unused, it was condemned – once 2000 lbs (907 kg) was destroyed. But the British government had to pay for it. Boothman forged receipts, was suspected, absconded, caught and confessed, but nothing happened. Fosbrook continued to pay on the receipts and fabricated transactions to cover them. He stole spirits and kept for himself a payment for government cattle. John Wade, the chief constable, was paid four times the going rate for 200 kangaroo skins which were never delivered to the store. All these frauds were 'committed with impunity, thinking the Distance secures them from Detection'.[7] Horrified London authorities instructed Macquarie to investigate.

Governor Macquarie, Van Diemen's Land's overlord, arrived in Sydney in 1810. An honest, competent man, for the next decade he tried to enforce law and order in the island, endeavouring to make inadequate governor after inadequate governor do his duty. He quickly replaced Lord with a man from his own regiment, Captain John Murray. Macquarie instructed him to stop smuggling, observe strict economy, build a barracks, establish a police force, enforce religious observance 'and exert yourself to the utmost in exciting the Inhabitants to Sobriety and industry, religion, and Morality'.[8] Murray ignored him, starting by permitting smuggling. Then his wife left him, first for a lieutenant, then, when Murray sent the lieutenant to Sydney, with the judge advocate – who was described by Macquarie as 'much addicted to low Company, totally Ignorant of Law, and a very troublesome, ill-tempered Man'.[10]

One of Murray's clerks told Keston that no accounts were kept. He (the clerk) had nothing to do but make out a few bills, draw the money, give some to his master and keep the rest himself. Instead of governing, Murray enjoyed drinking, gambling and paying with regimental money: 'continually in a State of Inebriation & Stupidity & allowing all manner of Vice to be carried on'.[11]

Gossip (via Keston) had it that Edward Lord accused Fosbrook of paying his mistress, Fanny Ankers, for over nine tonnes of wheat that had not been received in the store. Fosbrook was ordered to Sydney for trial, but he took two settlers who swore they delivered the wheat, and two clerks who swore they received it. It cost Fosbrook more to bribe the witnesses to lie than the price of the wheat, wrote Keston, 'but you can get plenty in this Country to swear Black is white & that white is no Colour at all for a few Pounds'. Fosbrook was acquitted. Lord's friend Matthew Bowden told Lord (his underlining): '<u>Murray utterly denies any knowledge of the transaction</u>' (so Bowden and Lord believed Murray was involved in the scam).[12]

Understandably wanting to know what was happening at the Derwent, Macquarie paid a visit. After several dinners with local gentlemen – so he heard all the gossip – Macquarie replaced Murray. In 1814 Murray's regiment was ordered away and he sailed off, leaving huge debts.

Major Andrew Geils came next, another officer from Macquarie's regiment whose honour and integrity Macquarie praised. Alas, Geils'

"THIS IS THE SPOT FOR A BARRACKS"
Governor Macquarie to Captain Antill, on the site of Anglesea Barracks, 2nd Dec. 1811.

The British Empire takes over. Governor Macquarie visited Hobart in 1811. This painting shows him choosing a site for a barracks but also, generally, depicts the might and confidence of the British Empire, doing what they like with someone else's country
(Army Museum of Tasmania, Anglesea Barracks, photograph by Rob Blakers)

main interest turned out to be his own career. He was granted and bought land, appropriated vast amounts of spirits, hardware and grain from the government stores and had no fewer than 29 convicts working on his property, while making no progress in public works. 'A Man of weak judgement, extremely venal and rapacious', wrote Macquarie, 'and always inclined to sacrifice the interests of the Public to his own sordid and selfish views'.[13]

Geils and Fosbrook quarrelled, charging each other with embezzlement. In 1814 they appeared in Sydney for trial. Fosbrook, a civilian, was court-martialled for embezzling large quantities of material from the store and, specifically, giving Daniel Ankers (his mistress's husband) 270 pounds of iron, thus defrauding His Majesty of £553. Fosbrook defended himself. How could he, a gentleman with the King's commission, be guilty of fraud? Why would he endanger his career for 'the trifling object of 270 Pounds of Iron'? He was found guilty, dismissed and ordered to repay the £553.[14] If all, or even some, of the claims again him were true, he got away lightly with years of serious fraud for which a working-class man would have been executed.

Geils was tried by a military court, judged by five brother-officers. His defence was masterly: long, rambling and numbingly boring, not answering the question, throwing dust in the judges' eyes, blaming others, appealing to the wisdom of the court and stout denial – though with the same basic argument as Fosbrook: how could he, a gentleman and an officer, be guilty of such crimes? He was acquitted without a stain on his character, but Macquarie did not believe it.[15]

Meanwhile, at **Port Dalrymple**, Governor Paterson also established a successful colony. Himself honest, he was easily led and more interested in botany than administration. Of his subordinates, Dr Mountgarrett was shady, taking advantage of any

One of the many little beaches down the Derwent estuary where illicit goods could be landed unnoticed
(Mary Morton Allport, Beach below Sandy Bay, TA AUTAS001139593768j2k)

An unnamed man painted by Thomas Bock, looking like a well-to-do member of the elite, confident that whatever he does, his punishment will not be too severe (TA, AUTAS001124066788)

opportunity; Kemp was a rogue; Anderson had a convict mistress and was ineffectual; and admirable and honest Lieutenant Piper did most of the actual work.

In 1809 Paterson was succeeded by Captain John Brabyn (1809–10), an able and honest man who followed instructions and pressed on with government buildings – the best of a poor lot, but only briefly in office.[16] Then came Major Gordon (1810–12), a gullible, none-too-bright officer who believed chance arrival Jonathan McHugo in his preposterous claim that the British government had appointed him governor. Gordon actually handed over power.[17] When McHugo continued to Sydney Macquarie quickly had him declared in a state of 'Outrageous Insanity', and as quickly replaced Gordon with Captain Ritchie – but only for a few months, for in 1812 the north and south of the island were united. The capital and therefore the governor were at Hobart, with a commandant running local affairs in the north.

There were scoundrels among the northern officials. Keston claimed that Richard Dry, ex-convict storekeeper, 'knew how to make Hay while the Sun shined', but if so he was certainly not alone.[18] Corporal John Jubal Sutton became commissary, but died in 1812 leaving huge debts to the government from overdrawing bills on the commissary far beyond his purchases. There were no accounts, so nothing could be checked.[19]

Peter Mills, a naval midshipman, became surveyor at Port Dalrymple in 1807 and married Jennifer Brabyn. A poor surveyor – fair enough, as he had no training – he made mistakes and Macquarie, visiting in 1811, received many complaints of bad surveying leading to boundary disputes and even litigation. This was embarrassing – Mills was not only a senior official but was Brabyn's son-in-law. Macquarie dismissed him but allowed him to become a settler on his land grant.

By early 1814 Mills was deeply in debt. To escape their creditors, he and commissary George Williams formed a bushranging gang with some convicts. They were 'active and desperate', Macquarie told London, plundering settlers' houses and driving off their cattle: 'atrocious robberies and depredations'. However, tiring of life in the bush, after eight months they gave themselves up. They were gaoled, but escaped after Jennifer Mills plied the guard with rum. Mills was discovered hiding under a heap of straw in a stable. He was tried in Launceston – when he gave information about officials misusing government stock – and then in Sydney, but the Launceston commandant had omitted to send evidence, and he was discharged. Macquarie let him return to his family, but in 1816 he left them and went to sea – where he vanished, presumed drowned.[20]

Meanwhile, Macquarie was appalled at Mountgarrett who was associated with 'many doubtful activities' – cattle stealing, misappropriating stores and medicine, not repaying debts and helping Mills, the bushranger. In 1815 Mountgarrett too was tried in Sydney and (as usual) acquitted. 'There is not a more despicable man in the

Colony', wrote a newcomer in 1825; 'every person despises him.' He died insolvent in 1828.[21]

Were there *any* honest officials in the colony? Even the Quaker George Harris joined the rest of them, signing (with the Rev. Knopwood) a claim for expenses for Collins' funeral which they must have known was wildly exorbitant.[22] The most I can say after reading every source I can find is that some men, like Brabyn and Piper, were not mentioned as involved. But in the absence of both accounts and most other records, it is impossible to say.

FLIGHT OF FANCY: GOVERNOR DAVEY LEAVES ENGLAND

'His intended departure from England he concealed from his family, by whom it was discovered accidentally: they reached the vessel by extraordinary exertions, and in neglect of all the usual preparations for the voyage.' West, *History of Tasmania*, vol.1, p.50

Scene: The deck of the Minstrel, *Southampton, 4 June 1812.*
Captain Reid and Lieutenant-Governor Thomas Davey chat on deck.

Captain: A fair day, sir, tide and wind just right. The women – the prisoners – are all on board, and we can weigh anchor in half an hour.
Thomas (*exuding wafts of rum*): Excellent, excellent!
Captain: Hallo, what's this? A boat coming out? That'll be last-minute despatches for you, sir.
Thomas (*cheerfully*): Work, work, work, that's my life!
Captain: No, it's a woman and a child.
Thomas: Oh, da – ahem. (*gloomily*) My wife and daughter.
Captain Reid darts him a quizzical look.
The boat reaches the ship, and the women scramble up on board.
Thomas (*used to making the best of things*) Margaret! And, er …
Margaret (*sotto voce*): Lucy.
Thomas: Lucy, that's right! Welcome, my dears! Come to bid me farewell?
Margaret (*meekly*): We'd like to come with you, Thomas. There's no money left and my brother can't afford to keep us on a clergyman's stipend …
Thomas (*hastily*): Yes, yes, well, better come along, I suppose.
Captain: We have no spare room, but – (*resignedly*) where is your baggage, madam?
Margaret: Just this little bag. We only just heard, accidentally, that Thomas was leaving …

Thomas (*hastily again*) We can buy things on the way.

Captain (*appalled*): But the first stop is Rio, months away! And the only other women on board are convicts! They have nothing suitable for ladies!

Thomas: Don't worry, they'll cope. They always do.

5. THE NADIR: GOVERNOR DAVEY

One of the few sagacious moves of the next governor, Thomas Davey, was to make friends with Robert Knopwood. The colony's only diarist, Knopwood showed him sympathetically: doing his duty as a magistrate, hosting balls, inviting the diarist to dinner with his family, going to church, praising the sermon. On New Year's Day Knopwood preached on the death of the old year and the birth of a new one, a comfortable topic with no calling of sinners to account or any other upsetting ideas. Knopwood knew on which side his bread was buttered. (Another popular sermon was 'Submission to Governors'.)[1]

Thomas Davey in his younger days. Sadly, there is no portrait of 'gaudy' Margaret Davey
(TA, PH30-1-640)

Davey was the son of a provincial mill-owner so not of the elite, but he had one enormous advantage: the patronage of his member of parliament, Dudley Ryder. With his help Davey obtained a commission in the marines, so rose socially to be an officer and gentleman. I see him as a charming, unprincipled conman, excellent at his role of kindly old buffer. He married Margaret, who in 1799 gave birth to their only child, Lucy.

Ryder rose to prominence and power, holding important political positions, made Earl of Harrowby. A word from him saved Davey from being cashiered as a bankrupt. After Collins' death, Davey asked Harrowby for the position of governor of Van Diemen's Land. Macquarie wanted an experienced officer capable of 'improving and Conducting an infant Colony to Maturity', and recommended competent Joseph Foveaux.[2] But Harrowby, much more influential than a mere colonial governor, recommended Davey. 'I understand that the situation which he sollicits, is one in many respects so disagreeable, that he is not likely to have many competitors', Harrowby wrote frankly. 'I shall feel much gratified in being instrumental in procuring [him] an honourable and what he considers a comfortable retreat.'[3] Davey was appointed.

Davey happened to be in gaol for debt, but charmed his way out. Having misused funds while serving as paymaster, he owed the government a considerable sum. The Colonial Office heads must have sighed: another dud foisted on them by politicians. They stopped his salary until his debt was repaid, and took the extraordinary step of warning Macquarie not to let him abuse his authority. Macquarie was horrified to find Davey a 'frivolous buffoon' who enjoyed rough humour: 'his countenance was strongly marked, and, by a peculiar motion of the scalp, he delighted to throw his forehead into comical contortions'. Very humorous. Macquarie limited Davey's power as much as he could – but this had little effect since Davey took no notice.[4]

Colonists loved telling their 'Mad-Tom-the-Governor' stories, especially of his arrival in Hobart. After landing, Tom remarked that it was at hot as Hades and took off his coat. Scandalously, *in his shirt sleeves*, he walked to Government House, with one version having him pause for a rum at the nearest pub.[5] Gentlemen just did not appear in their shirt sleeves. The elite were shocked.

Later, defending his rule, Davey said when he arrived he found 'the most deplorable derangement': hardly any records, the commissariat pillaged, disunion among the officers, little regard to religion, no security in the goal, no barracks for the troops, no hospital for the sick, and the bush infested with bushrangers. How could he govern?[6] This was probably accurate. Could any governor have succeeded? On the other hand, could any governor have done worse? At least Foveaux might have tried.

Colonists were not impressed with Davey. 'We see no formality with him', wrote settler Thomas Keston. Many people asked favours,

> & he never sent any one away with bad Hopes for he told all that asked him for any thing that they should have it but he did not tell them when ... he seldom performed any promise, he was a Giant in Promises but a Pigmy in performances

To make matters worse, he was an alcoholic: 'he did not mind who the Devil governed as long as he got his Bottle & Glass':

> this amphibious Soldier after he had landed a week or two must mount a Horse to take a ride to New Town, two Miles from Hobart Town & his Honor having a midling Cargo of his well beloved Grog on Board & the young Steed not being used to have such a Composition at the Helm rolling on his Back, thought proper to spill him off without any respect to his Rank.[7]

The medical certificate agrees: fall at New Town at 10 a.m. a week after he landed, broke his right leg. Drunk at that hour! The only other colonist who wrote about this period, John Pascoe Fawkner, said much the same: Davey was kind but more engaged in planning drinking bouts than ruling, and completely led by his 'tools or toadies'.[8]

His drinking activities were legendary. On state occasions such royal birthdays he would stand at the gate of Government House with a cask of rum, handing out drinks to passers-by. Convivial, of course, but ... He was most famous for his carouses in the bush. No invitations: anyone could turn up, convict or free. Davey would sit in front of a roasted pig with a tub of his favourite drink, 'Blow-My-Skull'. This consisted of boiling water, sugar, lime or lemon juice, ale, port, rum, brandy or any other alcohol going. (It must have tasted dreadful.) Guests had to drink when Davey ordered:

"No heeltaps!" called out the governor in a voice of authority, and the unfortunate stranger was at once 'hors de combat'; while the governor having an impenetrable cranium, and an iron frame, could take several goblets of the alcoholic fluid, and walk away as lithe and happy as possible, attended by an orderly who could scarcely preserve his equilibrium.[9]

Another 'humorous' story told of how a drunk man unbuttoned his clothes and turned his bare flesh towards Government House. Davey 'fired at the naked part of the man and actually struck him not mortally but severely', and it was six months before the man could work again.[10] This barbaric deed was not at all funny from the man's point of view – but he was a convict, a peasant, a man the upper classes could laugh at.

Excusing Davey's antics, historian John West wrote that 'Character can never be fairly judged when separated from the circumstances in which it is developed'; 'etiquette of office' was folly in the infant society. Yet West also wrote that when Collins lived some order was maintained, but under Davey the British flag flew over a society unlike any other.[11] Nevertheless, West's history has encouraged historians to view the early settlement indulgently.

What were respectable Margaret and Lucy Davey doing during all this carousing? Presumably looking the other way, as ladies were meant to do. Womenfolk were responsible for entertainments, and the balls at Government House were praised, at least in the sycophantic government newspaper. So Davey's most successful actions were organised by his wife. West described her as meek but, rather surprisingly, an early settler told Jane Franklin that she was a 'very gaudy dresser'.[12]

Davey looked on his new job as a 'retreat': pleasant, involving no work. Macquarie tried his hardest to bring him to a sense of duty. He soon realised that Davey ignored instructions, did little governing, allowed people to smuggle vast amounts of alcohol, and far exceeded his powers by favouring his friends and spending public money extravagantly. Writing in 1831, journalist Henry Melville opined that though Davey was popular, that was no criterion of merit. He had too many eccentricities, and he permitted those he governed to hold the laws lightly.[13]

Bushranging was alarming, but Davey did little to stop it.[14] Michael Howe's gang was notorious: heavily armed, threatening people's lives,

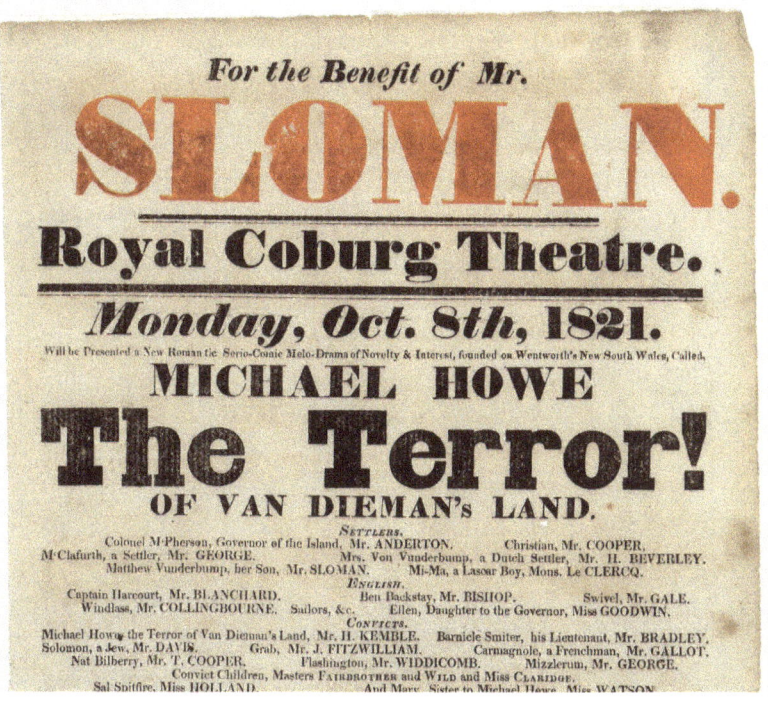

Michael Howe the bushranger fitted British stereotypes of lawless Van Diemen's Land (TA Allport Library and Museum of Fine Arts SD_ILS:1172914)

stripping houses of goods, raping women. Howe wrote to Davey as an equal, calling himself 'Lieutenant-Governor of the Woods', with Davey 'Lieutenant-Governor of the Town':

> We have Thought proper to write these Lines To You As we have Been Kept In the Dark so long And We find it his Only to Keep Us Quiet Untill By some Means or another you think you can get Us Betrayed. But We will stand it No Longer We Are Now Determined to have it full And Satisfactory Either for or Against Us... We think Ourselves Greatly Injured By the Country At large ...

An astonishing letter from an outlaw to the governor. Passing the buck, Davey told Howe that only Macquarie could pardon them: 'good conduct is the Surest way to Favor'.[15] This had no effect.

Smuggling too was notorious – avoiding paying customs duties, the government's main source of revenue. It was extremely difficult to stop.

The Derwent and the Tamar have many little bays and inlets where it was easy to land spirits, and the authorities did not have the manpower to patrol them. Macquarie told Davey:

> The series of notorious, disgraceful, and daring instances of Smuggling, which have recently taken place at the Derwent, far exceed anything that has ever yet occurred there or at any of the other Dependences of this Territory. This Traffick has arrived at a most alarming Pitch of late ... [you must check] that extraordinary propensity to smuggling, which appears to pervade all ranks and descriptions of People at the Two Settlements in Van Diemen's Land.[17]

One can visualise Davey tossing this letter in the fire as he reached for another glass of rum. 'In no part of the world is Smuggling carried on to a greater extent' than in Hobart Town, wrote its naval officer in 1817.[18]

Despite everything, no criticisms of Davey went back to London from the colony. Those benefiting from his misrule were not going to complain.

Van Diemen's Land was seen as the home of curious animals. Based on paintings by George Harris and Ferdinand Bauer (TA, AUTAS001131822348)

But by 1816 Macquarie had had enough. After three years of Davey's appalling government, or non-government, he told Lord Bathurst, his superior in London, that it was his painful duty to expose the man. He was idle, incompetent and totally incapable of carrying out the duties of his position. He spent almost his entire time drinking and ignored Macquarie's orders, his 'constant state of intemperance rendering him indifferent to them'. He was venal and corrupt, privy to smuggling. The government was brought into contempt. He should be immediately replaced. Not even Harrowby could save Davey now. In April 1817 Bathurst announced a replacement.[19]

Meanwhile, **Davey's subordinate officers** were under no sort of control. Corruption is insidious: if everyone else is doing it, unrebuked, unpunished, making money hand over fist, it can be hard to stand out.

Surveyor George Evans took bribes, as will be shown in chapter 6. Doctors were unimpressive: Dr Younge was 'the most unfit and disgraceful person in medical service', only just worse than Dr Luttrell, a 'wretched old man ...a very factious, seditious and unprincipled fellow'.[21] But the wooden spoon goes to Patrick Hogan, the commissary, 'addicted to inebriety ... so as to render him totally unfit for doing his Duty'. Negligent and dishonest, he used the commissariat as a milch cow to benefit himself. A scam was to issue receipts for his private expenses that looked like government documents, so their recipients expected the government to pay. He still ran up huge debts.[22]

Edward Lord was best friends with Davey and Hogan, and Davey protected them both. People outside the magic circle complained that Hogan would not pay their accounts, but Davey did nothing.[23] Then the captain of an American ship demanded cash for his cargo. Hogan had bled the commissariat dry and there was none. Lord lent him £400 and Hogan's storekeeper, ex-convict William Maum, signed vouchers claiming Lord had provided £400 worth of wheat for the stores when he had not.[24] The story came out and Macquarie dismissed Hogan, ordering him to pay his debts by selling his property, and to produce accounts for his time as commissary. Hogan could not.[25]

As acting commissary, Macquarie sent William Broughton to fix 'the shameful abuses that have so long disgraced the Commissariat

Department at the Derwent'.[27] Intelligent, honest and competent (a most unusual mixture), Broughton was shocked. 'The roguery, which has been carried on at this illfated Settlement, is beyond all calculation', he told Macquarie. 'Crimes are committed with the greatest impunity, while detection is most difficult to come at; but, how can it be expected otherwise, when the very heads, with but few exceptions, set the very worst examples.' He mourned 'the want of energy on the part of the Government of this Colony (if so it can be called)' and the lack of shame: people 'boast of their iniquity and glory in their misdeeds'.[28]

Lord tried to bribe Broughton to get him onside, but Broughton was no Fosbrook or Hogan.[29] He set about reforming the commissariat, announcing he would receive wheat and meat only from people who produced them. Middlemen like Lord were cut out. Lord was not going to put up with this. Discovering several minor mistakes, he accused Broughton of trading illegally. A court of enquiry, composed of Lord's friends, found there were grounds for an enquiry, and Broughton was sent to Sydney for a court martial. Macquarie, furious, exonerated him, but Lord had got rid of him.[30] The new commissary, Thomas Archer, became Edward Lord's good friend ...

A major problem for which Davey cannot be blamed, but in which he took part, was an irresponsible justice system. Those in power punished as they wished, since no one had the power to stop them. A magistrate tied a carter who mistreated his bullocks to the wheel of his wagon and inflicted 300 lashes. In Launceston, Mountgarrett ordered a blacksmith flogged for presenting his bill. When Davey ordered a free man to be lashed, his victim objected that free men could not be flogged. Davey answered with a 'pleasant jest' that he could try, and did. Officials, concluded John West, saw the limitations of civil government as absurd, 'and considered power as the standard of right'.[31] There were some fair magistrates but, with this capricious system, justice could never be certain.

Port Dalrymple was ruled locally by a series of commandants, the usual army officers. In 1814 Captain John McKenzie arrived. 'We are all as well as this Seat of Solitude and Dullness will permit', he wrote to Davey. 'Almost every one here, is, *I firmly believe, more or less, a Villain!*' Complaints swirled round: charges against this person and that – malicious charges, threats, reported perjury, unjustified dismissals – although not everyone, if indeed anyone, can be believed.[32] McKenzie sounds not far wrong in his assessment.

Macquarie, disgusted with McKenzie abetting the bushranger Mills, replaced him with Major James Stewart. Out of the frying pan into the fire: 'a perfect demon', Stewart quarrelled with everybody, stole police records, burned down the military barracks, ignored Macquarie's orders 'and in short, played the very devil'. He made illegal issues from the government store to 'worthless and undeserving characters', and illegally punished three soldiers without trial.[33] Macquarie speedily replaced him with Major Gilbert Cimitiere, a competent commandant.

With Davey, Hogan and Lord in the south and McKenzie, Stewart and Mountgarrett in the north, it was a dreadful time for the whole colony, a period of lawlessness, violence, fraud and unparalleled theft of all sorts. Probably the worst four years in Tasmania's history, it was a dark and grim example of appalling colonial misrule. It was an inversion of the ideal colony, a dark mirror image.

How ordinary settlers managed to keep going is hard to imagine. Presumably they retreated home in survival mode, doing their best to get by. Many joined in the corruption, because they wanted to share the proceeds, or were sympathetic or intimidated. The most laudable people in the colony, the honest and industrious ones, were ex-convicts and soldiers with smaller land grants, who worked away on their farms in just the way the British government wanted – despite the appalling examples set by their 'betters'. But because they were working-class, the elite took little notice of them.

A string of inadequate governors: why? From 1803 until 1818, British settlements in Van Diemen's Land were ruled by eleven lieutenant-governors or commandants. Almost all suffered from one or more of: weak character, dishonesty, drunkenness, incompetence, idleness, immorality, setting aside the laws or lunacy. The exception was Brabyn, whose rule was sadly short. Many of their subordinate officials were tarred with the same brush. Sorell, the next governor, was little improvement.

Why were so many so inadequate? Surely it was not just chance – Sydney, while not scraping the bottom of the barrel with a Davey, was not much better in its first two decades. The governors were all army or marine officers. They had a high opinion of themselves: they were the army, they could do anything. They scorned civilians, the people they were ruling. They were sent to govern without appropriate resources of infrastructure and personnel. They had little training or experience in civilian administration. They could be fairly certain that if their sins were found out, they would be treated leniently. Was this enough to explain their behaviour?

More than just poor governing, many of these men cast aside standards they might have been expected to maintain and plunged into hedonistic lives. Was it the lack of supervision, of anyone encouraging the type of upright life Jane Austen's characters were leading in England? Was governing a colony of criminals just too difficult, so they gave up? Did the British government, pre-occupied with the Napoleonic Wars, care so little about the colony that anyone would do to govern it – that did seem the attitude when Davey was appointed.

It seems amazing that the British Empire continued and even flourished when its colonies were so mismanaged. Perhaps the supreme and appalling irony is that one justification for its existence was that it was enlightened, bringing civilisation to the uncivilised – including the unfortunate Aboriginal inhabitants. Instead they were subject to misrule, chaos and brutality.

FLIGHT OF FANCY: GETTING A LAND GRANT

Scene: The Hope and Anchor pub at the Hobart waterfront, 1817
Jonathan Taylor walks in, orders a rum, and turns to the man beside him.

Jonathan: I've just arrived. How are things here?

Man: On the whaler, are you? Staying long?

Jonathan: Not sure. Bit of work to do on the ship. Not much to see here, is there?

Man: : Well, no. But there's pickings.

Jonathan (*ears pricking up*): Pickings?

Man: : You can get free land. You just ask for it.

Jonathan: What would I do with land here? I'm a sailor, not a farmer.

Man (*slowly, as to an idiot*): Sell it.

Jonathan: But why would they give me land to sell?

Man: Look. You go to the governor, say you're really impressed with the potential of this place [*Jonathan looks startled*], you'd love to settle and farm, could you have some free land? You might have to slip him a little something. Then you say you're just going back home to get the family, can't leave them behind, but you'll be back in a flash. You get the land, you sell it, you leave with the money.

Jonathan: Really? Would it work?

Man: Happens all the time.

6. SLIGHT IMPROVEMENT: GOVERNOR SORELL

The next governor was also a political appointment, but more able than the last. Like Davey, William Sorell became a close friend of Knopwood and featured positively in his diary. Every historian since has seen Sorell as a good governor – competent, much loved – but, looking closely into his term, cracks appear in the façade.

William Sorell was born in 1775 into an army family and joined up at fifteen. Family history depicts him as a wild young man, a friend of the notoriously dashing and extravagant prince regent. For years he carried on a 'rough trade' affair with a London fruiterer, Harriet, and sired seven children.[1] One imagines his father, appalled, laying down the law (presumably he held the purse-strings): William was to stop his dreadful way of life, marry this woman who had borne him so many children out of wedlock, and accept a position at the Cape of Good Hope, away from such ruinous influences. At any rate, William did marry Harriet, settled money on her and went to the Cape – by himself.

There he met William and Louisa Kent. Louisa was descended from King James II – on the wrong side of the blanket, but any royal ancestry gave one some cachet. She was raised as an aristocratic lady, elegant, accomplished and charming. But there was little money, and she married mere Lieutenant Kent. In 1807 she and their two children accompanied him to the Cape. Sorell, who posed as a bachelor, was kind to the young lieutenant and more than kind to his wife. Onlookers were surprised: Sorell seemed reserved and serious, 'a rather grave middle-aged man'. However, passion seethed behind the gravity. Louisa bore two more children, with Sorell at his special request godfather of the second.

In 1811 the Kents were posted back to England. Sorell followed, and Louisa left her husband for him.[2] Scandal! When the same thing happened in Jane Austen's *Mansfield Park*, written about this time, the culprits found themselves entirely cut off from respectable people. William had to resign from the army and lost his income. Louisa bore three more children and William, pushed for money, stopped supporting Harriet and their family.

Then Davey died and Sorell was appointed governor of Van Diemen's Land. Did the prince regent and/or the families involved pull

Governor William Sorell (TA LMSS754/1/91)

strings, only too keen to see William and Louisa to take their scandal to the other side of the world? 'When [Sorell] went to have his farewell audience of the Prince Regent, the Prince pulled a diamond ring from his finger and gave it to him as a keepsake. That ring was afterwards my mother's wedding ring', recalled a descendant.[3]

William and Louisa travelled as a married couple with four children (several had died). In Sydney, in early 1817, Macquarie was thrilled. Sorell had 'good Understanding Energy and Firmness', as well as honour and integrity. Everyone liked this affable, competent, 'gentleman-like' governor in Van Diemen's Land too: but then a bombshell arrived. Kent sued William for having a criminal conversation with his wife, as the terminology went. *The Times* reported the case in detail and when the newspaper arrived in Hobart in late 1817, the stunned inhabitants learned that their governor was 'living in Fornication with another Man's Wife'. There was great debate, wrote Thomas Keston, and 'some would have it that if he was not married to her his Majesty's Ministers would not have appointed him Lt Govr of such a Colony where the strictest Morality was wanting'.[4] But *The Times* report was irrefutable.

Governor Collins too had lived with another man's wife, unpunished; and nothing happened to Sorell either, at first. Able, friendly, he had had time to make himself appreciated, and no one in Van Diemen's Land complained publicly. Macquarie, himself strictly moral, kept silent. Possibly relief at having a competent man in Hobart at last overcame any scruples, with other thoughts running through his mind: Sorell's private life is his own affair; upsetting the prince regent's protégé would not be good for my career; they must know in London, they read *The Times*, it's up to them to act if they wish …

In Hobart Louisa lived with William and bore his children – altogether she had fifteen, of whom William sired eleven or twelve. In England his wife Harriet asked the government for help. In great distress, crippled by fire, she had to take the children to a dreaded workhouse and two daughters had to work in factories. Shocked, Lord Bathurst, the secretary of state for the colonies, gave her £100 from Sorell's salary. He was sure he was only anticipating Sorell's wishes, he told him. Forced into it, Sorell agreed that Harriet be given £200 annually. But Bathurst could do no more to the protégé of the prince regent. In Hobart, Thomas Keston was horrified at 'the whole account of the scandalous & ungentlemanlike manner [Sorell] seduced the young Woman from her Husband'. He set a bad example to young people, who said: 'have not we as much right to live together as they have we are not sent from England to teach Morality'.[5]

Undeterred – he never seemed to feel much guilt about Harriet – Sorell set about governing the colony. His first achievement was to put down bushrangers, offering rewards for their capture or information about them, punishing settlers known to assist them, increasing the number of constables. Bushranging was curbed, which respectable inhabitants greatly appreciated.

Described as patriarchal rather than despotic, Sorell established more firmly the rule of law – no more flogging free men, for example. He encouraged enterprise and industry, and instructed Major Bell, the engineer, to build the public works that Macquarie had wanted from previous governors. He established a settlement for serious criminals in distant, inhospitable Macquarie Harbour. When Macquarie arrived on a visit in 1821 he said he was thrilled with the progress made under Sorell's leadership. Or, with his career in mind, like Charlotte Collins in *Pride and Prejudice,* he mentioned nothing he could not praise. The inhabitants of Government House did not gain an entry in his diary.[6]

As well as top-quality patronage and competence, Sorell had two other helpful qualities: he was handsome, which never goes astray, and he was popular. The elite was sceptical of popularity – Governor Darling in Sydney wrote bitingly of Sorell, 'The convenient pliancy of his disposition made him a favourite at Van Diemen's Land'[7] – but there's no doubt it can be a huge boon. Sorell was affable, genial, thoroughly *nice*, even to ordinary people – standing by the Government House gate and chatting to people, listening to their problems. He had the gift of being all things to all people: to the prince regent, a fellow carouser; to Louisa, a devoted lover; to colonists, a genial governor; to Macquarie, a competent and obedient subordinate. But to Harriet and their children, who had no power or influence: faithless.

The one thing that would destroy Sorell's career as governor was the British government gaining official knowledge that he was living with another man's wife. Everyone knew this, from newspapers, but London's bureaucrats could pretend ignorance if no one told them *officially*. Sorell's patron outranked Macquarie's, so Macquarie would not complain; the only people likely to object were disgruntled colonists, the leading ones with the self-confidence to write to London. Sorell could not afford to have them offside, and he let them do as they pleased, with no attempt to rein in widespread corruption.

Charles Jeffreys' sketch of Hobart in 1817 with his ship, *Kangaroo*, anchored in the harbour – ready to land its illicit spirits (TA, LPIC147/3/141)

For the first time in the colony's history, however, several of Sorell's leading officials were honest: chief of police Adolarius Humphrey; commissary George Hull; and the officer commanding the troops, engineer and superintendent of convicts, Major Thomas Bell. As well, Bell kept a firm hand on his solders who (according to Keston) had no money-making schemes on the side and did nothing but their duty, '& that is more than can be said of any Regt that has been in these Colonies'.[8]

However George Evans, surveyor, was well known for needing bribes. John Hudspeth, a free settler arriving in 1822, was shocked. 'I understand it is impossible to obtain a satisfactory answer or any useful information from this man without a bribe', he wrote, 'and he is even so worthless that after he has got the money he pays often as little regard to the interest of those who have paid as those who have not'.[9]

Two years later, Roderic O'Connor was equally horrified. He was not prepared to pay a bribe and the Survey Department made choosing a land grant and settling on it extremely vexatious. Evans told him he did not care what the governor said; he, Evans, 'would do as he thought proper and that he could and would prevent any Person taking land, where he did not please'. All this was common knowledge but Sorell supported Evans, saying he entertained too high an opinion of him to listen to any complaints against him.[10] Was he gaining a cut? (There were other suspicious activities. Sorell was lavish with land grants, with some people gaining huge amounts, more than they should have done – why?)

The naval officer and treasurer, John Drummond, was meant to stop smuggling and collect customs dues, the colony's main source of income. He was unenthusiastic, saying he did not have enough resources. Like many people in this story, he had arrived under a cloud: after he married the daughter of a convict, his scandalised father had him posted to Sydney. In 1814 John and Elizabeth, their baby son and Elizabeth's two sisters, Lilias and Isabella, arrived in Hobart. Drummond obtained a land grant but complained he could not develop it owing to bushrangers.[13]

Looking utterly respectable – Isabella Lewis, sister of Lilias McKellar, by Thomas Bock (TA ALMFA SD_ILS:1253085)

In 1817 tongues started to wag as it became evident that Lilias McKellar was pregnant. Then she was 'divested of such appearance', but with no baby. John admitted that Lilias gave birth to a baby which died. An inquest found Lilias guilty of murder, and John and a servant of abetting her. They were tried in Sydney and acquitted for want of evidence (as usual) – but John had clearly had sex with his sister-in-law.[14] Utterly appalled, Macquarie dismissed him. Meanwhile, in 1830 convict Mary McLachlan was executed for the murder of her baby, on much the same evidence that saw gentleman John Drummond acquitted. (John and Elizabeth returned to England; Lilias married a respectable, well-to-do farmer and retired, gratefully I imagine, into private life.) Dr Bromley became the next naval officer, and was later discovered to have embezzled, or at least let be embezzled, a huge sum. Witnesses thought Sorell knew of it and was possibly involved in the scam (see chapter 18).

A few officers stood up to Sorell, but he dealt sharply with them – he might have liked to look merely patriarchal, but had an iron fist under the velvet glove. Surgeon Younge thought him arbitrary and despotic, suspending civil officials without enquiry. Unlike Macquarie's generally courteous letters, Sorell's tend to be pompous. When he felt crossed he sounds like a teacher upbraiding a kindergarten child. Hull tried to run the commissariat honestly and expose prior corruption. Sorell told him: 'If any act of neglect, irregularity, or malversation was known to exist to your predecessors, it was their duty to have reported it; as no such report was made', nothing need be done – as if they would have reported their own malversation! Sorell refused to give Hull a land grant and exiled him to Launceston.[15]

Sorell also quarrelled with the northern commandant, Major Cimitiere. An able and upright administrator (for a change), in 1818 Cimitiere inherited a neglected little colony, most of its population ex-convicts. Some were 'reformed men of good character', but most were an 'unprincipled Sett of people with no regard to morals or religion', according to leading farmer James Cox. Discipline was lax, too many convicts were under little or no control and robberies were frequent.[16] Cimitiere had inadequate supplies and finance, and the difficult problem of being subordinate to both Sorell and Macquarie. In particular, Macquarie ordered him to move the northern capital to George Town, but Sorell favoured Launceston and refused to sign off on construction bills for George Town.

When Cimitiere resorted to desperate measures to obey Macquarie and fund the works, Sorell accused him of abusing his powers. He wrote Cimitiere chiding letters then complained that Cimitiere found them unfriendly and sent 'insubordinate' replies.[17] (I would have too, had I received such infuriating letters.) Sorell said he could not work with Cimitiere; Macquarie found nothing to complain of, but in 1822 Cimitiere was promoted to command his regiment in Sydney.[18] A benevolent man, he received a laudatory address from his settlers, praising him for his impartial and upright conduct and his care for their welfare and the public good, so unlike his predecessors (as they wrote frankly). Keston too praised him highly for his justice and 'energetic Exertions for the Welfare of the inhabitants': he 'looks to nothing but his public Duty, he is not scheming to take away any poor man's farm to enrich himself' (unlike others, implied).[19]

One disgruntled colonist did complain to London: ex-army Captain Anthony Fenn Kemp, now a settler with a large land grant. In 1818 Sorell dismissed him as magistrate, and in retaliation Kemp told Bathurst that Sorell 'lived in Adultery with Mrs. Kent' and was not a fit and proper person to govern the island. But Kemp had been a notorious troublemaker in New South Wales, and Bathurst could accept an assurance from Sorell, the prince regent's protégé, 'repeling [Kemp's] falsehoods and calumnies'.[20]

Perhaps **Sorell's greatest achievement** in being all things to all people was to appear squeaky clean, aborting any effort to challenge this. Some doubted him, privately. Keston noted that Sorell had to pay William Kent £3000, and 'as he was very poor he began to look out which was the best way to make a few Hundreds in a Secret way'. He sold tickets of leave and other concessions.[21] No one else made these claims, but they wouldn't, would they? It's not clear whether Sorell ever did pay Kent.

Sorell could not live in this fantasy world for ever, unpunished for both scandalising contemporary morals and, at the very least, condoning large-scale embezzlement (at most, joining in). Lord Bathurst, his superior, was a strong and upright supporter of the Church of England. When he sent Bigge to enquire into the colonies, Bathurst asked him to look into Kemp's complaint.

Back in London in 1823 Bigge told Bathurst it was true: Mrs Kent 'received the attentions that could only have been claimed by his Wife' (not much to go by as far as Sorell was concerned). The prince regent, now King George IV, perhaps found it embarrassing to shield an adulterer; at any rate, not even his patronage could save Sorell. In 1824 he was replaced.

Outwardly, everyone in the colony grieved – and Sorell's governorship had provided a more settled environment for some progress to be achieved. When his recall was announced a public meeting asked London if he could stay. His supporters gave him plate worth £500, showing their regard for the man who had let them flourish.[22]

Not everyone remembered Sorell in this way. 'Seven years of misrule' was settler George Lloyd's description. The grandson of free settler Joseph Cato told of his family coming to the rugged, beautiful island of Tasmania: lawless and dangerous, the home of 'bushrangers, adventurers and the scum of the earth. It was administered by dissipated officials appointed under George the Fourth's regency, when British court life descended to an all time low'.[23] A review of the colony's history in 1827 recalled the period before 1824 as one of drunkenness and debauchery. People 'gloried in shame' and vice in the management of public affairs were apparent to every intelligent person.[24] Possibly exaggerated – but the author had lived through the period.

Sorell received a pension but no further employment and lived quietly with Louisa and their children – and refused to let a daughter marry, saying it was her duty to look after her parents.[25] What to make of him? My conclusion is: a competent and streetwise man, gregarious and pleasant when it suited him, but stopping at little to obtain his own ends.

7. ABORIGINAL TASMANIANS

In 1642 the earliest European to visit Van Diemen's Land, Abel Tasman, saw evidence of inhabitants, but decided the island had nothing to offer Europeans. The inhabitants were left undisturbed for another 150 years. From the 1770s various French and British explorers arrived. While some of the French saw the inhabitants as perfect examples of Rousseau's noble savage, 'primitive' people living in peace and happiness, uncorrupted by 'the vices caused by civilisation', the British believed in the Great Chain of Being, which ranked the world's people according to their activities and property. The Aboriginal people, nomadic, with few possessions, were at the bottom and therefore scorned.

Since they left little obvious impact on the landscape, the British government assumed the 'uncultivated' land was there for the taking. The invaders arrived in 1803–04 with instructions to treat the indigenous inhabitants kindly and live in amity, with everyone under the protection of British law. But it was just words. The British government must have known (had they thought about it, which they probably did not) that colonisation meant Europeans driving the original inhabitants off their land.

John West in his *History of Tasmania* called Tasman the 'harbinger of death', with Aboriginal people doomed the moment he sighted the island.[1] Possibly. But (as in Sydney) they were certainly doomed when the first Europeans arrived to settle: armed with guns, believing they were superior to 'savages', and thinking the land belonged to the first person to cultivate it. But at the same time they were afraid of the 'savages', only too trigger-happy if they felt threatened.

All too often, meetings ended with violence. In 1804 when a hunting group, including women and children, descended on the settlement at Risdon, the Europeans took fright and fired on them, killing at least three. Reflecting public opinion, West wrote that being shot at like this 'awakened irremediable distrust' in the Aboriginal people.[2] In the north a party led by Adolarius Humphrey met two Aboriginal men. They were friendly at first, but more men arrived and spears were thrown. 'We fired at them and they fled', wrote Humphrey. At least one Aboriginal man was killed. Governor Paterson described meeting about eighty Aboriginal people. He gave them looking glasses and tomahawks and all went

well. Then a group attacked three marines, who 'under the unpleasant alternative of defending themselves', killed one Aboriginal man. Paterson warned colonists to be well-armed – hardly living in amity.[3] We only have the Europeans' self-justifying descriptions and cannot know what actions by Europeans caused, for example, the men Humphrey met to change from friendly to hostile.

The Aboriginal people reacted by moving away from the settlements.

Aboriginal people meet Frenchmen, by an unknown engraver on the Baudin voyage, 1803. The Frenchmen admire a fire, play with a baby and apparently play some sort of game (TA, AUTAS001131822)

White settlement was confined to small areas around Hobart and Port Dalrymple, and there was plenty of land for the Aboriginal people to retreat to, including the excellent hunting grounds of the midlands. Collins was relieved that 'they are not inclined to come our way, which I do not much regret'.[4] This was a typical reaction: ignore them as much as possible.

Colonists labelled them gentle and affable, even shy, and right up until 1824 most took astonishingly little notice of them. The volume of *Historical Records of Australia* covering Van Diemen's Land from 1812 to 1819 has only five brief mentions of Aboriginal people in its 904 pages.[5] When Bigge made his extensive enquiry in 1820, he too barely mentioned the Aboriginal inhabitants, with only three mentions in hundreds of pages of evidence. Authors of books about the island seldom mentioned the Aboriginal population. When Sorell left the colony in 1824 he wrote a lengthy description for his successor – and he too did not mention them.[6]

There were some friendly encounters. The daughter of a settler was sometimes left in the Aboriginal people's care, she told West, and remembered their kindness. Chaplain Knopwood gave food to those near his house; Hugh Germaine, a kangaroo hunter, often met them in the bush about Bagdad, and described them as people 'in whom there was then no harm'.[7] George Lloyd, a teenager living with his uncle Charles Jeffreys near Sorell, recalled (perhaps through rose-coloured glasses, especially about his throwing ability) playing with Aboriginal boys, with many happy days following the chase with them. They taught him to throw 'the quivering spear and whistling waddie' until he could aim as well as they. The tribe would meet others at a traditional trysting-place under the full moon and hold corroborees, which George watched. He admired their ability to track men and animals, and would invite a friend, Beenac, to a breakfast of mutton chops, damper and tea, then take him to find missing sheep. Beenac could see a trace of sheep invisible to Charles, then follow the flock 'at quick-march pace', no matter what the country, until he found them. It sounds quite egalitarian, George and

An Aboriginal group with a canoe near Schouten Island, also from the Baudin expedition (TA SDILS:641290)

'my dark-skinned friend Beenac' – but George kept his distance. Beenac addressed him as 'Mister Lloyd'.[8]

Collins ordered that anyone firing on Aboriginal people would suffer the penalty of the law. Some people who abused them were punished, according to West. 'A man was severely flogged for exposing the ears of a boy he had mutilated; and another for cutting off the little finger of a native, and using it as a tobacco stopper.'[9]

These crimes point to the dark side of the situation. Some people, out of sight of the authorities, abused the Aboriginal people appallingly. Bushrangers, stockmen, sealers, almost all convicts, ex-convicts or soldiers, who often came from much the same background. Yes, they had brutal lives, enduring not only the hardening effects of squalor, poverty, and violence in Britain and then, unable to knuckle under as convicts, suffering the worst of the convict system. No one had ever treated them well: why should they in their turn?

That might explain but does not excuse their shocking treatment of Aborigines. 'In their intercourse with the natives', wrote West, 'licentious and cruel outlaws committed every species of atrocity which could be suffered by the weak in contact with the wicked.'[10] As we've seen, bushranger Richard Lemon tortured and murdered Aboriginal people, and such activity led to explorer John Oxley writing in 1810: 'from the many atrocious cruelties practised on them by the Convict Bush Rangers', Aboriginal peopled avoided whites.[11] There are plenty more stories of atrocities, but frankly I cannot bear to repeat them.

As well as torturing and murdering, some men seized Aboriginal women and children. In 1815 William Stewart wrote to Macquarie in Sydney about 'a banditti of bushrangers' who worked as sealers in the Bass Strait islands. They robbed settlers, robbed and plundered as they could on the islands, and they captured Aboriginal women whom they kept as slaves:

> hunting and foraging for them, who they transfer and dispose from one to another as their own property; very few of whom ever see their Native Home, being away for numbers of years, and, if they do not comply with their desires or orders in hunting, etc., they by way of punishment half hang them, cut

their heads with Clubs in a Shocking Manner, or flog them most unmercifully with Cats made of Kangaroo Sinews.[12]

('Cats' means whips, cat-o-nine tails.)

But it was not only convicts. Even educated Europeans abused Aboriginal people. Governor Paterson sent Governor King natural curiosities: the skin and bones of a newly discovered animal and 'a very perfect Native's Head, with some birds, etc'.[13] A settler was horrified to see Dr Mountgarrett, a leading officer, 'chasing a well-built young black woman through the shrub on his property with a musket. His horror was not diminished when he saw the doctor, who was being outdistanced, use a charge of shot to bring his victim to a halt.' The settler professed horror; but he was telling the story long afterwards, when this was the correct attitude. It was obviously not always the case. All settlers felt superior towards Aboriginal people, and many treated them brutally. The government occasionally ordered good treatment but, wrote West, 'was either too weak, or too indolent, to visit the guilty'.[14]

Had European settlement remained confined to a small area, perhaps the Aboriginal people could have continued their traditional way of life. Until 1820 they were able to do this, more or less, though their numbers were drastically reduced with some tribes suffering severely – north-eastern people, for example, had a majority of their women abducted by sealers. But in his biography of Aboriginal leader Tongerlongeter, born about 1795, Nicholas Clements estimated that this man grew up living traditionally.[15] It was still possible.

Events on the other side of the world were about to change this. The Napoleonic Wars ended in 1815, leaving Great Britain with unsettled economic conditions, demobbed soldiers flooding the labour market, and rising crime. The government decided to enlist its colonies in a neat solution: transportation and emigration. It increased the number of convicts it sent to Van Diemen's Land, and encouraged free settlement by offering free land grants. Settlers began to flood in. From 1820 onwards, settlement expanded exponentially, driving Aboriginal people off their land. There was nowhere left for the First Tasmanians to go. Conflict was inevitable.

FLIGHT OF FANCY: BIGGE CONFRONTS SORELL

February 1820, and Commissioner Bigge has just arrived in Hobart. Governor Sorell visits him in his lodgings to finalise arrangements for his travel and interviews.

Sorell: My staff have made a tentative list of men to be interviewed, and they will discuss the list with your secretary. To start in, say, a week?

Bigge: Most suitable, thank you.

Sorell: Have you interviewed anyone already, about Van Diemen's Land?

Bigge: I spoke to Mr Kemp in Sydney.

Sorell (*knowing Kemp probably spilled the beans about his domestic situation*) Oh dear! That troublemaker! As man to man, I wouldn't put too much reliance on what he told you.

Bigge: Ah.

Sorell (*feeling his charm is not having the usual effect*) I hope you like our little town. So picturesque, between our beautiful harbour and the majestic mountains! (*desperately hoping the convict gang remembered to clear away the dead dogs on the shoreline*) You'll have noticed our new church. We're very proud of it.

Bigge: : Very creditable, I'm sure.

(*It's hard going but Sorell ploughs on*)

Sorell: I hope you'll join us at Government House for dinner this evening.

Bigge: Is it true that you are not married to the woman with whom you live there?

Sorell (*gulping, not used to such blunt speech*) Well, ah ... that is to say ... well, in a word, yes.

Bigge: In that case, I cannot enter Government House or undertake any social activities with you.

Sorell: But – but – my relationship with my, er, with Mrs Kent is long-standing! To us it is as if we had received the most solemn sanction of matrimony!

Bigge (*coldly*): But you have not done so.

Sorell: No one here minds! They can see past it to appreciate all the benefits I've brought to the colony!

Bigge: I hope we can work together on the commission but I reiterate, I cannot enter Government House.

Sorell (*swallowing*): I am sure we can work together profitably.

Bigge: Ah.

Sorell: Well, er – good afternoon. I will see you tomorrow to show you the town. (*Escapes with relief*)

8. THE BIGGE REPORT: VAN DIEMEN'S LAND IN 1820

In 1817 Lord Bathurst, in charge of the colonies, was worried. New South Wales had been set up to rid Britain of criminals and deter others from crime, but appalling stories were coming back to Britain of convict labourers being treated too well by masters and, even worse, of ex-convicts making fortunes. Transportation was no longer a deterrent. To find out what was going on in the colonies, and how to make transportation more severe, Bathurst set up a commission of enquiry under John Bigge. Bathurst instructed him to examine not just transportation but the colonies' administration, law courts, church activity, trade and revenue.[1]

John Thomas Bigge, looking bland and superior (SLNSW IE546247)

Bigge, an upper-class, professional lawyer, was an intelligent, conscientious man with high moral standards; but he was not brilliant, not a lateral thinker, and was constrained by the prejudices of the upper class. Most of his enquiry concerned the larger colony of New South Wales, where Governor Macquarie had incensed those wishing transportation to be punishment by encouraging convicts, thinking that humane treatment was the best method of reform. He also 'wasted money' on impressive government buildings. Bigge found much to criticise. Historians, admiring Macquarie's policies and loving his buildings, tended to treat Bigge harshly.[2] They also tended to overlook Van Diemen's Land, but the report is a milestone in its history: the evidence Bigge collected gives a picture of the colony in 1820, and his recommendations were important for its development.

Bigge arrived in Sydney in September 1819. He spent three months in Van Diemen's Land, February to May 1820.[3] Knopwood described in his diary how Bigge arrived, was introduced to leading colonists, and spent a week inspecting the colony, going to church and attending dinners held by those leading colonists – Knopwood enjoyed three. Doubtless Bigge heard a mass of enlightening off-the-record information. Sorell did not attend any dinners because of his adulterous liaison, which Bigge quickly discovered. He told Sorell (privately) that he could not enter Government House where Sorell lived in sin.[4] The two men co-operated in the enquiry but were distant socially.

Meanwhile, others (presumably Sorell's staff) were organising Bigge's work schedule. In three months he interviewed eighty witnesses, some more than once. The interviews produced an average of 3.7 pages of evidence each, as reproduced in *Historical Records of Australia*. Knopwood was interviewed four times. The first took 'all the morning' (four hours?), resulting in four pages of transcript. The second, four hours: one page. The third, four and a half hours: nothing – so Bigge and his secretary ignored superfluous information. Later, investigating a dispute between superintendent of police Adolarius Humphrey and merchant Roland Loane, Bigge interviewed Knopwood in the presence of both.[5] Again, nothing.

All eighty witnesses were men except for one woman. Their backgrounds varied from esquires – gentlemen – to ex-convicts but almost all were at least respectable, that great middle- and upper-class desideratum. Their status had often changed from the time they arrived in the colony:

Arrived in colony as	(%)	Interviewed as (%)
Convict	44	0
Free arrival	21	22
Government employee	19	72
Army officer	16	6

Overwhelmingly, interviewees were government employees. Some had other careers such as farming, but it was as government employees that they were interviewed. It is not surprising: Bigge was on government business, and Sorell's staff considered that the colony comprised convicts and their administrators. Free settlers were secondary.

Witnesses answered questions Bigge put, so the enquiry was driven by him. The longest interviews were with senior government functionaries Bigge found competent, honest and intelligent. With seventeen pages was commissary George Hull, clearly honest since he could not afford to educate his children properly, removing one son

What Bigge saw: George Evans' painting of Hobart Town in 1820 (TA ALMFA SD_ILS:95300)

from school at age ten to make way for younger brothers.[6] The other seventeen-pager was Adolarius Humphrey. He had arrived in 1804 but apparently remained honest during the extremely corrupt early period and was now an effective leading public servant. Third with fifteen pages was Major Thomas Bell, in charge of the military, convicts and public works.

Bigge was a shrewd man, able to make sense of a mass of often conflicting evidence. Mild-looking, unthreatening, he seemed to treat all witnesses alike, questioning ex-governor and ex-convict in the same courteous manner ('Be so good as to inform me ...') – even when he must have known, from other evidence, that they were telling him a pack of lies. His questions were wide-ranging. Some were personal ('Your period of Transportation has expired some time I believe? ... Are you married and have you a family?'). Others were direct: to Governor Davey, 'What were the reasons that induced you to permit Mr. E. Lord to import and receive 15,000 Gallons of spirits in the year 1816, taking his Bond for the Duty?'[7] The answers were often clearly false, but Bigge did not challenge them.

Naturally, no witness admitted to any wrongdoing, though many were guilty. They gave excuses. It was someone else's fault. I forget ... I do not know ... I cannot recollect ... I did not think the order applied to me.[8] It's not clear whether they were on oath, but some at least of their words were written down and they signed the transcript (or, if illiterate, made their mark). In New South Wales Bigge was blamed for using evidence in his reports that he did not record and this probably occurred in Van Diemen's Land, much perhaps coming from those dinners.

The first interviewee (in Sydney) was Anthony Fenn Kemp, who provided fifteen pages of evidence in what sounds like a breathless jumble: Sorell had wrongly imprisoned him; magistrates favoured Sorell and his friends; robberies were frequent; sheep-stealing was rampant; smuggling was widespread; many shopkeepers received stolen goods; drunkenness was rife; everyone including the governor used spirits for barter; Sorell was living with another man's wife.[9] Kemp was a well-known troublemaker, but all this must have given Bigge food for thought.

The information colonists gave Bigge must be seen in the context of the population figures:

Van Diemen's Land's British population 1820[10]			New South Wales
Adults			
Came free	16%		7%
Born in colony	4%	Always free 20%	8%
Ex-convicts	13.5%		24%
Convicts	66.5%	All convicts 80%	60%
Total adults	4448		18271
Children	1020		5668
Total population	**5468**		**23939**
Women	20% of adults		21% of adults

A heavily convict, heavily masculine community. Bigge was given these figures but when they were published locally, the breakdown into convict and free was omitted, with only the total given. The colony was sensitive about its convict population and not keen for outsiders to see how overwhelmingly convict the colony was. (The New South Wales figures were reasonably similar – though it had four times the island's white population. Being twenty years older, it had more people born in the colony and more convicts whose time had expired.)

So what was the information colonists gave Bigge? Was it accurate? My impression is that when people were reporting the general situation, they were reasonably accurate, in that most answers seem probable and agree with information given by others. However, if witnesses' interests were involved and, particularly, if their jobs were questioned, they were (naturally) on the defensive, and some omitted facts or told downright lies.

The convict system was the main aim of the investigation. Major Bell told the official story.[11] On arrival, convicts' trades and descriptions were noted. Bell took the most useful for government work, and settlers chose from the rest. Government men worked from five to six hours a day, then worked privately to pay for their accommodation, as there were no barracks. At least Bell hoped they worked. 'Notorious thieves and London Pick Pockets and Housebreakers, do not work at their after hours [which] are principally spent in lounging about the Streets, gambling

An activity Bigge disapproved of: drinking in small pubs like the Black Snake Inn, by Charles Tomkins (TA ALMFA AUTAS001124072919)

and robbing at night.' He punished convicts with a fine, a night in the watchhouse, or a period in the gaol gang making roads; only magistrates could order flogging, a maximum of 200 lashes (down from the 500 of early years).

Convict rations were a pound (440g) of meat and a pound of flour a day, with tea and sugar for good workers. After Bell realised there were 'great mistakes' (corruption) in issuing rations, he kept the list himself. He did not say explicitly but it seems he found little order and method, or records, and installed an organised system, as did Hull in the commissariat.

Bell appointed overseers from convicts who appeared to know their work and behaved well. But they were seldom competent to control other convicts, being 'so connected with each other in feeling ... that they are unwilling to exert proper authority' and rarely informed about robberies. 'If an overseer made himself troublesome by vigilance or activity, he wd. be a marked man amongst the bad Prisoners.' Wouldn't free men be better? asked Bigge. 'Not the Free people, who are in this Country now', replied Bell drily – meaning, they were ex-convicts.

Were ex-convicts good masters of convicts? asked Bigge. Middle-class ones tended to be severe, but 'the Poorer ... live in common with convict servants and make little distinction'. How hard did convicts work? Taking into account their short hours, 'the want of ability in many and of inclination in all', about a third as much as a free man. Even so-called skilled mechanics were indifferent; only a quarter were of any real use. Convicts who behaved well could apply for a ticket of leave, which Bell used as an incentive to encourage work.

Instead of working, convicts robbed. They constantly robbed each other, witnesses told Bigge though, one added, most were not cruel. Government tools were often stolen: 'lost', 'broken', the king's mark erased or cut off. Ticket-of-leave men in particular committed robberies, being under less superintendence. John Wade, chief constable at Pittwater, said many were 'very bad characters'. Because wages were high, they had to work only two days a week.[12] At George Town there was no shop so boat crews brought goods from Launceston. 'This produces a great traffic in Stolen property, which it is very Difficult to prevent', said the lieutenant in charge. 'There are some Lime Burners on the Shores of the River who are supposed to assist in this Traffic.'[13]

Convicts got drunk 'whenever they can get liquor'. 'Last night I found 12 or Fourteen in a Public House near here after Hours', said a constable. In places without a pub, like Pittwater, they were more sober. When they could, they gambled, quarrelled and fought.[14] Private employers found assigned labourers of little use. Some took a pride in their job but it was impossible to get work out of others. Mechanics were sometimes better, but not always. A wall of the new church had already swerved fifteen inches (38cm) and brickwork was badly done, partly because the bricks were badly made.[15]

Most witnesses thought assigned convicts were treated well. One witness allowed a convict to work for himself on payment of five shillings a week, handy income for his employer. Edward Kimberley said he treated his assigned convicts like family; they worked together and ate together.[16] Naturally no one admitted to treating convicts badly, but no one said anyone else did, either.

Could convicts be reformed? asked Bigge. Sensible Humphrey thought many had been, and 'the most abandoned may be made to conduct themselves well by making it in their Interest to do so, and enabling them to acquire Property, so they may feel have something to lose when they commit crimes'. He knew many ex-convicts who 'can be considered as reformed'. Knopwood agreed. He did not think ex-convicts 'would attempt now to do any thing wrong. [They say] "I will not throw a Chance away" '. James Gordon at Pittwater was more sceptical. When ex-convicts became settlers owning land they became more respectful, but in the point of morality there was not much difference, he said. He did not mention the many who did not own land. Everyone agreed that children of convicts were much better behaved and more deserving than their parents.[17]

Did many convicts escape? asked Bigge. No, said officials Bell and Humphrey: all ships leaving port were searched. Yes, said Captain James Kelly, a whaler. Many prisoners escaped on sealing vessels. On four occasions men, sometimes prisoners, had escaped on stolen ships. Others plotted but someone dobbed. Kelly told of how, when a ship was taking on spars at the Huon River, convicts in Hobart planned to sail there and seize it. One of his assigned servants told him and he was working out how to stop the plot – but Superintendent of Police Humphrey had also been told and beat him to it, surprising fourteen of the convicts hidden in the bush.[18]

Female convicts gained a poor press. They were few, with no provision made for them. If settlers requested them, they were assigned; otherwise they were left to their own devices. So they lived with male convicts, which observers thought appallingly profligate; no one considered that they had no other way to support themselves.[19] If they broke the rules, they were punished, at worst by wearing a six-pound (2.7kg) iron collar. In Launceston, convict Alice Blackstone left her husband for the superintendent of convicts, William Leith. Gilbert Cimitiere, the northern commandant, determined to 'crush Vice' and ordered her to walk from George Town to Launceston (53km) wearing the iron collar. Justifying himself, Cimitiere told Bigge that Alice was a 'profligate adultress', a thief who disobeyed his order. Besides, it was only a small iron collar, she was well able to walk to Launceston, and this was 'the usual punishment thro' the Colonies for woman of infamous Character'. (An enquiry exonerated Cimitiere, blaming Leith for seducing Blackstone; Leith said he took her in from purely altruistic motives, to escape her husband's 'Brutal and fatal treatment'.)[20]

While Bathurst might have approved of this punishment, most of the rest was hardly what he wanted to hear: convicts being treated leniently, even well; doing little work, going to pubs, drinking and gambling, eating plenty of meat, robbing, enjoying themselves, even escaping. It does not sound like a deterrent.

Bathurst and Bigge were particularly interested in the social position of ex-convicts, a divisive topic in Sydney. In Van Diemen's Land there were not the commercial opportunities for ex-convicts to amass fortunes, and the few that did made no attempt to create a faction, as in New South Wales. Were they received into 'society'? – an important question for the elite. Judge Edward Abbott named four ex-convicts who lived respectably on their estates, but said he would never 'willingly meet them any where as members of Society'. He had seen one, George Gatehouse, at Government House, at a dinner on a royal birthday. Bigge asked Knopwood whether admitting ex-convicts to 'the Society of Free Persons' had been discussed. Collins had prohibited it, said Knopwood, but governors Murray and Davey 'sat in Company' with ex-convicts. Knopwood defended Gatehouse strongly: 'nobody conducts himself better', 'I shd. have no objection to visit him myself'.[21] Knopwood actually 'sat in company' with many ex-convicts but did not tell Bigge this.

Nor did anyone else. Ex-convicts were part of the fabric of society but no one was going to say so. People skirted round this topic, giving careful answers. Sorell wrote that he followed Bathurst's advice: well-behaved ex-convicts should be readmitted to society, as fair to them and better for the community; but should not be made magistrates, which encouraged a hostile spirit between 'always free' and ex-convicts.[22] No one claimed that Sorell did not 'sit in company' with ex-convicts (the wife of his great friend Edward Lord was one – did he socialise with her?). Bigge himself did not state how many ex-convicts he interviewed, though these included two chief constables, John Wade and Thomas Massey. Bigge knew Wade had been a convict, having asked him directly.

Bathurst asked Bigge to enquire about the administration of justice. All witnesses agreed that the colony needed a criminal court, instead of having to go to Sydney. Wade said bushrangers could only subsist by their links with settlers, but no one was punished because there was no criminal court. Thomas Hayes of Bagdad, for example, 'was the very life and soul of the Bushrangers at one time' but was never punished and was now a constable. Wade and Massey described a weak system, where they knew what was going on but were powerless to act.[23]

Bigge did not ask direct questions about the colony's administration – largely because he did not interview Governor Sorell. Out of what I feel was exaggerated reverence for senior government officials (or their patrons) these were treated leniently. Despite his many failings Davey was barely questioned, his lying answers allowed to stand; Sorell merely replied in writing to accusations against him, with plausible, bland answers. However, Bigge found plenty of material in the commissariat, whose officers had been fleecing the system from day one. He spent much time examining John Boothman, clerk to the commissary, who had admitted to forging receipts and was suspected of much more. 'My conduct has been irreproachable', Boothman assured Bigge.[24]

Bigge tried to get to the bottom of the Hogan affair. As we have seen, Commissary Hogan used commissary funds to pay his debts. He was tried, found guilty and dismissed. But it was not clear how much he embezzled as, scandalously, he could provide no accounts for eleven months. He and his storekeeper, William Maum, blamed each other. Bigge questioned both but could get nowhere as they prevaricated and lied. Undoubtedly other sources told him both men were thoroughly corrupt. Both lived in the colony to ripe old ages, Hogan becoming a respected elder citizen and devoted adherent of the Church of England.[25]

There were few of these in Bigge's day, and he must have realised that the one clergyman, Robert Knopwood, had done little to advance morality, reform convicts or encourage Christianity generally. Yet he questioned him gently, more about what he observed than what he had actually done. For example, was there concubinage? Yes, said Knopwood, a great deal. There was no follow up: no, 'what did you, as the clergyman, to do stop it?' Recently arrived Youl in the north said there was much depravity and dissipation among the convicts and ex-convicts – 'they cannot be worse'. Again, Bigge did not ask him what he did about this. Neither did he take any notice, however, when witnesses said concubinage and adultery were not as great as could have been expected.[26]

As far as trade and industry went, the colony's main product was wheat, with exports to Sydney from 1816; but unless land was close to Hobart or Launceston, wheat did not pay as transport was expensive. The price varied, dropping at good harvests, and most farmers were indebted to merchants. Wade estimated that two-thirds of the farmers in his district, Pittwater, were insolvent. From their dissolute and expensive habits of life? asked Bigge. No, replied Wade: because of the sudden fall in the price of wheat and farmers' difficulty in obtaining cash.[27]

No other enterprise was very successful. Whaling was lucrative but only one local ship took part, owing to heavy British taxes. Sealing had been good but seals were disappearing due to overfishing. People prophesied that Van Diemen's Land would be good for wool, but this trade was not organised. Sheep were kept for meat, with wool thrown away. Could it be made into coarse cloth? Bigge asked. Yes. Had this been done? No. One man boiled down wattle bark to make a substance used for tanning leather – but failed to find a market.[28] Hops and barley grew well; had brewing been tried? Only on a small scale. Had butter or cheese been exported? Never. What about salted meat? A little had been sent to Sydney, but overall, apart from wheat, exports were negligible.[29]

Bigge was no economist. He asked little about merchants, and what he heard about them was negative: their profit was high, many settlers were in debt to them, and they looked after their own interests.[30] He ignored their important role in building up the economy, and also asked virtually nothing about transport, or the problem of having no bank and no stable currency. People bartered for goods, with rum the main currency. Workers were paid with rum, rewarded with rum, gained rum as part of their ration – constables received a pint (600 ml) a week. Was there much intoxication in Launceston, Bigge asked Massey. Yes, Massey replied, but it was not caused by pubs as much as by people being paid in spirits. Sly grog houses were a problem but it was useless to prosecute because of the difficulty of gaining evidence.[31]

Revenue came from customs dues, collected by the naval officer who was also meant to stop smuggling. Since 1818 John Beamont, ill-educated and easy-going, had held the post. Do you send an account of the duties you collect to London? Bigge asked.

A: I do not ...

Q: There are no persons who are specially charged with the Duty of protecting the Colonial Revenue?

A: None; but I have given a Verbal order to the Coxswain of the Lt. Governor's boat to prevent and seize all he may find smuggling.

Q: Have any seizures of smuggled spirits been made during your time?

A: None, except a cask of Spirits ...

Q: No person in the Settlement has any interest but yourself in the protection of the Colonial Revenue ...?

A: None.[32]

Did Beamont recall any smuggling? There was an instance in 1814 ... Has a governor allowed spirits landed without payment of duty? I have known it ... Others told Bigge smuggling was rife, whole cargoes at a time, with perpetrators paying no duty at all or owing the government large sums.[33]

As for leading officers' private lives: Bigge was told about three men 'living in sin'. At Launceston, Captain Barclay and Commissary Walker lived with female convicts, and in Hobart the governor introduced another man's wife as Mrs Sorell. Yes, these instances caused some friction with colleagues though most people did not publicly object.[34]

So much for the topics Bathurst asked Bigge to enquire about. Others came up in general discussion. Bigge heard a great deal about land grants, especially the sins of the Survey Department: unfair treatment at the expense of someone else, grants never measured, illegal sales. Abuses of grant conditions (reside, cultivate and no sales within five years) were so common people told Bigge about them without trying to defend themselves. Knopwood explained that he had sold a grant without cultivating it; Judge Edward Abbott had a 2000-acre grant though 'I never intended to farm Land, and have not done so'. Selling early was widespread, but when Bigge asked about this Evans replied, blatantly lying: 'Several have attempted, but I have always checked it'.[35]

Bigge asked about farming. The climate was favourable, warmer than England and with more rain than Sydney, and some land was fertile but there were problems. People had not cultivated farms at any distance from Hobart because of the danger of bushrangers and of losing cattle and sheep to thieves, for stock theft was 'carried on to a very alarming extent'. Much land lacked water.[36] Are smaller farmers good cultivators? Bigge asked Evans. 'All those who have been industrious have been successful', Evans replied. Were many free settlers who had been in the colony for some time doing well? Only Henry Thrupp, was the discouraging reply. (Thrupp farmed at Old Beach, having arrived with his family in 1817.) Do free settlers from England make useful settlers? 'Very few have come till lately, and I have not much idea of the others doing well', said Evans gloomily. He named four men with large land grants, 'all of whom have been here a considerable time and have done nothing'.[37]

Bigge asked about schools (see chapter 11) but ignored other important topics, like the effect of the enormous imbalance of sexes. The one female witness, the wife of a farmer, was only asked to explain how she was cheated when she sold wheat to the commissariat.[38] Nor did Bigge comment on the large amount of corruption in the elite described in the evidence he collected. Surely, tightening regulations about paying invoices would have been a sensible recommendation.

Bigge asked remarkably few questions about the Aboriginal inhabitants. He was told that seven or eight years ago they had been 'troublesome', but they were 'easily frightened', and 'pretty quiet' now more settlers had arrived. Intercourse between female natives and stockkeepers was rare, he was assured, though another witness said Aboriginal men disliked the English taking their wives. Captain Kelly sounded a note of caution: he did not cultivate his grant on Bruny Island as the Aboriginal natives were hostile there. Ominously, farmer Edward Kimberley defended himself with 'I never did them the slightest injury nor did any of my people' – implying that others did.[39] But Bigge did not explore this topic. His time was limited, and he felt obliged to spend much of it investigating petty grievances people brought up, like the Humphrey–Loane dispute.

Something which shocked me, a historian, was the lack of records. There were hardly any. People gave all sorts of excuses: records had been stolen, sent to Sydney; Davey sent them to his patron Harrowby in England (never to be seen again); the inspector of public works operated on verbal instructions, not written; the chief constable did not make a list of settlers convicts were assigned to because he was not allowed the paper. Even when there were records, they were not necessarily correct. Bigge asked Hull about the government herd of cattle (kept to provide deserving settlers with stock). It had existed since 1804 but, said Hull, the earliest record was dated 1818, and even so 'It is very incorrect and no reliance can be placed upon it. It was written ... on the verbal dictation of G. Salter'. Salter, the government stockkeeper, said when he arrived the good stock had all been removed (so any deterioration was not his fault). Yes, he had kept records, but they were destroyed when his house burnt down. No, he had never received written instructions, nor been ordered to make returns to the commissariat – until Hull arrived and required weekly returns.[40] This disgraceful state of affairs explains why historians can find so few records for this period.

Bigge spent seventeen months in the colonies, then returned to England. He wrote up his reports – plain, straightforward descriptions, with guarded suggestions for the future. As expected, New South Wales dominated but Van Diemen's Land was included in some general recommendations, especially that convicts receive stricter treatment and that salaries not be paid in rum.

Bigge presented a gloomy picture of Van Diemen's Land. The state of farms indicated the poverty of owners and bad cultivation, inferior to New South Wales. Sheep-stealing was a great evil; wages were high (another evil as far as Bigge was concerned). Penniless convicts had little chance of success as farmers. Land should be given only to those with the means to cultivate it. On the positive side, Bigge thought rules were more strongly enforced in Van Diemen's Land than New South Wales and settlers were more orderly, with less 'excessive use of spirits' in country areas. But the economy was unpromising and there were insufficient churches, clergymen and schools. The Aboriginal natives were hostile but rarely seen and, Bigge thought, would not seriously oppose extension of settlement.[41]

Bigge had a host of minor suggestions for Van Diemen's Land, such as having a larger gaol, and three major recommendations: that it be made a separate colony, equal to New South Wales, with its own court system, and that adulterous Sorell be replaced.[42] All were put in place, paving the way for the rapid development that followed.

Bigge judged from the point of view of an upper-class English lawyer, who had probably never had to do a hand's turn of physical labour in his life, or seen an urban slum. He was mainly interested in the upper class, seeing lesser persons merely as workers. He had no idea of the difficulties of pioneering a new settlement and made no allowance for the fact that two-thirds of the population were serving convicts. He showed his prejudice in assuming that small farmers' problems were due to their dissolute lives rather than volatile prices, and ignored the fact that many of his questions about workers, drunkenness and petty crime would probably have been answered similarly in Britain, or were topics some people always complain about – for example, that employees are idle.

Bigge did not mention that over half his interviewees were former convicts, who had prospered at least moderately, since they were respectable enough to be interviewed. He ignored positive aspects of Van Diemen's Land: that many ex-convicts and soldiers were doing well in their small farms or businesses, which were perhaps not neat and tidy but which supported themselves and their families. He ignored the way such people were establishing a new community, building up networks of friends and relations by marriage. Surely it was promising that children of convicts were better behaved than their parents – but Bigge did not mention this in his report.

To me, the evidence given in the Bigge report shows that six thousand people, most of whom were convicts or ex-convicts, convicted criminals, and with hardly any women, had done astonishingly well in establishing a functioning community. There might be a large amount of crime but so there was in Britain – and much of the colony's crime was committed by the elite, including governors. Convicts might not toil hard but at least they did some work and there were enough of them to do it. Many of the complaints were about activities that today seem minor offences or no offences at all: being in the pub after hours, living together unmarried, working slowly.

Richard Bradstreet, a London dock labourer transported for pocket picking, might have had a view typical of convicts when in 1824 he told his family:

> The hardships that we undergo is far beyond telling [but] a Prisoner are very near as well of as a free man ... we work for

the King and the rest for yourself so by that a man may obtain a living if that he is a mind to work and keep good company[43]

'To work and keep good company': enough people had that attitude to forge a stable community.

Bigge and other officials, such as Governor Collins, saw people in black and white: law-abiding or law-breaking. But many colonists were in and out of these categories, law-abiding when it suited them, law-breaking when that was advantageous. Thomas Hayes, described earlier as in league with bushrangers, became a constable. After his death he was remembered as an upright pioneer of the Bagdad district, engaged in agricultural and pastoral pursuits (very praiseworthy).[44] The list of benefactors to the Auxiliary Bible Society in 1819 includes the names of many less-than-perfect citizens mentioned in this book – Dr Luttrell, Dennis McCarty, George Salter, William Maum. Ex-convict and embezzler Maum settled down as a reasonably law-abiding farmer.[45] As did many others, when community values changed in the 1820s.

From his elevated position Bigge might have thought Van Diemen's Land a hotbed of crime, but this was no *Lord of the Flies* situation, with everything dissolving into feral cruelty and anarchy. Enough ordinary people wanted to live more or less respectable, more or less law-abiding lives to form a community which worked, and which was the basis of the astonishing development of the next decade. The really serious crime was one Bigge did not confront: treatment of the Aboriginal inhabitants.

Drawn on Stone by T. O. Ommanney Esq.

Jetty and Warehouses.   Commercial Tavern.

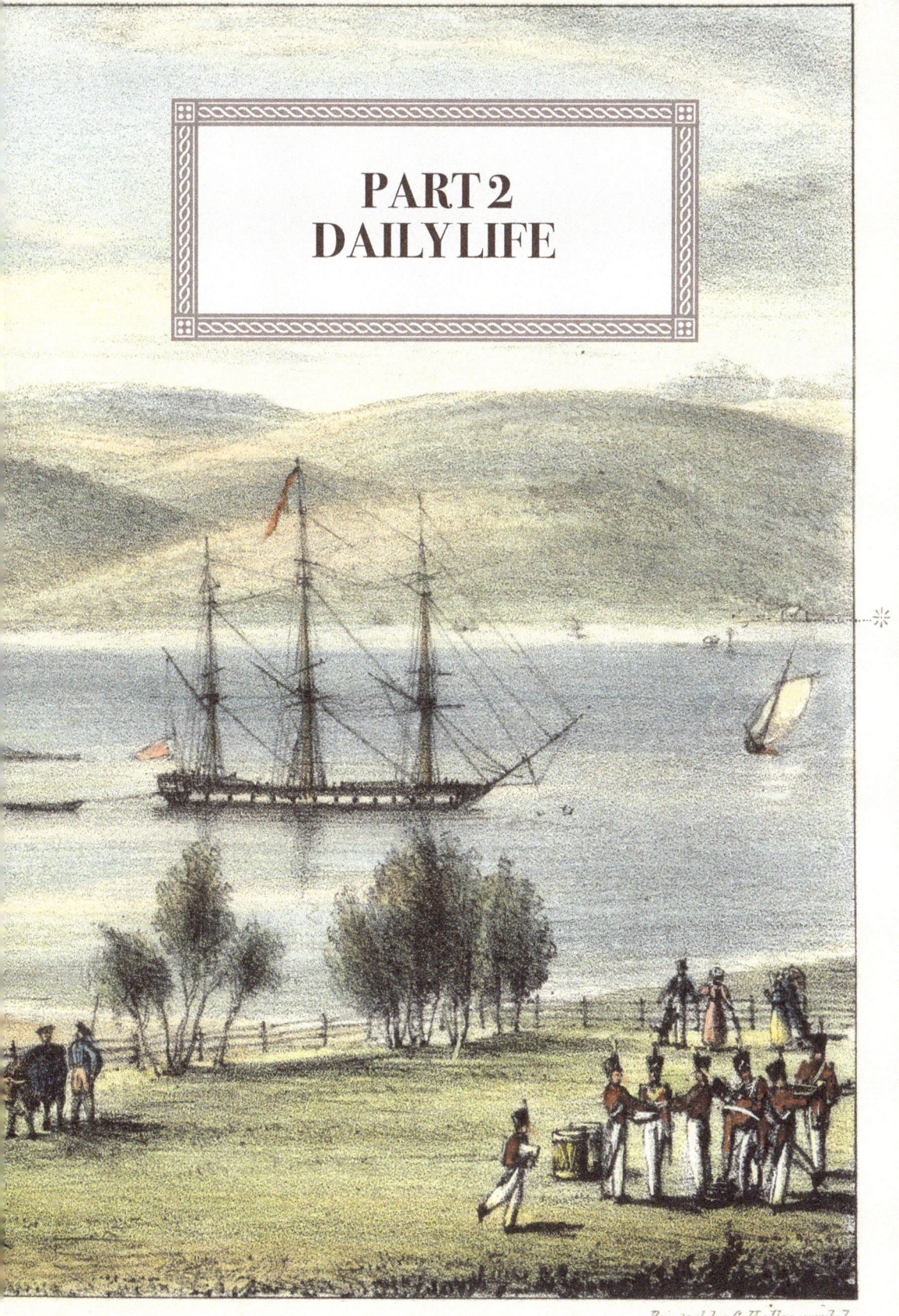

PART 2
DAILY LIFE

9. FOOD, CLOTHES AND HOMES

'How did people *live* in the colony?' asked a friend. 'I've read such-and-such a book but it didn't tell me how people *lived*.' This section discusses his question. How did people go about their daily lives? They needed much the same as we do – food, shelter, company, remunerative work, health care, recreation and so on – but what were these necessities like in early nineteenth-century Tasmania?

Food

The basic ration for British settlers comprised meat and flour – typically one pound (440g) of each per day – and smaller amounts of tea and sugar. Van Diemen's Land provided plenty of meat, mainly kangaroo, but also from other animals and birds, as well as fish. The diary of chaplain Knopwood shows that he and his servants hunted kangaroo, emu, ducks, snipe, wattle birds, swans, pigeons, quails, partridges and lorikeets (just about anything that moved) all for the pot. They went fishing and caught flathead, perch, cod, mackerel, crayfish, oysters and eels. For example, in January 1806 a party explored up the river. The gentlemen went up to the cataracts sightseeing while 'the men that were left behind' caught eels, 'which we had for dinner, and a very pleasant eve was had'.[1]

Meat from domestic animals was uncommon at first because these were few, but in October 1804 Knopwood gave a grand dinner for the eight other officials: fish, kangaroo soup, roast saddle of kid, two fowls with rice and bacon, pig ... The rest of the menu is missing, but this was a feast, heavily protein-based.[2] When herds and flocks grew, mutton and beef were the favourite meats. Presumably there were no vegetarians, let alone vegans; they would have had a hard time of it.

The other staple was flour, made into bread in towns where there were bakers. Otherwise, people made damper. James Ross gave instructions: mix flour, water and salt with 'a little leaven from the last batch' (moistened and left to ferment, or did he have some yeast on the go?). Knead it until you have a 'good manageable lump of dough'. Let it stand an hour or two, as long as your hunger will allow; rake a hole in the ashes of the fire, clap your dough down and cover it with hot ashes. In an hour it will be baked and fit for any emperor with the good fortune to visit the banks of the Shannon River (where Ross lived).[3]

Those without leaven or time made a simpler version. Charles Jeffreys' five assigned convicts arrived on his property in mid-afternoon. While four cut down timber and built a shelter, the ploughman cooked kangaroo steamer: diced meat cooked over a fire in its own gravy with a few rashers of salt pork. He also cooked potatoes, probably roasted in the fire, and a large damper made of flour and water kneaded together and baked in the ashes. The grog went merrily round and the men 'declared that they never in their lives ate a meal with greater relish'. That was dinner: meat and carbs but no vegetables except potatoes.[4] Another version of kangaroo steamer had meat packed in a jar with any spices available and steamed in a Dutch oven – a lidded pot on three legs that stood in a low fire.

Out in the bush, men ate 'sticker up'. After killing a kangaroo they cut steaks from the haunch. They lit a fire, cut a small bough with a little fork at one end, stuck the steak on it and thrust the stick into the ground near the fire. The meat by its own weight leant towards the fire and was 'cooked to perfection'.[5] (But it's easy to imagine a few disasters.)

What pleased working people was the abundance of food. Many had

Dinner in the bush: Lycett's painting of men camping by the South Esk. (NLA 65279647)

gone hungry in Britain – it was often the cause of them being transported to Van Diemen's Land – but here they could eat meat three times a day, an indication of extreme abundance. The few letters home from convicts often dwell on the food: plenty of it! One employer told Bigge that he let his men eat as much meat as they wanted, and weighed it: three pounds (1.3 kg) a day, which he thought was usual. Another witness told Commissioner Bigge that ex-convicts' food was pork and mutton, 'good wheaten bread', tea and sugar.[6]

Green vegetables were rare. In 1804 some men died of scurvy from the lack of vegetables at Port Phillip, but at the Derwent, said Fawkner, they ate wild parsley, 'a vegetable like sage', and Botany Bay greens, which they boiled and ate. Botany Bay greens, or Warrigal greens, grow luxuriantly and are pleasant though not delicious. If it was the choice of them or scurvy, I'd choose them any time. Seaweed was also eagerly sought after – ditto.[7] Henry Widowson said tea made from tea tree leaves was a pleasant beverage (presumably how it got its name), and bandicoot meat was delicious.[8] However, none of these items became part of the everyday diet.

Instead, people planted British fruit and vegetables. Knopwood started a garden as soon as he could and in November 1806 ate the first products: strawberries and peas.[9] How exciting, the first fresh fruit for years! As gardens developed vegetables became more plentiful, but only potatoes were sold commercially.

When people described meals, meat was prominent. As a constable carrying a summons to a bush hut, John Hudspeth was pleased to find the convicts there did themselves well. 'A famous saddle of mutton was smoking before the fire, a large pot contained vegetables and in another was digested a quantity of tea to work down the more substantial viands. I made a hearty repast.' In Hobart, George Boyes' dinner consisted of 'a fine leg of mutton which had been exposed to the cold drying winds for the last seven days and … at least a pint of good Port wine'. Vegetables were missing or not mentioned.[10]

Other types of food were rare. Dairy produce was expensive but available: Catherine Kearney sold butter and milk at her Hobart dairy and in 1820 Coal River butter was advertised. Desserts were seldom mentioned, though surely a 'sumptuous and splendid dinner' at Government House included a sweet course. George Boyes only mentioned dessert at social dinners: blancmange, jelly and cheesecakes.[11] Just before Christmas in 1823 plums and currants for puddings were for sale: let's hope people enjoyed a traditional Christmas pudding.[12] And let's hope it tasted better than Peter Harrisson's puddings. He wrote back to Britain advising emigrants to learn to cook before they arrived, so they could make bread without yeast and puddings without suet or butter. They would find them palatable once they had 'shaken off their English nicety'. Something missing from the diet was sweets and lollies; the only form advertised was sugar candy, perhaps a form of barley sugar.[13]

Overall, it was a diet with plenty of protein and carbohydrates, and enough vegetables to ward off scurvy, since no more cases were reported. People had sugar in tea but, with sweetmeats rare, the consumption of sugar was a fraction of what it is now. Hardly anything was processed, except imported foodstuffs which were too expensive for most people. So, generally, a healthy diet which allowed some people to live into their eighties and nineties.

Tea was the staple drink. Coffee was rare, a drink only for the wealthy. It's not clear whether ginger and spruce beer were alcoholic; 'cordials' definitely were, like ratafia.[14] If people did not drink tea, beer or rum, they had a choice between water and possibly milk. But since water was often polluted, boiling it for tea or brewing it for beer made for safer drinking.

Most food was produced locally but ships bringing speculative cargoes from Britain often included delicacies – though only preserved foods, due to the long voyage. Even the trip from Sydney was too long for most perishable goods. From 1817 newspapers advertised imported foods: preserved herrings, tongues, pickled tripe (!) and sauces such as 'walnut and mushroom catchup'. Spices included cloves, mace and nutmeg but they were expensive: a nutmeg cost more than a loaf of bread, so was a luxury for most people.[15] The 1820s saw English cheese and ham, dried and preserved fruit and curry powder but, like nutmegs, such food was expensive.[16] Most people continued to eat local products.

How did people cook their food? At first over an open fire, using a frying pan or a Dutch oven. Enclosed ovens were used for baking. In 1805 Knopwood's servants' kitchen (so they had a separate one!) caught fire and he lamented losing a very fine stove. Sanders van Straten, a convict, built him a new oven, stove and chimney, and later a mason 'set up' another oven, perhaps in Knopwood's own kitchen.[17]

Some houses advertised for sale had ovens. A Norfolk Islander sold his property at Crawfish Point (Taroona): it had a fine view over the sea, and included a good house with two chimneys and an oven. Four years later a 'small genteel Family' was offered a cottage at New Norfolk, with parlour, closet, bedroom, 'good kitchen with a large brick oven', and sleeping places above for the family and servants (the parents had the bedroom?).[18]

Factory-made imported ovens, stoves and ranges – all versions of enclosed stoves – were offered for sale from 1821. There were many sorts: register (with a plate to stop smoke escaping into the kitchen), elliptic, convex, hedagonal (hexagonal?), gothic, organ fronted, a Bright Register Stove with bow front and burket bottom ... What was a gothic oven, or a burket bottom? Even Google is no help here, but clearly many sorts of closed stoves were available for baking. Some sound sophisticated: 'a kitchen range, with oven, boiler, and steamer complete'.[19] With little coal available they mostly burnt wood, which meant a good deal of work, felling trees, chopping them up and frequently feeding the fire.

Clothing

Convicts' outfits show what sort of clothes the working class wore. In 1820 each woman was issued with a brown serge (wool) jacket, a petticoat, a linen shift (dress), a linen cap, stockings, shoes and a neck-handkerchief. For men: in 1826 the field police were issued with trousers, red waistcoats, jackets, shoes and leather hats, and other lists include shirts.[20] No underwear or nightwear in either list. Did they all sleep in their clothes? Clothes were expensive and the working class could afford few, just basic garments.

As ever, wealthier people could fuss more about clothes. On the voyage out, Adolarius Humphrey wrote to his parents that 'The greatest attention is paid to dress'. Most men wore two shirts a day, changing for dinner. 'I have to put on a clean shirt and neckcloth when I dress for dinner, which shirt I make serve me next morning.'[21]

From the earliest days shops sold clothing, probably pretty basic, but advertisements started only with newspapers in 1816. A merchant offered ready-made shirts and nankeen (strong cotton) trousers, broadcloth (dense, plain cloth) of different colours, and strong shoes for

George Augustus Robinson in his 'bush dress':
striped shirt, neckerchief, jacker, trousers
buttoned to his shirt, shoes and a fancy hat
(TA W.L. Crowther Library AUTAS001131821274)

men.[22] Later that year, more clothes were available, jumbled in a long list among soap, tea and artificial flowers:

> Ladies Bonnets, of the first fashion; Satin for Ladies Dresses; Ladies Dress Boots, Ribbons, and Gimp [braid] Trimmings ... Ladies Shawls ... a Variety of Muslins ...Women and Children's Shoes; Children's black worsted Stockings and Gloves; a Ladies' handsome black silk Cloak; a Ladies handsome blue Mantle [cloak]; black muslin Handkerchiefs ... Men's blue Jackets and Trowsers; Waistcoat Pieces ... Ladies Dress Caps ... Crimson Cloth ...[23]

Imagine reading this advertisement, hastening to the store and finding the one handsome black silk cloak had been sold! Notice that while some clothes were ready made, fabric was sold for clothes to be made at home, or by a dressmaker.

By 1831 a great variety was available for the well-to-do: silk shawls and scarves, dressing gowns, long dress kid gloves, velvet waistcoats, sealskin caps, French silks, gauzes and gloves, silk hats, as well as stock keepers' strong felt hats for employees.[24] Local newspapers gave fashion advice from London, only six months old, so those who could afford it could be as smart as any Londoner. Some people clung to old fashions, though. Young Sarah Mather described ex-convict John Fawkner as the only man in Hobart who still wore old-fashioned knee breeches; all the other men wore newfangled trousers.[25]

Hugh Hull, born in 1818 and son of commissary George Hull, remembered going to spend an afternoon at the Barracks with the colonel's children. Aged about four, he was 'dressed in a white frock and red morocco [soft leather] shoes. I remember the grapes given me with strict injunctions as to not spoiling my frock'. (Little boys wore 'frocks' – dresses – until they were considered old enough to wear trousers.) When Hugh was six he was sent to boarding school, where he wore 'a blue cloth jacket and trousers with lots of buttons on them and a wide broadbrimmed leghorn hat – with a crimped white frill round my neck'. His father had a 'very showy' uniform of 'deep blue cloth, the breast covered with gold embroidery, large gold epaulettes, cocked hat and steel sword, with spurs on his heels'. He cut up the spurs later to make fishing lines, recalled Hugh.[26] There was no need to lecture colonists about recycling; materials and money were both in short supply and nothing was thrown out unless there was absolutely no use for it.

Those who could afford it enjoyed dressing up. A concert in 1831 was attended by 'all the beaux, belles and fashion', wrote a journalist. 'With the exception of seven (out of about 150) ladies, who were not only in dishabile [casual wear?], but wore bonnets, the dresses betokened a taste and elegance not to be exceeded in any British Colony'.[27] Alas for the seven who did not know fashion's decree that bonnets were not worn in the evening!

Homes and furniture

At first, settlers found shelter where they could: one slept under a blanket supported by sticks, then in a hollow tree. As seen above, Charles Jeffreys' servants could cut timber and make a rough shelter in an afternoon, but soon people built more substantial huts. Edward Lord built the first house in Hobart of wattle and daub, with windows like the port-holes of a vessel. 'That it was the first, constituted its chief claim to distinction: it was considered as an achievement of civilisation – a trophy gained upon the wilderness', he told John West.[28]

John Pascoe Fawkner described how these 'wattle and daub' houses were built. Upright posts were rammed two feet (60 cm) into the earth, two feet apart, and the spaces were filled with 'lathe or wattles worked in' – thin boughs woven together – and plastered over with mud mixed with straw. The roof had round poles for rafters, with wattle crossed on top, then a thatch of grass. Doors were made of canvas. There was no glass for windows, which were covered with oiled paper or thin cloth. When sawpits were set up and boards were available, wooden doors and shutters were made.[29] Houses were also made from sods, clumps of earth, and out in the bush stockmen made bark huts.

As the community developed, weatherboards were cut and bricks were made for more substantial houses. Both these skills were fairly easily learned, though early bricks were not of top quality. Some early brick buildings which survive, all built around 1810, are the Bond Store and the private secretary's cottage (both part of the Tasmanian Museum and Art Gallery) and, at Glenorchy, Pitt Farm, a two-storey house built by free settler Richard Pitt. The earliest weatherboard building mentioned

Mary Morton Allport arrived in 1831 and her group started to farm at the Black Brush. They lived in 'Our Winter Quarters': a rough shelter, with an outdoor fire for cooking and a fallen log for seating (TA ALMFA AUTAS001124060575)

in the *Gazette* was a four-roomed house in central Hobart in 1818.³⁰

The most impressive houses were made of stone, which had to be quarried and shaped by skilled stonemasons. Some time after 1817, Thomas Davey built Roseway Lodge at New Town. In 1821 he had to sell it: 'a commodious, genteel, and comfortable Stone-built House', which contained 'a handsome Parlour, a Drawing Room, a neat Vestabule, or common Kitchen, and two Bed Rooms, with several Out-houses for Servants'. No dining room (did they eat in the parlour?) – and no mention of bathroom or sanitary arrangements. No doubt one of the outhouses was a dunny. The property also contained a stockyard and a garden with fruit trees, flowers and 'almost every kind of Kitchen Vegetable' – comfort indeed.³¹ However, only someone like an ex-governor who never admitted to money worries could afford such luxury.

In the north, someone sold an elegant stone house (unfinished) at Norfolk Plains, with barns, stables, a granary and sixty acres of land, all cultivated.³² How disappointing for someone: gaining a grant, cultivating his land, building his dream home, only to have to sell it before it was finished. Did he over-reach himself?

The private secretary's cottage in Hobart, still to be seen inside today's Tasmanian Museum and Art Gallery: four small rooms and a lean-to at the back. A roof of wooden shingles was steep to allow rain and snow to run off. Artist: Mary Morton Allport. (TA ALMFA AUTAS001131821985)

When Elizabeth Fenton arrived in Hobart in 1829, she reported that most houses were made of wood. Some merchants' houses were 'brick-nogged', a mixture of wood and brick; a few houses were made of brick and fewer of stone. They looked very English, except that most had verandahs to provide shade in summer. Elizabeth loved the gardens, 'gay with hedges of scarlet geraniums, stock, wallflowers, and an unknown variety of native shrubs'. So colonists were planting local flowers, especially wattle, 'sweet-scented almost to excess'.[33]

What furniture was inside dwellings? Little at first, with scant room for furniture in the initial ships. In 1820 William Williamson wrote that 'there is hardly a chair in the colony' and very few beds. 'Almost all sleep in cribs or on the floor.' By 'bed' he probably meant four-posters and 'cribs' were probably basic beds, sacking stretched on four legs. In his mud hut in the country, Peter Harrisson had a packing case for a table, a box to sit on, and as a bed his sea-cot (a type of hammock). Passers-by asking for shelter for the night slept on the floor by the fire, rolled up in their cloaks.[34]

Those with more money could afford more comfortable furniture. In 1818 a gentleman in Launceston was selling a feather bed, a mahogany bedstead, cedar tables, chairs, a chest of drawers and sofas. Down the social scale, a farmhouse at Clarence Plains contained two chests of drawers, four tables, ten chairs and three bedsteads. A man who lived in a hut in the bush slept on a grass bed. Most people, however, could afford a mattress: a sack of ticking (strong tightly-woven cotton) stuffed with straw, chaff, coarse wool, horsehair or, best of all, feathers.[35] But feathers varied. John Wedge, a surveyor, was given a bed with a mattress stuffed with muttonbird feathers, 'the effluvia of which was such as will by no means make me anxious to regale my olfactory nerves with again'.[36]

No house had a bathroom (the first one was mentioned in 1842).[37] If people had baths, it was in a hipbath in front of the fire in the kitchen, but it was a nuisance heating enough hot water and mostly people just washed faces and hands (if that). To get clean, men could swim, naked, in the river. Women did not have this option. It is difficult to gain information, however, as newspapers, diaries and letters seldom mentioned anything so mundane as washing.

There were few amenities as we understand the term today, either in Britain or the Australian colonies. People provided their own light and heating with candles, lamps and fires, usually wood but sometimes coal. There was no official street lighting, though lights were sold for people to put up outside their own houses.[38] There was no rubbish collection – and not a great deal of rubbish. Much would have been burnt, or perhaps buried or left lying about. There was little public transport. Ships took passengers to Launceston and Sydney, but the first stagecoach service, Hobart to New Norfolk, did not start until 1833.

The one amenity was a postal service. Mail arrived by ship, lists of letters were advertised and people collected them. The government in Hobart had to be able to communicate with Launceston; the journey by sea was slow, and at some stage an overland service started. By 1816 this involved a government messenger making the journey once a week on horseback, taking official documents and possibly private mail. He also brought news – of bushrangers, for example.[39]

In 1818 this service was extended: messengers left Hobart and Launceston every alternate Monday, setting out at daybreak and reaching York Plains on Tuesday evening. They exchanged mail, were allowed a day off, and returned. In 1820 this service became weekly. Branch messengers took mail to Sorell, New Norfolk and Bothwell.[40]

There were titivations to this scheme and by 1830, mail posted in Hobart or Launceston on Friday was available on Monday (as fast as today!). There was no delivery, however; recipients still had to pick up letters at a central office and the system was not always efficient. According to Ann Weston at Longford, letters and packets were often lost.[41]

10. JALOP AND TRAGACANTH: HEALING ILLNESS

Forget your twenty-first century ideas of illness, medicines, medical treatment and equipment. Two hundred years ago knowledge of all these was extremely limited. Many diseases of today were not even named, let alone recognised or treatable. Doctors could set or if necessary amputate bones (without anaesthetic) but they had little equipment and few effective medicines: only quinine for malaria, digitalis for the heart, magnesia for indigestion, and opium for pain relief.[1] If a patient had an obviously broken limb, diagnosis was more straightforward, and doctors could make a fair guess about a patient with spots, but vague internal symptoms – how was a doctor to tell, with nothing but experience to go by? They tended to take one of three paths: soothing (bedrest, care, calm and hopeful words), heroic (violent purges and drastic blood-letting) or 'nothing to see here', let nature take its course. This chapter made me, and I'm sure the reader, extremely glad to be living in the twenty-first century.

Fortunately, Van Diemen's Land had a healthy, temperate climate. The small population did not produce much pollution, many people worked in the open air, and there was (mostly) plenty of relatively healthy food. People with strong constitutions could live long lives. Diseases were another matter. In many cases patients would get better naturally – if they were not poisoned by medication. Treatment often actually hastened death.

There was no shortage of medicines of one sort or another. Before anyone considered banning harmful substances, chemists could stock anything they liked. Some sound harmless (if not necessarily beneficial): liquorice, cinnamon bark, turmeric, vinegar, grains of paradise (a spice). Some were relatively harmless laxatives: Turkey rhubarb, jalop (made from the roots of the aptly named *Ipomoea purga*), gamboge, tragacanth. Not so harmless was mercury, particularly dangerous for the unborn or infants and liable to cause damage to the kidneys, lungs, skin, eyes, nerves and immune systems of adults.[2]

Enterprising pharmacists produced patent medicines. Most were

MESSRS. MATHER and HOPKINS, at Pullen's House, Potter's Hill, Hobart Town, respectfully inform their Friends and the Public, that they have received, per Caledonia and other recent arrivals, the undermentioned useful and general Assortment of Goods, viz.—

Hosiery, of the very best Quality.
Women and children's cotton, worsted, lamb's wool, and Vigonia hose; also a few ladies' silk hose; men's pantaloon half-hose, and children's socks; men and women's lamb's wool, worsted, and cotton under-waistcoats; cotton and worsted drawers; net braces, and worsted pantaloons; comforters, single and double cotton caps.

Ready-made Clothes.
Men and boy's toilonet and Valentia waistcoats, at 8s. 6d. and upwards; gentlemen's black and corbo coats, at £3 and upwards; gentlemen's brown & mixed surtout coats; kerseymere trowsers at about 25s.; children's plain and rifle dresses; blue cloth jackets and trowsers; duck and drill trowsers; red flannel and cotton shirts; Scotch plaid, wrappers, buttons, silk, and other tailors' trimmings; rugs, leather caps, gentlemen's travelling caps, ladies' parasols, silk, & gingham umbrellas; painted table mats, and Doyles; parlour and library bellows.

Boots and Shoes.
Ladies' Denmark, satin and jean boots & shoes; gentlemen's Wellington and top boots; men's very strong laced boots, proper for stock-keepers and others; gentlemen's boot legs and tops, of very superior quality.—Shoemakers' thread, heel balls, and hairs.

Brushes.
Scrubbing, dusting, bannister, painting, white-washing, shoe, and clothes brushes; wisk, carpet, and long brooms,—various sizes of each sort.

Turnery.
Bushel, half-bushel, peck, half-peck, quartern, and half-quartern measures; hair sieves, wheat sieves, and riddlers; and wooden porridge dishes.

Fowling Pieces, &c.
Single & double-barrelled fowling pieces, pocket pistols, gun flints, bullet-moulds, japanned and copper powder flasks, with and without improved screws; leather shot-belts and bags, metal drinking bottles with cups.

Optical Instruments.
Telescopes of various sizes, reading glasses, spectacles and cases, watch glasses and keys.

Ironmongery.
Batten and shingle nails; cut and billed brads of several sizes, for flooring and other purposes; rose-head, broad gate, clasp, fine wattle, clench, and other nails, of many different sizes; wrought tin tacks; screws of all sizes; and steel dog collars.

Hinges.
A various assortment of butt, cross-garnet, and hook hinges; iron frame pullies, staples, locks, bolts, &c.; draw-back, plate, and Banbury stock-locks; pad-locks, various, with screw hasps and staples; and thumb latchets.

Tools and Husbandry Implements.
An assortment of bricklayers, carpenters, and cooper's tools; coach-wrenches, lath renders, choppers, cleavers, bill-hooks, chids, pick axes, mattocks, garden rakes, and hoes; 2-prong forks, sheep-shears; Charley, forest and other stones; curry combs, melting ladles, spades, and shovels; fine knotted traces, long linked chains, land chains, halter reins, hay knives, cross-cut saws, wrought iron wire for corn screens, & unwrought iron wire.

Domestic Utensils.
Cast iron pots and saucepans, of sizes; frying pans, oval and round; tea, table, and desert metal spoons; Italian and French irons.

Copper Stills.
Two small copper stills, with cock, charging screw, head, pewter neck, and worm, complete.

Paint.
Very best white lead and linseed oil.

Medicines.
Purified Epsom and Cheltenham salts, in pint bottles; calcined magnesia, in pint bottles; powder Turkey rhubarb, in half-pint ditto; calomel, in bottles; essence of peppermint; and Dalby's carminative.—These are particularly well adapted for family and private use.

Vinegar, Fish Sauce, &c.
Best vinegar, anchovey, fish, and salad oil; Harvey, Reading, Pitt, Quin, and Coratch sauces; walnut and mushroom ketchup, and essence of anchovies.

Books.
An elegant copy of the Encyclopædia Perthensis, 23 vols. royal 8vo. with maps and plates; the Rev. J. Wesley's Commentaries on the Old and New Testament, 4 vols. 4to.; Nicholson's Encyclopædia of Arts and Sciences, with very fine plates, 6 vols. 8vo.; several Copies of Atmore's Sermons on the Lord's Prayer. 12mo. recently published; Burns's Poems, 4 vols. 8vo.; a complete Set of the Evangelical Magazine. 26 vols. 8vo.; a few Grammars, Spelling Books, Geographies, and other school books.—Also black lead and slate pencils, quills, pens, &c.

Furniture.
A very elegant and curious mahogany cabinet, with solid curls; a pair of beautiful Pembroke tables, with pillar, block, and claws; a set of elegant mahogany chairs, with satin hair bottoms — All the above articles are quite new, and made of fine Spanish mahogany, and by one of the first workmen in London.—A good mahogany 4-post bedstead, with furniture complete, nearly new; also paper hangings of several patterns.

Family Chaise, &c.
A very neat and useful family one-horse chaise, very strongly made, and capable of accommodating 6 persons, with two patent lamps, a complete set of new harness, extra collars, whips, &c.—Likewise, coach-springs, axle-trees. &c. equally suitable for gigs and light carts; saddles and bridles.

☞ MATHER & HOPKINS respectfully assure the Public of the Colony, that the above Goods are generally of very superior Quality, and as they purchased them on very advantageous Terms, they intend to offer them at moderate Prices.—Having been accustomed to the Wool Trade in England, and being desirous of carrying it on in Van Diemen's Land, they take this Opportunity to inform the numerous Stock owners and Settlers of the Island, that they not only receive that Commodity as well as Wheat in Exchange for Goods, but also purchase it at a fair Price.

HOBART TOWN: PRINTED BY A. BENT.

Mather and Hopkins advertise medicine for sale, including calomel and Dalby's carminative for infants. Both contained opium but they were advertised as 'particularly well adapted for family and private use'. (*HTG* 30 November 1822) either of little use or so effective they could be toxic and have since been banned: calomel, a purgative (mercury chloride) for general pain, like panadol today; laudanum (opium) for pain relief, coughs, diarrhoea anxiety and virtually everything else; Dover's Powders, Dalby's Carminative and Godfrey's Cordial (all opium) to soothe babies (!!!); Hooper's Female Pills of senna and ferrous sulphide (abortifacients), myrrh and aloe (possibly anti-inflammatory and antioxidant) for period problems and 'irregularities' – often used to encourage abortions, probably with not much effect.[3]

Many 'medicines' sound alarming: sulphuric acid, white lead, antimony, corrosive sublimate, elixir of vitriol. In 1830 a chemist published an enormous list and added 'Prescriptions & Family Recipes carefully dispensed': so people had their own favourites.[4] I can imagine Aunt Emily's mixture for indigestion, Grandfather's infallible elixir for lumbago. All these medicines appeared accepted. The colony's senior doctor, James Scott, recommended that fellow-practitioners always carry with them calomel, opium, tartarised antimony (emetic) and lancets. With these they could keep the most urgent symptoms at bay until more help could be procured, 'and often check the disease'.[5]

In 1820 Commissioner Bigge questioned three doctors about their work: Jacob Mountgarrett in Launceston, Edward Luttrell and newly arrived James Scott in Hobart. Mountgarrett listed his 'useful medicines' as opium (in the form of laudanum), different preparations of mercury, 'bark salts' (quinine), cream of tartar and purgatives such as castor oil, rhubarb and jalop.[6] The internet is doubtful about the medical benefits of cream of tartar. Perhaps it relieves migraines or helps quit smoking, but this last was not seen as a problem in the early nineteenth century. Medicines were less effective if they were badly packed, said Mountgarrett. Some of his vitriolic acid had oozed out, almost entirely destroying the contents of its case. The internet doesn't suggest any medicinal use for vitriolic (sulphuric) acid.

As far as illnesses went, Luttrell said the most common were rheumatism, dysentery ('bloody diarrhoea' – often bacterial), catarrhal fevers (colds), diarrhoea, hepatitis and scabies. Mountgarrett named venereal disease and ulcers from old wounds received by soldiers and sailors. He thought dysentery was mainly found among newly arrived people, and was due to 'immoderate use of Spiritous Liquors'.

Few caught the dreaded disease of consumption (tuberculosis), and many of those who arrived with it were cured. So pure was Van Diemen's Land's air that officers came from hot, tropical India for their health. The *Hobart Town Gazette* boasted that infectious diseases, such as measles, whooping cough, smallpox and scarlet fever, did not exist, wearing themselves out on the long voyage from Britain.[7]

Mountgarrett's mention of venereal disease is the only suggestion that this was a problem – but it was widespread in European societies and was probably just as rampant in Van Diemen's Land. However, it was not socially acceptable, so was not mentioned in newspapers. It was usually treated with mercury, which was certainly available, widely so in the patent medicine calomel. Possibly some taking this were treating their syphilis.

When people were ill, often the doctor had no idea of the cause. One Saturday morning Henrietta Bowen, aged nineteen, was ill enough for Knopwood, a close family friend, to visit and read prayers. That evening he returned:

> She knew me and said, 'sit down Mr. Knopwood. Read.' I read 1 prayer then followed commendatory prayer [commending her soul to God]. She put her left hand to her head, afterwards her right for 2 or 3 minutes. She then took them down, closed her hands before her for a minute, and put them behind her and died instantly without a struggle. Thus died one of the finest girls on the earth.[9]

How was a doctor to know what disease Henrietta had, let alone treat it? David Collins died suddenly, with doctors unable to help. In 1812 George Harris had a 'short but severe illness of three days'. Three doctors attended him and everything as possible was done, but nothing helped and he died, as his brother-in-law (one of the doctors) wrote to the family.[10] He did not name the disease, probably because he did not know it.

One day, Knopwood called on Mr Ayers, 'very well and myself very unwell'. Later that day he was asked to visit Ayers again; he found him dying and read the last prayers to him. Leaving the house, he met Dr Hood and they returned, to find Ayers dead.[11] The morning situation dramatically reversed, implied Knopwood. His friend Edward Lord suffered from asthma, for which there was no remedy. Sea voyages helped, so Lord went to England and back for years. But not everyone could afford this cure, and the first clergyman in Launceston, John Youl, died of asthma.

There were hospitals in Hobart, Launceston and later New Norfolk, but nursing was rudimentary. Anyone who could be, was cared for at home; hospitals were for those with no one to care for them, mainly the poor. Conditions were notoriously terrible, as they usually were in institutions for the poor, where economy won over inmate comfort every time. At Launceston, Mountgarrett said he often had inadequate bedding and clothing. Patients had to bring a fortnight's food, and were then fed from the government stores – though the meat often had to be thrown away as it was flyblown. In summer it only lasted three days, he added. The hospital staff comprised a clerk, wardsman, a cook, and 'an old man as an orderly and a barber who is almost disabled'. Mountgarrett kept a register of patients' diseases and treatment but it had been stolen, so he had no records. At Hobart, Luttrell did not keep a register at all. He said there were usually about 25 in the hospital and ten outpatients, mostly with ulcers and contusions (bruises). Launceston's single ward generally housed about twelve male patients, reported Mountgarrett; he occasionally let a woman with a venereal complaint stay in the dispensary, and for other female patients the commandant let him hire lodgings.[12]

Dr Scott was horrified by the Hobart hospital. One patient had a broken leg, and Scott saw nests of maggots between his skin and the bandages, which had not been changed for five or six days. The orderly told Scott he only wiped off the discharge with a sponge and had not noticed the maggots. Dr Luttrell ordered him to use ammonia and vinegar to stop the smell. The next day the bandages were still not changed, Luttrell telling Scott it was not necessary as the leg had to be amputated. 'I told him the irritation would be much improved with new bandages and care, and until the irritation was improved there would be no amputation', said Scott firmly. What happened to the unfortunate patient was not recorded. Luttrell was described as negligent, deficient in humanity, sordid and unfeeling, and Governor Sorell dismissed him as soon as a replacement arrived.[13]

Three other doctors provided information. In 1826 Dr William

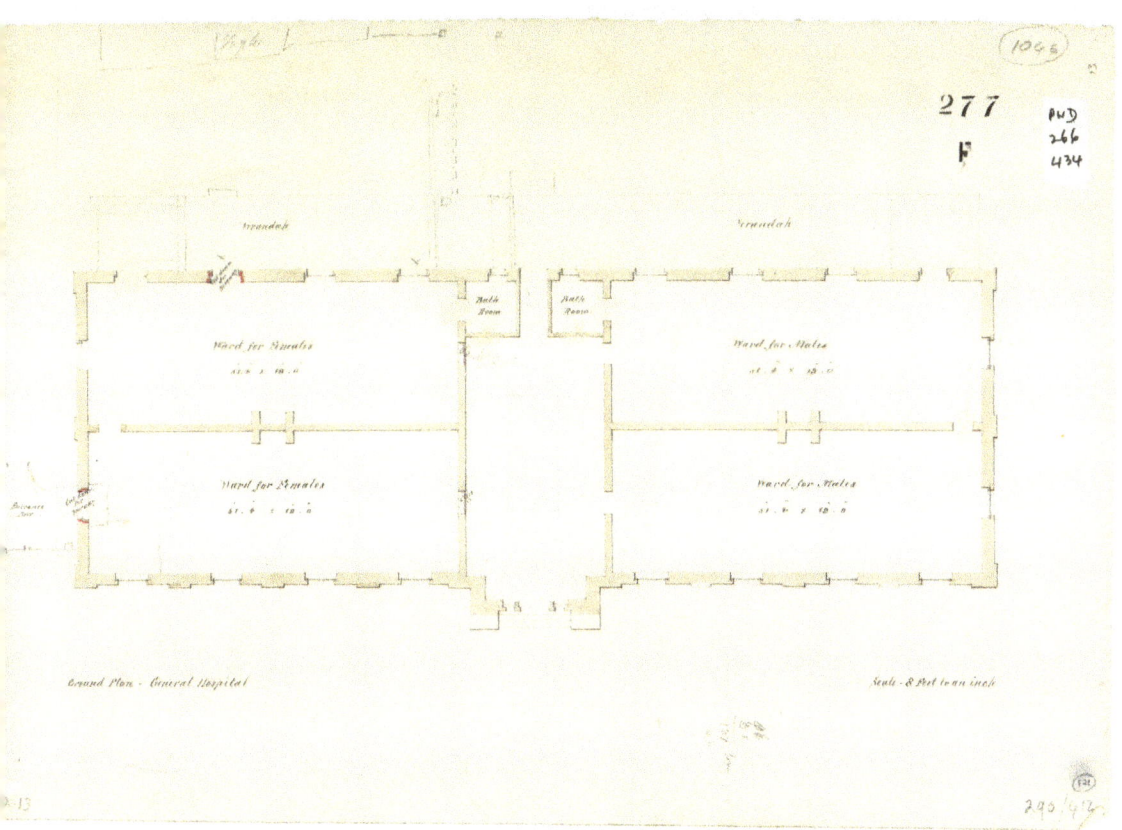

A plan for developing the Hobart Hospital, 1828: two wards each for men and women, verandahs in front, and two small bathrooms. (TA PWD266/1/434)

Crowther advertised his treatment of a female assigned servant suffering from 'violent purging and pains in her bowels', which she attributed to wearing damp clothes. Crowther found her delirious, shivering, grinding her teeth. He bled her (900 ml) and gave her a strong emetic, calomel and a laxative (covering all bases). In the next few days he gave her 'two scruples of jalap powder', Epsom salts and a blister, and bled her until she fainted. Despite this medical care she recovered, which Crowther put down to his use of emetics which discharged the 'acrid and pent up bile from the gall bladder, through the cystic ducts'.[14]

Dr John Hudspeth, surgeon and accoucheur, settled at Jericho as a farmer but advertised that he would be happy to provide medical services for neighbouring settlers.[15] He noted his few cases in his diary: a gentleman 'ill from hard drinking'; a man at Spring Hill 'seized violently with lumbago whilst at work'; the overseer of a road gang whose eyes were burnt from an explosion of gunpowder. Overseers of convict gangs asked him to examine convicts they thought were

The hospital at New Norfolk, at first a general hospital, later for 'lunatics'
(TA, W.L. Crowther Library, SD_ILS:655252)

feigning illness and Hudspeth generally found 'little or nothing the matter'.[16]

Dr James Murdoch arrived in Hobart in 1822. He set up as a 'physician accoucheur', practising for many years and becoming a well-respected family doctor. His journal survives, giving brief details of patients, diseases, treatment and charges. His day-to-day practice involved bandaging fractures and dislocations, removing troublesome teeth, scarifying teeth and gums, letting blood and treating dog bites. (No specialist dentists were mentioned at this period.) Murdoch prescribed opium for pain, valerian as a sedative and quinine for fever, but most medicines were purgatives. He grew medicinal herbs and made some remedies himself. Little could be done for severe injuries.

Operations were rare but Murdoch did operate on a child. His entry runs: 'Anurism [sic] by Anastamosis on the left side of the upper lip broad base double ligature'. This was most likely closing a cleft lip.[17]

Other information comes from colonists describing treatment. At Hugh Hull's boarding school, the headmaster went in for heroic treatment. To keep them regular, boys were given doses of 'Salts and Senna, and Brimstone and Treacle', and the headmaster treated an enormous boil on Hugh's leg by bringing it to a head with a poultice, then cutting off the top with a pair of scissors – unsterilised, of course. Hugh was left with a large scar.[18]

Others reported working out their own treatment. When George Harris suffered from ophthalmia, he avoided direct sunlight. George Boyes, colonial auditor, arrived in 1826. His diary shows that for mild ailments such as a cold he took calomel. Otherwise he used common sense. Ill with 'cold, fever pain in the limbs', he had a dinner of 'boiled mutton and Toast and water' and went to bed early. Next day he was much better.[19] For a bad back he had a bath and lay on the sofa. To cure some unspecified sickness he stopped eating animal food and took calomel and 'a draught' (doctor's medicine?). Next day he felt extremely ill. 'I try this and that but without any defined acknowledged object – it is all a matter of experiment. I am inclined to think the Doctor's pills powders and draughts have never been of the least service to me.'[20]

Dr Bryant was Boyes' neighbour and friend, and his prescriptions sometimes worked:

> A headache with a slight degree of fever has been hanging about me nearly a fortnight and Dr. Bryant who came up to see me last evening recommends 8 grams of Calomel a tureen of mutton broth and … a ride in the country in the afternoon. I feel the benefit of his advice already.[21]

Boils are usually caused by bacteria, which Bryant could not have known. When Boyes developed boils, Bryant recommended he work less and play more, and buy a horse for exercise. He did and was 'completely restored'.[22] From these pieces of information it seems that medicine was largely a hit-and-miss affair, with Dr Bryant's knowledge limited. Both he and Boyes relied largely on common sense; exercise and rest seemed the most effective treatments. (Boyes eventually died of 'continued fever' in 1853, aged 67.)

Knopwood's diary shows he was often ill 'of the stone', kidney stones, and frequently recorded that he was 'very unwell' for several days. Sometimes the pain faded, but once 'my death was expected'. Doctors' treatment varied: they bled him ('which reduced me very greatly'), 'blisterd' him, 'fomented' him with hot water, put warm flannels on the pain and put him under a 'solavation' (?). To relieve pain they prescribed calomel, and occasionally laudanum and 'oether' – ether, not yet used as an anaesthetic.[23]

In 1816, when Knopwood was having a bad bout of pain, three surgeons consulted and 'passed bougees a very little way down' (the penis). A bougie is a thin flexible medical instrument; some were caustic, which sounds alarming. In 1820 Knopwood calculated that caustic bougies had been applied 118 times and ordinary ones at least four hundred. Presumably this painful procedure brought relief, but he kept on suffering, so badly that again his life was despaired of: 'the inquiry was, how is Mr. K. now, is he likely to live'. Finally in 1825 'a very large stone came from me', and after this he had fewer attacks.[24]

Knopwood occasionally suffered other illnesses: bad colds, dysentery (for which he took castor oil) and liver disease, not surprisingly considering the number of alcoholic dinners he enjoyed. He fell from his horse, for which Dr Westbrook bled him 'profusely for fear of an inflamation' – Westbrook seemed to bleed him whenever he visited.[25] But in general, apart from his alcohol intake, Knopwood's lifestyle was healthy: he walked and rode, spent much time in his garden, and ate mainly meat, plentiful vegetables from his garden and (presumably) bread. He died aged 75, cause unspecified.

In the north, **Ann Weston** suffered some unspecified illness which confined her to her bed for three months, but then her doctor recommended a cold vinegar bath (fortunately this was in summer). 'I already feel much strengthened by it', she told her sister, 'and hope soon to be able to attend to domestic affairs. I can hardly sit still and see a number of things which I know will be left undone till I do them but I must mind what my husband and the Dr say.'[26]

Another woman to record medical details was Elizabeth Fenton, who arrived with her husband Michael, an Indian army officer, and their baby daughter Flora. Michael was in delicate health and doctors said the Tasmanian climate would cure him (which it did; he died aged 85). In Hobart, Flora became ill. 'My baby, the very light of my eyes, was then quite despaired of and given up by all but myself', wrote Elizabeth. The first doctor left Flora to die, and Elizabeth sent for Dr Bryant who 'adopted a different mode of treatment'. Flora survived.

In July, mid-winter, they moved to their land grant at Plenty. They spent the first night at New Norfolk, and sent the servants ahead with the luggage including the clothes. Michael, Elizabeth and Flora set out in the buggy. Caught in a snowstorm, they sought shelter in a house where a bachelor was drying himself in front of his fire. Startled, their host gave Elizabeth and Flora his bed and himself slept on the floor in front of the fire with Michael. In the night Elizabeth found Flora flushed with a rapid pulse. She dosed her with calomel – mercury chloride – for a baby! Towards morning Flora woke 'very sick', so Elizabeth walked to and fro with her until dawn, then possibly gave her more calomel.[27] I'm relieved to report that Flora survived.

Eliza Hammond's story was grimmer, possibly because it involved more doctors and more medicine. She arrived with her businessman husband James in 1824. They went back to England, then returned to Hobart; but James caught a fever on the way, and Eliza gave birth to a third child only five days before they landed. James then died, as did the baby. Eliza, 26, was left a widow with two small children and little money. She had to sell her house; then another child died. A friend described her, not surprisingly, as broken-hearted. The respectable version of her story, as reported by a newspaper, ran: Eliza caught a fever, recovered, but relapsed and died.[28]

The *Colonial Times*, not so reticent, published every detail. Dr Westbrook said he treated Eliza for fever, disclaiming all knowledge of her drinking (perhaps tactfully keeping quiet). The Rev. Richard Yaldwin, who arrived to find himself Eliza's only relation (his sister was married to her brother), took care of her. He was unhappy at Westbrook's treatment, thinking his powders were killing her. Since, horrifyingly, they contained opium, mercury and antimony, a toxic purgative, he was right. Yaldwin called in another doctor, who arrived drunk, then Dr Bryant. He realised Eliza was drinking heavily; the landlord found in her room sixteen spirit bottles and a five-gallon (19-litre) keg of rum, nearly empty. Bryant stopped Eliza's access to spirits and recommended moving her to the country, away from temptation. She was extremely ill – agitated, delirious, with hallucinations and clammy hands, all symptoms of delirium tremens. Yaldwin felt he should follow Bryant's advice – 'I am not a medical man', he told the inquest, helplessly – and drove her to New Norfolk. She took one of Westbrook's powders and immediately became much worse, her bowels continually open. The New Norfolk doctor was called in, but having never seen the patient before he had no idea why she was obviously dying. 'Owing to my total ignorance', but presumably feeling he had to do something, he prescribed cutting off her hair and bathing her scalp with vinegar, with a mustard poultice for her feet. Eliza fell into a stupor and died the next day.[29]

Several points emerge from the evidence at the inquest. One was that convict servants knew what was going on and acted as they thought for the best – either helping their mistress (and joining in the drinking), or alerting their master. Another was the helplessness of doctors, who had nothing useful to prescribe for fever, alcoholism, delirium tremens or indeed a broken heart. The third was the appalling use of toxic 'medicines': Westbrook, defending his dreadful powders, said he had often given them to a girl of twelve. The fourth was Eliza's lack of family; she was lucky to have even a distant relation, a virtual stranger, to help her. The fifth was that everyone in this story, by their own account at least, meant well but did not know how to do anything helpful. Even Westbrook possibly did not realise how harmful his powders were, since the ingredients were all accepted medicines.

Afterwards Westbrook continued to practise but died in 1839 of 'a long and painful illness'; Bryant returned to England; the unfortunate Yaldwin, pitchforked into this imbroglio, died three years later.[30] The surviving Hammond child, three-year-old Maria, was granted 1000 acres and taken in by the wealthy Grants of Ballochmyle. Brought up apparently happily, she married, had many children and died aged 85, the only member of this whole saga to live a long and fruitful life.[31] The moral of all these stories is: if you were ill in Hobart in the 1820s, consult Dr Bryant, not Dr Westbrook.

Medical operations were necessarily few, given the lack of anaesthetics. Naturally, they were dreaded. Richard Priest, a surgeon, came to the aid of his neighbour Richard Dry, who was attacked by bushrangers. The bushrangers shot Priest in the knee. He refused to have his leg amputated – and died.[32] In Sydney in 1815, Dr Jacob Mountgarrett consulted Dr Joseph Arnold about a badly wounded finger, gained from a saw wound when assisting in an amputation. His whole hand was badly swollen and covered in purple spots (a symptom of gangrene). Arnold recommended 'an application of charcoal and hot fomentations'. This did no good and, unlike Priest, Mountgarrett agreed to have the limb amputated. He lived another decade.[33]

Poor sanitation and polluted water caused some diseases. Sanitary arrangements were rarely mentioned. Presumably people went at first in the bush, then dug a cess pit with a dunny building over the top. Those living along the Hobart Rivulet built toilets over the stream. Water closets were first advertised in 1829 and were probably only for the wealthy, though the convicts in the Female Factory had them. This building had the advantage of being beside the Hobart Rivulet, so the results flowed into it.[34]

Water mainly came from rivers and creeks. Some people had water casks to collect rainwater from roofs, but these were not large enough for a permanent supply. Hobart's water came from the Hobart Rivulet. In 1804 Collins ordered that, since this provided 'that great comfort of life, a permanent supply of pure running water', it was not to be polluted. By 1820, however, three mills had been built on it and their waste drained into it, as did people's household waste, and there were complaints of polluted water. Also, in summer there was not enough water. In 1828–29 there was public outcry against pollution:

> Need we call the attention of the inhabitants of Hobart Town to the present state of the Creek, with scarcely a sufficiency of water to supply their tea-kettles – much less their washing tubs ... the impossibility of washing with the water from the effects of the *quantities of filth* allowed to be continually emptied into it.

Hobart would not have pure and wholesome water until 'a stop is put to the creek being made a cess pool'.[35] But it was many years before Hobartians had a reliably pure water supply.

In the north, Launceston also needed a supply of pure water. There were two possible sources: the basin of the South Esk, up Cataract Gorge, hard to access because of the rocky gorge and floods; or about a mile up the North Esk, where water was easier to collect but brackish and muddy. As in Hobart, citizens had to wait years before they obtained a pure supply.[36] Those outside the main towns had to do the best they could with water from rivers, creeks or, sometimes, wells.

What did people die of? Until the end of 1831, colonial records show the deaths of 2553 people. (Given the poor quality of record keeping, this is certainly not the real total.)

	Percentage of all deaths
Children under 5	22
Children 5 to 14	3
Young adults 15 to 24	13
Adults 25 to 34	24
Adults 35-44	15
Adults 45-54	12
Adults 55-64	6
Adults over 65	5

Notable is the high number of deaths of infants – 14 per cent of all deaths were babies under one year old. This was usual at the time, when many babies died of diarrhoea and dysentery.

Hobart dominates as the place of death: 81 per cent of deaths occurred in the south, with three quarters in Hobart alone – though people about to die often went there to hospital, for medical advice or for their executions. The oldest person to die was John Waters, aged 97, described as an invalid. Mary Hammond, aged 95, was a 'poor woman'. I can find nothing else about her, no convict called Mary Hammond, nothing. How did she find herself in Van Diemen's Land and how, a 'poor woman', had she managed to keep alive for so long? Perhaps by being unable to afford the medicines of the day.

Cause of death was given in only a quarter of cases. The most common, astonishingly, was execution with 109 men executed – for murder, bushranging, stealing sheep. As well, 63 people were murdered: by bushrangers, by soldiers, 'killed fighting', 'killed by Mr Humphrey's shepherd', 'killed by a blow on the head'. Aboriginal warriors murdered 27 people, though their murders by Europeans were not recorded.

Another large group died by accident. They were drowned, burnt or had the equivalent of road deaths: falling off a horse, run over by a cart. There were industrial accidents: killed by a falling tree (probably

Burial registers had no column for cause of death, though sometimes this was included under 'Ship's Name' (a neat way of avoiding the word 'convict'): 'Found dead in ye Bush', 'Killed by ye Aborigines', 'Murdered', 'Executed for sheep stealing' (TA RGD34/1/1 p.48)

when cutting timber), killed when blasting stone, fell from the masts of ships. One unfortunate person 'died in consequence of injury received in saluting judge' (how was not explained). Boyes described how three people ate poisonous toadfish and 'two or three hours after were corpses'.[37] At least one person died from snakebite, and more were bitten. When Matthew Goulder's wife was bitten by a snake at York Plains, he cut the affected part, sucked poison from the wound and rubbed it with salt, the recommended treatment. 'Mrs Goulder is now in a fair way of recovery, and out of all danger, though weak' – not surprisingly! Hugh Hull and some employees were burning down trees at night when a tree fell on one man, 'old Paddy', smashing him to a heap, as Hugh wrote. He raced over only to see 'a mass of matter which two minutes before had been my man ... I was dreadfully shocked'.[38]

Though many people must have died of disease, this was rarely mentioned, perhaps because doctors were unable to diagnose. Three people died of apoplexy, two of 'visitation of God' and one dropped dead in the street, all possibly heart attacks or strokes. Eight died of the effects of alcohol and two of poison – whether taken accidentally or on purpose was not stated. There were eight suicides (usually by cutting the throat or shooting), with 14 'found drowned' and 11 'found dead', which could mean suicide or accident. Some 'found dead' were lost in the bush, with 'gully New Norfolk' the place of death. Two men were 'found dead supposed to have died of cold and hunger' and 'found dead in the bush'. Van Diemen's Land could be a place of promise, but could also be home to lonely, even anonymous people.

Women had their own sad cause of death: dying in childbirth. Pregnancy must have been terrifying, with women knowing that death was a strong possibility. In Britain the maternal mortality rate was around 20 per thousand births, and probably colonial figures were similar.[39] Experienced midwives could help with normal births, but could do little for abnormal ones (no caesareans) and, as well, too many women died of puerperal fever caused by septic conditions, post-partum haemorrhage or eclampsia.

From 1819, some midwives, man-midwives or accoucheurs advertised their services in Hobart. The first, William Boston, claimed training as a 'surgeon and man-midwife' from the University of Edinburgh and was ready 'to afford every assistance and relief to the afflicted', but no more was heard of him. Then came Dr Murdoch, whose journal mentions delivering many babies but with details in only one case. When in 1826 Mrs Mary Bignell of Tea Tree Brush had a life-threatening adherent placenta, Murdoch recommended a manual removal of the placenta, which remains current practice.[40]

Miss Field and Mrs McTavish advertised as midwives, both mentioning experience and qualifications as well as 'respectability of character' to obtain patients. This last was possibly code for 'sober', for a drunken midwife was little help. In 1826 Mrs Baker of Lake Plains died in childbirth owing to the midwife being 'rather intoxicated'. The husband was so distraught he cut his throat, leaving five young children orphaned. Another distressing death in childbed was that of Mrs Balfour, wife of the

Launceston commandant. There was no danger apprehended only two minutes before her death, reported surveyor John Wedge.[41]

Robert Knopwood adopted a young orphan, Elizabeth (Betsy) Mack, and brought her up dotingly. After she married they remained close, with Betsy often visiting, bringing her little boy Robert. When Knopwood was ill she stayed with him, caring for him. In 1830 she was pregnant again and on 20 October, her wedding anniversary, Knopwood planned to dine with her. But that morning he received terrible news. The night before she had been delivered of a daughter and was doing well, so that her attendants did not think there was any danger (there was always fear for women in childbirth). But a few hours later 'she was taken in a fit and expired in it'. Knopwood was devastated. For the rest of his life he mourned 'my dear and ever regretted Elizabeth', 'my sole comfort', 'my dear and ever lamented girl'.[42]

John Hudspeth described the experience of his patient and neighbour Elizabeth Gregson. When she went into labour, 'I was in attendance all day'; he delivered a baby daughter at midnight. Three days later Elizabeth was 'taken alarmingly ill', but John and his wife Mary nursed her all day and night, and she pulled through. When the baby was five days old, Elizabeth was so well that John did not feel he had to stay with her all night, so went home. 'We took this opportunity of weaning the child by me taking her home, away from her mother.' Five days old! John obviously cared for the baby well, for she became fretful and would stay with no one else.[43] He did not record what he was feeding her, or when he took her back to her mother. The little girl survived to grow up.

Another description of childbirth comes from James Sutherland, on a farm near Campbell Town. On 30 March 1825 his wife Lucy 'had some pains', so James went for the doctor and for their neighbour, Mrs Cox. Lucy's pains were 'very great', but the baby, 'our sweet Mary', was born safely. Lucy's milk was slow to come in so Mary lived on panada (bread boiled in a liquid, let's hope milk). By the time Lucy had milk in abundance the baby was used to a spoon and would not suck, but Mrs Cox was determined and soon Mary was sucking – so, unlike the Gregson baby, she was breastfed. Four days after the birth, Lucy was doing so well she was able to sit up. Three months later, wrote the proud father, 'our dearest baby becoming very engaging'.[44]

Though women must have dreaded childbirth there was nothing

they could do to avoid it. Someone asked George Boyes his advice on contraception. 'I have no advice to give', he replied. 'I know of an instance where the apparently obvious remedy of sleeping alone failed altogether'. That was it for contraception in the 1820s.[45]

With all these diseases, the wonder is that anyone lived into old age. But, like Knopwood, most people lived reasonably healthy lives, if they survived infancy. As in Britain, a high infant mortality meant that those with health problems tended to die early. The diet was fairly healthy and there was little pollution, at least in the air. Daily life involved plenty of exercise. Dr Mountgarrett told Commissioner Bigge that the people were generally healthy, particularly those born in the colony, 'more robust' than emigrants. A downside was the huge amount of alcohol too many people drank. However, those whose livers could cope, and who were not too much subject to doctors' drastic treatment, could remain well. In 1829 John Headlam wrote home that his family had not had a day's illness since they left England nine years earlier.[46]

As with other aspects of the colony, from 1824 Governor Arthur organised a more efficient medical system. By 1831 there were eight surgeons in Hobart and six district surgeons, who like John Hudspeth were often farmers as well: at New Norfolk, Jericho, Campbell Town, Bothwell, Norfolk Plains and Great Swanport on the east coast. Melville's *Annual* claimed that at the Hobart hospital, patients were 'treated with the utmost possible attention'.[47] Let's hope so.

In 1831 James Ross commented on the health of the colony.[48] It was good, generally, with higher longevity than in England. The most common diseases, fever and dysentery, were not usually fatal. He did notice cases of a protuberance on the neck around New Norfolk – most likely goitre, common in Tasmania and caused by the lack of iodine in the soil. Many convicts arrived with 'emaciated and diseased frames', wrote Ross, owing to their dissolute and irregular lives (and poverty), but the control under which they lived (limited access to alcohol) and good and wholesome food often restored them. The major problem was drink: over half the deaths were due directly or indirectly to drink, with drunkenness causing disease, accidents or fatal fights and murders. (However, puritanical Ross did exaggerate; he also said many deaths were caused by overeating, due to the stimulation of the 'dry and elastic' atmosphere.)

11. EDUCATION AND CULTURE

Education

Many European children in early Van Diemen's Land, especially from poor families, learned the life-skills they needed from their parents. However, to earn a living some people needed academic skills, particularly reading and writing, and it was most convenient for a teacher to instruct children at school. Some parents in the bush gave academic teaching to their children, but it must have been difficult to fit in with their busy lives.

Schools had existed in Britain for centuries and were replicated in the colony. There were two types, government and private. Government schools, like government hospitals, were for the poor – but the authorities were keen to educate these children, to improve them, raise them above their mainly convict parents. In both Hobart and Port Dalrymple, the government paid schoolmasters from an early date. It was hoped that they would teach not only the three Rs but also good morals and behaviour.

Thomas Fitzgerald, a literate convict, opened a school in Hobart in 1807, earning what he could persuade parents to pay. From 1812 the government paid him a small salary, providing he taught convicts' children gratis. Governor Sorell was happy to remunerate Thomas's wife Mary (with a little over half Thomas' salary) as 'she pays much attention to the female scholars'. Thomas also worked as a clerk, from which Sorell dismissed him for drunkenness, though he thought him 'well qualified as schoolmaster'. In 1818 the Fitzgeralds' school was described as the best and largest in the colony. It operated until Thomas died in 1824.[1] In Launceston, in 1810 Macquarie appointed convict Thomas Macqueen as a paid teacher. The Rev. Youl described him as 'a very dissipated man', but he continued teaching until 1822, then retired on a pension.[2]

Sorell wanted to improve education for the children of 'poor free people' and set up small schools at Clarence Plains and New Norfolk. In 1820 Commissioner Bigge asked about schools generally. People agreed that many colonists wanted their children educated, but schools were

A bored child at school? Sketch of a girl by Thomas Bock (TA ALMFA AUTAS001124060799)

few and badly conducted: teachers were not capable of teaching children, most were convicts and ex-convicts, one was dismissed for misconduct, others were drunk and dissipated. There were three government schools and five small private ones. Only two teachers were praised.[3]

Knopwood told Bigge that government schools were under his supervision (though he did little about them). Children learnt reading, writing and arithmetic, and girls were also taught sewing. Bigge was unimpressed. He thought scholars' progress and teachers' qualifications inadequate. Only 193 children out of 1021 (19 per cent) were at school, though this was probably much the same as in England. Bigge recommended more, and more competent, teachers and use of the Bell system of teaching: learning divided into small segments which pupils mastered before progressing, and older children instructing younger ones, so fewer adult teachers were needed.[4]

As a result, in 1821 Peter Mulgrave, who had no experience beyond briefly observing the Bell system, arrived as superintendent of schools. By this stage, Sorell had set up 15 schools, though only nine had teachers, all ex-convicts. Mulgrave was competent, active and effective and in 1822 established a central government school in Hobart.[5] It flourished, particularly when Thomas and Ann Stone (free settlers) took over in 1824. Soon they were teaching 100 children. In 1828, in the presence of daunting local luminaries, the children were examined, largely on religious knowledge. Medals were awarded to girls and boys, and onlookers were impressed:

> The intellectual improvement which [the pupils] evinced, and the orderly conduct which they preserved, redounded very greatly to the credit of the master and mistress of the Institution, (Mr. and Mrs. Stone,) and the excellent discipline they maintained.[6]

Order, discipline and progress: just what the authorities wanted.

One Aboriginal boy attended the school. A journalist had seen 'among the boys let loose from Mr. Stones school, a native black boy playing with his school-fellows at marbles'. He was George Van Diemen, an orphan sent to England for his education but since returned. He had made considerable progress at the school, continued the report, but regrettably he had just died of consumption (tuberculosis).[7]

The Stones' school was a bright spot in an otherwise gloomy picture. Because of his inadequate salary, Mulgrave resigned and moved to Port Dalrymple, where he combined superintendence of the school with three other government jobs. In 1827 a newspaper deplored the decline of schools, and a parent at the Black Brush complained that since the school closed, 'our children are left to degenerate into barbarism'.[8]

In 1826 Archdeacon Scott of Sydney reported on Van Diemen's Land's schools. Of the colony's 1086 children aged between 5 and 15, only 312 were at government schools and 130 in private ones (41 per cent in total), and their education was 'most imperfect'. Parents claimed to be eager to have their children educated, wrote Scott, but did little in practice. He was not surprised, with inadequate schools and low salaries which did not attract 'a competent person of character'. Besides, free people were prejudiced against sending their children to school with convicts' children. He recommended more teachers and higher salaries: financial considerations should not matter compared with the good which would result. This was not London's view, of course, and though some individual teachers were successful, there was little overall improvement by 1831. That year there were eight government schools: at Hobart and Launceston, and in the country at Campbell Town, Sorell, New Norfolk, Back River, Glenorchy and Norfolk Plains.[9] The government had also opened the large King's Orphan Schools for boys and girls, where orphans and children of serving convicts were housed and educated.

John Headlam's story illustrates the difficulties teachers faced. Called 'a fine scholar', from 1825 he taught at the Launceston public school, but it was dilapidated with no fireplace, broken windows and a partly collapsed ceiling. The government pay and rent allowance was £76, and though pupils were meant to pay a fee of £2 a year, of his 67 scholars only a dozen paid anything. Headlam paid £125 rent a year for his family's home and had to open a private school for young gentlemen to make ends meet, and his wife opened a young ladies' school at well. But their income was still not enough, and in 1830 Headlam gave up teaching and took over an inn.[10]

Sunday Schools

When effective clergy arrived in the early 1820s, they were keen to educate children, as well as train them in behaviour and morals. Sunday Schools – classes for children (and adults) after church – were popular in Britain. Open only on Sundays, they could teach less than regular schools but they were free. From 1821 the Wesleyan church in Hobart ran a Sunday School. It had its ups and downs but persevered, and in 1830 a newspaper praised its 'very gratifying' procession of over 150 children to a Christmas function. Their 'neat dress and orderly manners were a soothing contrast to the disgusting scenes of drunkenness which had disgraced the streets' on the holiday – a telling comparison between old colonial habits and what authorities and the middle class, including this journalist, hoped were the new.[11]

The Presbyterians and Launceston Methodists ran smaller Sunday Schools, and in 1828 there was even one at the Oatlands prison for the chain gang. Most prisoners volunteered for lessons.[12]

Private schools

From 1806 to 1831, I found 47 private schools in Van Diemen's Land (though there were probably more).[13] Most started after 1820, once the population had begun to increase rapidly. Almost all (37) were in Hobart, by far the largest centre of population; most of the rest were in Launceston (from 1825) and two were in the midlands. Almost half (21) were mentioned just once, and only eight lasted three years or more. So schools came and went, and running one was a precarious business.

There were two types: either for young children of both sexes, teaching the rudiments; or the far more numerous and expensive schools for 'young ladies' and 'young gentlemen', teaching not just literacy, numeracy and some geography and history but a smattering of, for boys, Latin and possibly Greek; for girls. accomplishments such as music, dancing and drawing. Occasional teachers offered other subjects: science, accounting, elocution, astronomy, 'foreign exchange'. Holidays were short: in 1831 one boarding school provided two weeks in mid-winter and four in summer.[14]

It was easy enough to open a school. The teacher had to be literate and numerate but no other qualifications were needed (only a few advertised prior experience). A room in the teacher's home became the school room, furnished with a table and chairs. The teacher provided some textbooks, pencils and paper or slates, and advertised for pupils. Most schools remained small, with perhaps half a dozen pupils, easy enough for a competent person to manage. Opening a school was particularly attractive to middle-class women in difficult financial circumstances, such as widows, abandoned wives or young single women.

A successful school could bring an adequate income. A government teacher earned at most Headlam's £76 a year. Private teachers had to pay the costs of a home anyway so had few overheads. They charged day pupils anything from £8 to £20 a year.[15] At £8, to earn £50 a year they would have to be sure of seven pupils; at £20, only three. But the real money was in boarders, who paid from £35 to £60 a year.[16] Teachers had to provide living accommodation and food, but six boarders a year would bring in say £240, a good income, with expenses relatively small.

However, there were problems, firstly in attracting enough pupils to open a school, secondly in keeping them. A family withdrawing say three pupils might make a school uneconomic. A negative report, even a rumour, might be disastrous. In 1823 Knopwood withdrew his ward from Mrs Speed's school because of ill-treatment, which would not have helped her reputation.[17] She closed the school at the end of the year.

Another problem was collecting fees. Bitter experience must have led Mrs Headlam to advertise in 1822 that she 'finds it absolutely necessary to state, that no young lady can be taken into her Establishment without a Quarters Payment being made in Advance'.[18] A fourth problem was inability to teach, which must have made the job daunting. Running through this section is an emphasis on kindness; teachers who were not kind might not have lasted long. Though Hugh Hull did not find James Thomson kind (see below): perhaps kindness was considered more desirable for girls.

Why did people open schools? Some were frank. Mr and Mrs Chorley were dismissed as master and mistress of the Orphan School for improper conduct so, 'Circumstances [financial] not admitting of their leaving the Colony', they opened a school. Everyone must have known, in gossipy Hobart, that Caroline Dawes' lawyer husband was an alcoholic who had abandoned her and their toddler, so they knew why she opened a school 'for the support of herself and little family'.[19] Miss Bamber might have been relying on people's love for gossip when she advertised that prospective parents could visit her to find out what had induced her to open her school. Widow Mary Fitzgerald was 'left for some years to struggle with difficulty to maintain a large family. Numerous misfortunes have oppressed her, and she is now under the necessity of taking to the above Employment as the means of Support' – not out of love of teaching or any more acceptable motive. Though Mr Hobson, advertising that he was induced to open his grammar school in Hobart because of the difficulty of gaining an education there, had no more success.[20] None of these schools lasted long

Three schools were notably successful. James Thomson from Edinburgh opened one in Hobart in 1823, for day boys and boarders,

Ellinthorpe Hall, by Henry Grant Lloyd, painted long after the school closed – but the scene had barely changed (TA ALMFA AUTAS001124062795w800)

teaching reading, writing, arithmetic, Latin, and as extras French and geography. It ran until 1838.[21] As a little boy, Hugh Hull attended a small school run by Miss Pitt, who was kind and gave him bread and honey. The family moved to Launceston, which had no schools, and in 1824 Hugh was sent to board at Mr Thomson's. This had 92 boys of whom 25 were boarders. Thomson was severe and frequently caned boys, while Susan the servant used to wipe her greasy hands in Hugh's curly hair – less brutal but demeaning. Hugh's one happy memory was of swimming in the river, but otherwise it was 'the usual routine of work, floggings'. He left aged ten to make room for younger brothers and started work in his father's office. Aged ten (!), he 'counted out dollars and issued slops and rations to the Military and convict establishments'. After only four years' schooling, he went on to function perfectly well as a senior public servant.[22]

In 1823 Hannah Davice and her apprentice Elinor Binfield opened their 'establishment for the INSTRUCTION of YOUNG LADIES' in Hobart. Having experience in England, they advertised, they were confident they could combine 'useful and solid acquirements' (the three Rs) with 'all that is necessary to form and adorn the female character'. When Hannah married grazier George Carr Clark she moved the school to his home, Ellinthorpe near Ross. It became the colony's leading school for girls, surviving an attack by bushrangers – and negative gossip. In 1829 landowner James Cox publicly stated that 'From my long experience (5 years) of the kind attention you invariably give your pupils, and the excellent management of the estate in general', he had no intention of removing his daughters from the school; he had only taken them home for a short holiday while Mrs Clark had a baby.[23] In one version or other, Hannah's school lasted seventeen years.

More ambitious but less successful was the Cornwall Collegiate Institute. In 1826 sixteen leading northern men decided to establish a school for 'the liberal and scientific education of youth' (meaning male youth). As schoolmaster they appointed the Rev. Richard Claiborne who had a degree from Oxford and had started a school in Hobart. The Institute opened in early 1827, the fifty pupils learning Greek, Latin, English, history, geography and algebra. At an examination in July they 'evinced astonishing progress'. However, Claiborne resigned, not finding it as lucrative as he expected (it was rumoured). Unable to find a replacement, the board closed the school. Claiborne, a competent teacher, opened the Norfolk Plains Grammar School, which he ran until 1832.[24]

People tried other types of school. Evening classes, dancing classes: for a period Mr Knight ran a dancing academy in Launceston. Some people took individual pupils. Clergymen often did this, for they had attended university, an attractive qualification: Governor Arthur's son boarded with a clergyman who educated him as a gentleman.[25] George Boyes, planning on bringing his family to the colony, told his wife that his friend Robinson (another clergyman) could undertake the education of the boys, but 'I am not quite sure ... that Nature intended him to be a schoolmaster'. Besides, he would charge the exorbitant sum of £100 per boy per annum.[26]

In 1831 there were seven private schools for boys in the colony (including one for Catholics in Hobart). Thomson and Claiborne both taught classics and could prepare boys for university. (No parents appeared to require this before 1831 but William Dry, born in Launceston in 1820, attended a school run by a clergyman and then went to university in England.) There were also seven schools for girls, for which the most flattering adjective was 'respectable', clearly the main requirement.[27]

Sometimes it was cheaper and more convenient for a family to employ a governess or tutor, though little is known about such arrangements. Such people were not well paid and candidates' calibre was not notably high, though James Ross, with a Doctor of Laws from Aberdeen university, tutored Governor Arthur's children when he needed a job.[28] Some immigrants brought governesses from Britain but, in a colony short of women, such eligible young women tended to marry.[29] On the whole, privately educating children in Van Diemen's Land must have been a difficult and expensive business, what with large families, high fees and schools opening and closing.

Culture

Music was the most popular art form in Tasmania until 1831 and long afterwards – and may be still. Everyone can have a go at singing a song and almost everyone enjoys listening to music. Aboriginal singing and dancing, going back tens of thousands of years, continued into the British era. Camping with groups of Aboriginal people, George Robinson often spent his evenings 'in conviviality, singing and dancing until a late hour, making the woods to echo with their song'.[30]

The first British music was similar: singing round a campfire or in a hut, or at men's dinners, especially after a few drinks. Casual music like this persisted: perhaps someone had a fiddle and could play a few tunes, perhaps someone tried a dance. No one wrote it down though, so there's no evidence. Musical instruments were for sale from 1818: pianos, violins and cellos.[31] In 1820 Mrs Headlam was providing the young ladies at her school with 'instructions on the Piano Forte'. Pianos became remarkably common. James Ross's wife had one in their hut on the Shannon, and in 1831 James Backhouse reported that most prosperous settlers had a piano, 'from whatever rank they had risen' (not just the gentry).[32]

Collins and Paterson each brought two drummers with them but nothing was recorded by way of musical performances for years. Balls were held from 1814 and someone must have provided music for dancing

The military band preparing to perform in Hobart, by John Ommanney (TA ALMFA AUTAS001139593909)

– a few fiddlers perhaps? In 1821 Hobart's bachelors gave the first public ball, to honour Governor Macquarie. The 150 guests danced till 5 am – but no one described the music.[33]

In 1822 Hobart's first serious musician arrived: John Philip Deane. At first he opened a store (where among many other things he sold a grand piano) and a bakery, then in 1824 he advertised lessons on the piano forte and violin. He also sold sheet music.[34] Churches were a source of music, with congregations singing hymns and psalms, sometimes led by a choir. In 1822 Hobart's first church, St David's Church of England, was opened, and had a choir accompanied by a small band of wind instruments. Three years later the church gained Australia's first pipe organ, with Deane as organist.[35]

Deane co-operated with the second notable musician, Joseph Reichenberg, bandmaster to the military band of the 40th regiment, which arrived in 1825. The band performed at public events such as a dinner in honour of the king's birthday, and when a detachment of the regiment left for Launceston, it accompanied them along the road through Hobart, so 'silvery tones of musical instruments enlivened the town'.[36] The band played in the open on Sunday evenings, despite complaints that this encouraged undesirable familiarities in the audience – probably code for non-convicts mixing with convicts.[37]

In 1826 Reichenberg and Deane organised Hobart's first concert. The music was mainly classical – a Mozart overture, a clarinet concerto, Haydn's *Surprise Symphony* arranged for string quintet – but included band music and a glee, 'The Witches'. It was a great success, delighting the audience of about 250, and would have astonished the most fastidious ear of a London critic, according to a local newspaper. A second concert was not as successful, partly because people applying for tickets had to pass a respectability test. A newspaper claimed this 'party feeling' was deplored by 'every real friend of the colony': an attempt to keep out ex-convicts?[38] But in 1828 the 40th regiment departed. The new military detachment's band gained less praise, though Knopwood was pleased that it often played in his paddock on Wednesdays. People came to visit him to hear the band: 'very great attendance of ladies and gents'.[39]

Reichenberg remained in Hobart, and both he and Deane gave lessons and published music, 'Hobart Town Quadrilles' by Reichenberg, 'Tasmanian Quadrilles' by Deane.[40] Then Reichenberg went to teach at Ellinthorpe Hall. A letter-writer mourned the way concerts had fallen into oblivion: Hobart was 'out of tune'! Deane was at the forefront of what musical activity there was, for example presiding 'as usual' over the music at a ball at Government House.[41]

In 1830 Deane started his own concerts. The first showed the skills of ten musicians and seven singers, including three Deane children aged six, nine and ten. Deane was praised: unrivalled as a musician in the colonies and performing the duties of a citizen, father and husband to general esteem, despite meeting 'the gale of adversity' (probably financial).[42] By late 1831 he had given five concerts, all praised: excellent performances (considering the limited material, added one review), large, enthusiastic audiences – not surprising, since the concerts were Hobart's only public entertainment:

> Nothing but music seems the fashion, children were taking lessons ... There is something indeed in the clear elastic atmosphere of Van Diemen's Land which seems to improve the tone, and to add to some degree to the charms of music.[43]

Meanwhile, Launcestonian music-lovers had, apparently, nothing.

Reading was a favourite recreation among literate people. Arrivals in 1804 brought books, though not many: in 1808 George Harris deplored the lack of books, saying he had read those there were again and again. When people died or left the colony and their estates were sold, purchasers could buy books (one gentlemen left 800), and in 1818 books appeared in Hobart stores, though sellers did not always sound particularly literate ('a great variety of choice books').[44]

Libraries began in Launceston in 1825, when John Fawkner, innkeeper, opened a circulating library ('circulating' as books went from borrower to borrower). Three years later the Rev. Browne established one at St John's Church and encouraged its use 'by convict and free'.[45] In 1826 the Wesleyan church in Hobart began a library, and the next year John and Rosalie Deane opened a circulating library, offering children's books for spelling, reading and ciphering, as well as 'dictionaries, tradesmen's assistants, histories, domestic cookery, religions books, &c'. They built up a large stock (2300 volumes), and set up Hobart's first bookshop.[46] Scientific societies (see below) also set up libraries, or planned to. As schools developed and more people were educated, the demand for books grew. By 1831 readers were quite well catered for.

There were some local authors. Many people wrote privately – diaries and letters – but two, both convicts, had books published. An account of bushranger Michael Howe (1818), probably by convict Thomas Wells, was the first book of general literature published in Australia. Henry Savery's *Quinton Servinton* (1831), much of it set in Van Diemen's Land, was the first Australian novel. Newspapers published poetry by local writers, notably verse by visitor Mary Leman Grimstone. Naturally, for a visitor, the convict presence was dominant. 'On visiting the cemetery in Hobart Town' she found 'This scene neglected, naked, and unkind ... Oh! Here where all is young save grief and crime'.[47]

Tasmania, as a curiosity, began to feature in English plays. In 1831 a three-act melodrama, *Van Diemen's Land* by a Mr Moncrieff, was staged in London. Characters included Michael Howe; Bennelong, actually a mainland Aboriginal man; as heroine, a female convict unjustly condemned (of course); notorious convict Ikey Solomon and dozens more. The *Colonial Times* thought the play gave 'ample scope for laughter'.[48]

Some private groups enjoyed intellectual activity. Charles Arthur described a debating society of six young gentlemen who met once a week. He took part in a discussion on duelling, which he had to justify, difficult when he thought it could never be justified. His next activity, to defend 'The importance of speaking the truth', was easier as he could not see any argument against it. Months later the club was still 'going on very well', with Charles having to argue against the topic, 'Whether Plays are beneficial to the morals of the people'.[49]

Interest in science developed rapidly from the mid eighteenth-century, as did interest in educating the masses. Mechanics' Institutes, which encouraged education among the working class, were first established in Scotland in 1821. Astonishingly, in 1827 'respectable master tradesmen' opened an Institute in small, distant Hobart. They made the mistake of inviting gentlemen, who took over. At the first general meeting, attended by over a hundred people, Dr James Ross took the chair – a university-educated teacher, newspaper editor and keen promoter of intellectual activity. Enthusiasm came and went, but the Institute often held regular lectures. Most were about modern science: Astronomy, Chemistry, Matter and Motion, the Diving Bell, Mechanics, the Steam Engine. Audiences were good – overall an astonishing achievement for a small convict colony.[50]

In 1829 a visitor, Dr Henderson, established the Van Diemen's Land Society, modelled on London's Royal Society. It was similar to the Mechanics' Institute but (unstated) for gentlemen only – excluding tradesmen who interrupted the Mechanics' Institute lectures by drumming with their feet. The first lecture drew an audience of a hundred, who heard Henderson suggest they invent one system of nomenclature for plants throughout the world (not having heard of Linnaeus's work in this field).

Problems arose when the society blackballed four prospective members. The reason was not publicised, but newspapers called them gentlemen high in the esteem and good will of colonists. The *Launceston Advertiser* asked, 'Has not Botany Bay a right to be considered elect?', so they were probably prosperous, respectable ex-convicts. This caused a huge sensation both outside and within the Society, with much criticism and several resignations, and it soon faded out.[51]

On the whole, societies and activities in the colony tended to be short-lived, whether intellectual, sporting or recreational. In 1830 the

Portrait of artist John Glover, paintbrush in hand, by Mary Morton Allport (TA ALMFA SD_ILS:85047)

Colonial Times bemoaned that 'all public bodies' came to an untimely end. 'Look at the Turf Clubs – the Whaling Club – the Chamber of Commerce – the Philosophers, &c; they all died nearly as soon as they were born.'[52] The Mechanics' Institute was an exception, though even it came and went. For the most part, there were just too few people to support these communal activities.

Europeans started sketching the Van Diemen's Land scene as soon as they arrived. Two surveyors were artists, with such skills part of their training: George Prideaux Harris painted watercolours of birds and scenes, and George Evans painted landscapes.

There were also artists among convicts. Thomas Bock, artist and engraver, was transported for administering drugs to a young woman. Arriving in 1824, he engraved plates for the Bank of Van Diemen's Land and various almanacs. As Tasmania's first professional painter, he had a gallery from 1831 and became well-known for his portraits of wealthy settlers. Charles Costantini (theft) arrived in 1827 and painted watercolours of scenery, though mainly after 1831; William Buelow Gould (also theft) arrived in the same year but for further theft was sent to Macquarie Harbour. He also completed little painting before 1831.

Probably best-known from the 1820s are the works of convict Joseph Lycett, who almost certainly never visited the island but published 24 reasonably accurate, pretty landscapes in his *Views of Australia* (London, 1824).[53] George Boyes who arrived in 1826 was another talented artist and often went sketching. He was thrilled to meet the artist John Glover, who arrived in 1829. 'He intends to reform the Convicts (no trifling labour) and to direct the views and regulate the conduct of the rest of the population' through art, wrote Boyes.[54] This was a grand objective in which he was not really successful, but Glover did produce major and much-loved paintings of Tasmanian scenes.

From 1822 imported paintings were sold in Hobart and, later, Launceston, though no title or artist was named: 'oil paintings', 'a few water paintings', 'fine oil paintings' and even 'paintings, handsomely framed'. In 1828 'a variety of English and Colonial Paintings' were offered, though the latter were probably from Sydney.[55] Overall, general interest in art remained slight until 1832 and afterwards.

12. SPORT AND RECREATION

The first sport among the British in Van Diemen's Land was hunting, though it was as much to obtain food as for enjoyment. Hunting remained popular beyond the early hungry years and 'kangarooing', hunting kangaroo, was a common activity in the bush. Going out with a gun to shoot something for the pot remained common; in 1827, for example, public servants John Montagu and Charles Arthur went hunting quail at Pittwater.[1]

As recreational activities developed, most sports were, naturally, those popular in Britain: foot races, swimming, boat races, horse races, boxing and cricket. Four things stand out, much as in Britain. Firstly, just about any activity attracted a large crowd, showing how limited public entertainment was. Secondly, sports were extremely male-oriented, with women relegated to watching – except for (possibly) two donkey riders and two swimmers (see below). Thirdly, there was often a great deal of drinking among the spectators. And finally, sports nearly involved gambling, with bets ranging from trivial to extremely high amounts. When reading figures, remember that a teacher's annual salary was about £50.

Swimming was not so much a sport as a way of crossing rivers or saving yourself if a boat was upset. It was also a way of getting clean. Some men (not usually women) could swim, if they had grown up near the sea or a river, and one article implied that most 'native-born' boys could swim (meaning Europeans born in the colony).

Newspapers mostly reported swimming only in connection with dramatic events, often when someone drowned while trying to cross a river, or bushrangers threw inconvenient people into rivers and left them to sink or swim. A man reported that as he was walking down Argyle Street in Hobart he fell into a hole, so large and deep that the water completely covered him. Had he not been able to swim he might have drowned. Or so he claimed.[2]

In 1826 the schooner *Sally* with 23 people aboard was wrecked opposite Waterhouse Island on the east coast. A survivor recounted that people clung to the mast and the rigging in misery and despair. After being beaten about by waves for nearly two hours, this man tried to reach the shore. Finally, he was washed up, exhausted. Altogether, thirteen people drowned. Ten managed to struggle ashore – all men.[3]

Some people swam for pleasure. On a hot summer day in 1820 two young men went into the Derwent to bathe. One who could not swim stood watching the other, who swam out into the river and back a few times, then dived off a rock – but got entangled in a branch and did not surface. Two bystanders, non-swimmers, ran for help but it arrived too late. Again, swimming in connection with a disaster, but presumably many men went bathing and swimming without drowning – though they were warned not to go out of their depth.[4]

Two women were not afraid of this. One winter's day, reported a newspaper, 'Fat Catherine' and 'Carrotty Kit' decided to swim across the Derwent for a wager of some rum and tobacco. When they were halfway across, two immense whales were reported in the river and a whaling crew went out after them. When the first harpoon hit Catherine's shoulder she roared out, 'By Jesus, what are you at?' and Kit with thunderous lungs bellowed, 'Pray what are you arter?' – completely astounding the disappointed whalers.[5] Or so this extremely improbable story went.

John Wedge told of an Aboriginal boy who, terrified of whites, ran into the sea on seeing Wedge's party. He stayed in the water as long as he could, swimming in the very heavy surf, to Wedge's admiration. Finally his apparently lifeless body was washed ashore but Wedge 'restored him to life by friction'.[6]

Boat racing was limited, perhaps surprisingly for a colony dependent on shipping and with so much maritime activity. There is not even any mention of vessels racing upriver to reach Hobart. The first recorded race was in 1815, between two boats for a wager of £52. In 1819 a visiting ship's captain challenged a local boat-owner. Crews rowed boats from Hobart to Kangaroo Point and back, 4.5 miles (7 km): the locals won in 31 minutes. In 1824 'numerous spectators' watched a similar race, in beautiful weather. This too was won by the locals – despite the visitors' boat being propelled by a machine 'working four paddles, and also pulling three oars'. The loser paid for a group dinner.[7]

From 1820 there were a few more races: passengers on a ship versus men from the sheriff's office; a race at Launceston; a rowing race across

Sailing boats off Kangaroo Point, by Charles Atkinson (SLV wp010256)

the Derwent by two local crews.[8] Then another visitor, Captain Rous of HMS *Rainbow*, with a crew never beaten around the world (claimed the Tasmanian press), challenged a local side to row to Kangaroo Point and back for £200. *Rainbow*'s beautiful gig looked imposing, manned by six hand-picked sailors and a steersman, all dressed in white and blue. The local entry, an old whaleboat hurriedly repaired and 'by no means watertight', was manned by six Tasmanian youths. Large bets were placed, £2000 altogether, and interest was intense among the huge crowd who, with immense excitement, watched the locals completely outstrip the visitors. How the inhabitants enjoyed their little colony's defeat of outsiders!

'Born in the country & whalers', exulted Knopwood. Locally built, owned and rowed! Rous issued a second challenge. Again the locals won. They offered to exchange boats for a third race but Rous declined, admitting that a finer, more robust and active set of men he never saw in a boat in any part of the world.[9]

In 1831 an 'immense concourse of spectators' enjoyed the first sailing regatta. Boats were specially built, and interest was intense. The weather was unfavourable with a heavy north-west wind, and one boat disqualified itself by going to save the life of a man who had fallen overboard. Still, it was a rare holiday: pleasure craft crowded the river, ships in harbour were decorated with flags, the band played, bets were laid, and the five thousand spectators were thrilled as the signal gun fired and they were off.

Several ran foul of each other in the gusty wind but most sailed clear, across to Kangaroo Point, down to Sandy Bay then back against an adverse wind to the starting point. The first boat won easily but there was an exciting duel between the next two. Journalists were mostly positive: 'On the whole, the inhabitants of Hobart Town never witnessed any sight that so generally excited interest'. People were brought together in a spirit of good feeling, 'the want of which is the bane of these colonies'.[10]

Cricket was widely played in England and was probably played casually by early settlers, especially at the Christmas and Easter breaks. 'Being Xms holidays the people were playing at cricket and other games', noted Knopwood in 1814 and 1816, and dancing and cricket were noted at Port Dalrymple at Christmas. Such games continued, but most were not thought worth mentioning in newspapers. In 1824 a letter-writer calling himself (or herself?) 'Censor' bemoaned as 'indecent and reprehensible' men and boys playing cricket on the government paddock on Sundays.[11]

Casual cricket games continued. In 1826 a gentleman whose house had been robbed recognised a pair of his new trousers on a cricketer – who fled when he caught the constable's eye. However, the villain turned out to be merely an innocent spectator.[12] (Probably many men in the convict colony fled when they caught a constable's eye.)

In 1829 a regular cricket game at Macquarie Point inspired an (atrocious) poem quoted in a newspaper. Meanwhile, a northern newspaper asked: where are the Launceston cricketers? In 1831 the reporter watched a game between 22 young men, mostly locally born youths. One or two were fair players but for the most part it was 'anything but cricket': why not establish a cricket club?[13]

Boxing (prize-fighting or milling) was a favourite sport in England and also in Tasmania – though until newspapers were established none was described, and even then many fights went unreported. The first known boxing match occurred near Hobart in 1817, when numerous spectators watched three bouts featuring two 'Israelites', two 'Hibernians', a Londoner and another man known as a 'muling cove' (thieves' cant for an obstinate person). Interest was intense with farms being wagered. The journalist regretted to say that the spectators at this 'disgraceful and indelicate' scene included several females who (he said sternly) would have been better pursuing domestic affairs.

A month later the largest crowd in the colony to date watch a prizefight for sixty ewes for the winner. It lasted 84 rounds, with nearly two hours of 'the hardest milling', and much money wagered. The next year a 'grand milling match' comprised four fights and an impromptu fifth between several boxers' seconds.[14]

After this, there was a lull in descriptions of boxing matches. Did they stop, or go underground, or were they just not reported? In 1826 a journalist frowned on another fight he thought shameful and brutal, but in 1829 a 'long-talked-of fight' took place at Launceston between a London prize-fighter and a local favourite, 'Jack's the lad'. It was even until the fifth round, when Jack planted his 'dreadful left' on the Londoner's kidneys, and he fell. 'He will come no more', shouted the numerous spectators, but his second got the Londoner to his feet. 'Let go the man', 'Don't strike him, Jack', rang out, but he fell at Jack's feet and the fight was over. Then came a fight between two lightweights, which lasted 34 rounds and afforded the spectators a high treat. How appalling! thundered a rival newspaper. Two men fighting 34 rounds for no motive but filthy lucre, described as a high treat![15]

Launceston was the centre of boxing – perhaps away from the capital's eye. In 1830, £1200 changed hands at a match. This time the combatants and some supporters were charged with disturbing the peace, but punishments were mild. Meanwhile, in Hobart a journalist was disgusted to see a very large crowd – not just the lower orders but 'respectable' men – watching two men half-kill each other.[16] Did journalists feel obliged to frown on the sport? Or did these middle-class men see it as lower-class and therefore inferior?

Legally, boxing was a grey area. Fighting was against the law, with a stream of convicts and ex-convicts punished for it, though not usually severely. Some fights were reported with amusement. A man and two women fought in a Hobart street, shouting and singing. One of the women grappled with the man and both fell into a cart – unhurt, as they were drunk. Two men fighting but separated by a woman provided a similar spectacle in Launceston – though it seemed not so much the fighting but the woman's participation that was so degrading (or interesting). But many convict women were good fighters – they probably had to be. In 1831 Mary Buckley was found guilty of 'fighting a pitched battle in the Red Lion Public House last night'. She was ordered to find sureties for good behaviour.[17]

Definitely illegal – and therefore seldom reported – was cockfighting. In the early 1810s a clerk who was a friend of Thomas Keston told him he had 'a fine sporting master. He is the Gentleman for Boatracing & Cock fighting, he sports the money, he thinks nothing of 50 or 100 £ at a Bet'. The first time cockfighting was mentioned in the press was in 1826, when it was claimed that four or five years earlier, cockfighting and dogfighting were 'the order of the day' but now, under Governor Arthur, hotel licensees were not allowed to hold cockfights. Making rules and enforcing them were two different things, and cockfighting continued well into the 1830s at least.[18]

In December 1826 Hobartians were warned to keep a watch on their poultry houses as 'abandoned characters' were stealing cocks for matches at Christmas. The warning was repeated in 1827 – but an enthusiastic journalist praised the improvement in the colony's habits and morals. Unlike in the past, on Christmas Day general conduct was excellent. People went to church, had rational enjoyments such as picnics, and in the evening groups of young people paraded round the town.[19]

F**oot races** were popular. They needed no equipment, and were light-hearted and easily organised, even spontaneously. The first recorded race – though surely there were earlier ones – took place in 1816, when twelve gentlemen ran two miles along the main road at New Town. The last six were to give dinner to the first six. This was typical – running races were a diversion, with only small bets. Some races were against time. In 1828 Mr Brest, a merchant aged 47, twice wounded at Trafalgar, bet $8 that he could walk three miles from one pub to another in 28 minutes. He took 40 minutes, submitted to his loss philosophically and 'enjoyed a glass of *good stuff*'.[20]

Horse races often ended up with spontaneous running races. In 1827 a broom-maker 'of singularly simple and dull appearance' (in those frank days, poor man!) offered to run the same distance as the horses for a small wager. The distance is not clear but the fastest horse ran it in 3 minutes 10 seconds, while the athlete took 9 minutes. He claimed he could run a mile in the amazing time of four and a half minutes (the first record time for the mile, in 1855, was 4 minutes 28 seconds). The first mention of training came in 1831, with two gentlemen racing 'for a considerable sum' from New Town to Hobart. The winner ran a mile in five minutes, due to 'superior training'.[21]

Horse racing was the really popular sport – probably also the most popular in England. It attracted large crowds and large bets. At first colonial horses were small, not bred for racing, but Governor Geils imported a 'celebrated stallion' which from 1816 was available to cover mares, and gradually more thoroughbreds were introduced. Races were usually between two horses, the best of several two- or three-mile heats. The first recorded race was at Cornelian Bay in 1813, and in 1816 wealthy Edward Lord hosted races at his property, Orielton, with large bets such as £300 and £500. One winner was ridden by ex-convict Thomas Tombs, said to be Lord Barrymore's former jockey.[22]

Parson Knopwood attended many races, noting events such as 'both gentlemen fell from horses'. In January 1816 he enjoyed a grand day with a great crowd of people including Governor Davey, and a tent 'with every refreshment'. The Hobart races moved to Sandy Bay beach, and in 1820 Knopwood went to the New Year's Day races there 'as usual'.[23]

In the 1820s more horses were available and races were held 'more or less' annually in Launceston. In 1825 the road to the racecourse was 'literally covered' with riders and pedestrians, cars and carts, crowded with ladies eagerly pressing forward to see and be seen. Four fine young horses raced for a subscription plate of £120, followed by some boxing, out of sight 'in a sequestered spot'. Betting was inconsiderable, reported the local newspaper, which praised 'the growing rectitude of our moral character'.[24]

New Year's Day 1827 saw excellent racing in Hobart. A reporter noted Sandy Bay lined with boats, 'laden with beauty, youth, and fashion'.

Tents sold refreshments, and music from pipes, drums and fiddles provided 'mirth, festivity, and glee'. Over a thousand people watched the two races, which began once the tide was low enough. They went off well, with enthusiastic betting – despite the horses running 'under every disadvantage': a narrow course thronged with people, horses and dogs; heavy sand; and a sharp and sudden turn around the post.[25]

Races were mentioned at Sandy Bay three or four times a year, once attracting four thousand spectators. One race ended in tragedy, with one horse running at full speed into another. Both horses and riders went down, with one rider dying.[26] In 1831 a horse called Yabberly won his twenty-first race (out of 22 run in 12 years) at Sandy Bay. He was overmatched, 'but from custom seems to have won as a matter of course'. 'The little Sandy Bay races', wrote young settler George Lloyd,

> were looked forward to with a peculiar degree of excitement and delight ... so novel a sight as a well-contested horse race on the sands of the Antipodes, the majority of the limited free population invariably attended.[27]

Meanwhile, in 1826 a group of mainly northern landowners formed the Tasmanian Turf Club to organise proper, English-style races. The first were held at Ross in 1827 on a traditional circular course with white posts, and a handsome stand with seats. The large crowd enjoyed the six races and some impromptu bye-races, and a dinner that night displayed the greatest conviviality. By now three thoroughbred horses were available for mating.[28]

Betting was often heavy at these races. The highest sum mentioned for a race was £500, and there were many side bets. There were a few complaints, though not about betting: someone was selling sly grog at Ross, someone else was said to have lost a race in order to win a wager, and inebriety among the spectators was criticised. Some churches disapproved of racing's 'idleness, profaneness and drunkenness'.[29]

Standards were gradually rising. By 1831 the progeny of imported thoroughbreds were lifting the quality of racing, and there were new, better race courses. In the south a circular track was opened at New Town, and the Cornwall Race Course was set up in Launceston, with races commencing each March and an annual race ball.[30]

There were also casual races, such as one between two mares,

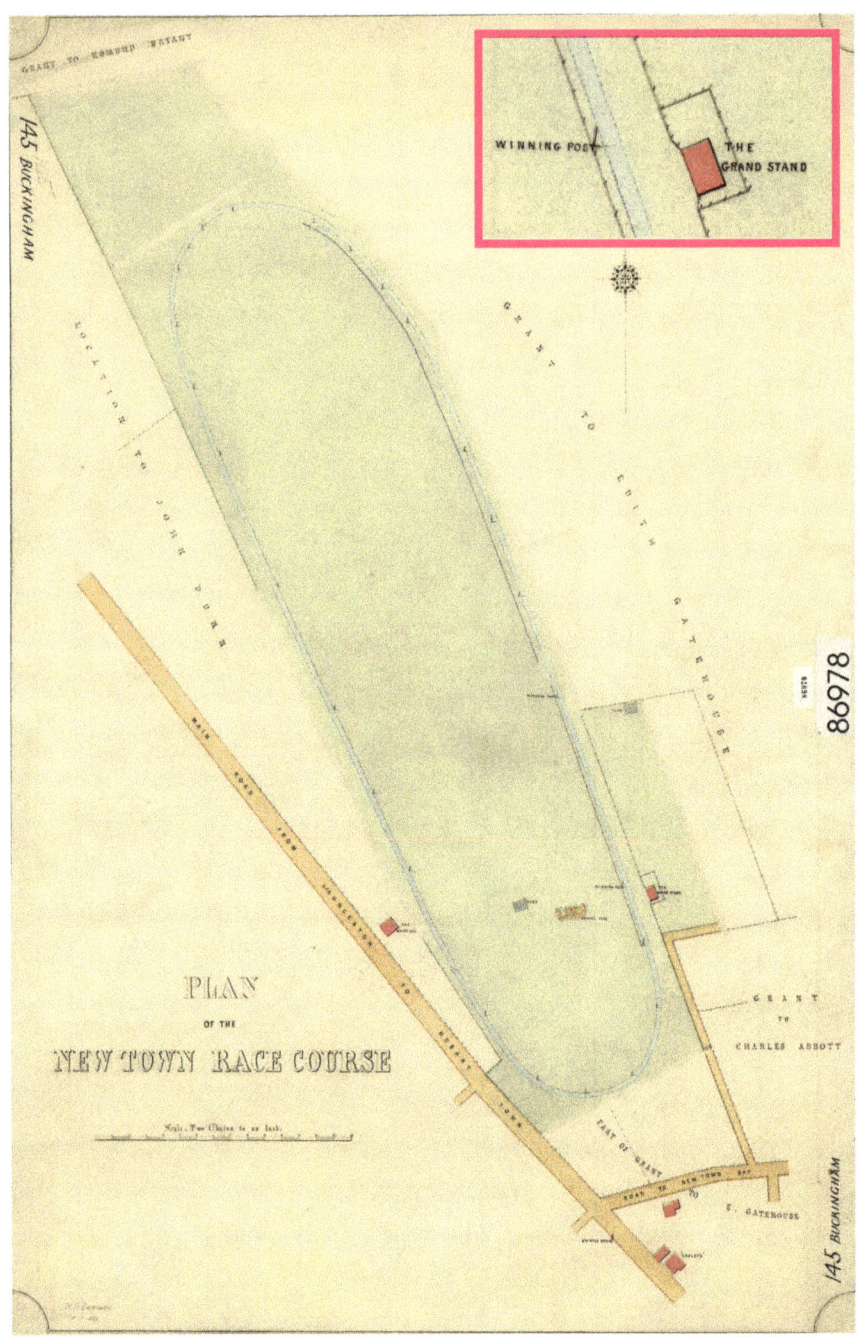

Plan for New Town racecourse, with three features: winning post and nearby grandstand (see inset), and distance posts dotted around the track (TA AF396/1/154)

locally bred and imported, three miles along the high road. (The local horse won.) In 1831 Judge Abbott challenged his horse to run against any in the island for £500 – a challenge no one took up. There were also a few trotting races, though one at Glenorchy had to be abandoned after one horse bolted into the bush. In 1825 heavy bets were placed on a donkey race involving 'two *fair* Equestrians' – women? Cranky won the race by a neck.[31]

The dominant note of reports about racing is enjoyment: people loved getting out, being part of a crowd, cheering the horses, drinking and gambling, winning or losing. Racing enlivened the monotonous round of the year, commented one enthusiast. Trifling as the amusement was, said a less keen racegoer, it brightened the dull monotony of Hobart where there was no other entertainment.[32] Racing brought the community together, probably more than any other sport.

Recreation for working people centred around public houses. There they could have a drink, yarn to their mates, play games such as quoits, skittles and, more excitingly, watch or even take part in fights or wrestling. For the many single men, the pub offered warmth and friendship, a pleasant change from their lonely, possibly cold and unwelcoming accommodation.

People worked from five to six days a week, but Sunday was always a holiday. People caught up with friends, did their washing, played sports of various types or, increasingly in the 1820s, went to church. There were public holidays at the Christian feasts of Christmas and Easter, and loyal occasions such as the king's birthday, but on the whole people spent far more time at work than in recreation.

Few diaries or letters mention recreation and they were written by gentlefolk. Parson Knopwood attended any races or other entertainment going, but his main pleasure came from dining with friends. No one has counted how many such dinners he enjoyed but they would have run into the hundreds. He loved putting a good dinner in front of neighbours, acquaintances, newcomers to the colony, any chance visitor. He also loved eating (and drinking) out.

Young surveyor John Wedge, camping out in the bush, also enjoyed a good dinner when any local inhabitant invited him. A 38-year-old widow, Mrs McAuley, invited him to a superb meal:

> A more hearty welcome or a more plentifully fil'd table no one ever met with – it was about 5 p:m. when I arrived and in about five minutes I saw before me a large cold round of Beef & one of the largest legs of Pork I ever beheld a bottle of wine & a Bottle of brandy – what more could a man wish for?[33]

In his diary, public servant George Boyes described his pleasures. Like Knopwood he enjoyed dining out, though the food was not always good:

> Dined with Captain Roe, a greasy mutton chop fried in its own fat – a half starved fowl and a slice of rusty ham, followed by an attempt at an apple tart, all sugar and rancid butter.

His own board was not always ideal. A manservant, Wood, did the cooking. 'Three gentlemen attempted to dine with me, a small round of beef, a pair of chickens and a beefsteak all spoilt' by poor cooking. More successful was a dinner of a pair of chickens, a loin of veal, and green peas from the garden. Clearly, a proper dinner had at least two sorts of meat, with vegetables coming a poor second, often not mentioned.

So that Wood appeared well as a waiter, Boyes gave him a 'drab coat and breeches of the same stuff and colour' ('drab' being dull brown) but was astounded at his next dinner party to see Wood in a green velvet shooting jacket, red waistcoat, yellow silk neckerchief, corduroy 'tights' (breeches) and brown leather gaiters. He explained, wrote Boyes in astonishment, that if he 'had gone about in the things I had given him the folk would have tuck [taken] him for a dandy'.

Visiting friends often involved entertainment, which Boyes did not always appreciate: 'Singing and playing as Hone & his daughters are pleased to call their crude inharmonious efforts with the voice and upon the old and out of tune piano'. Boyes preferred playing cards, usually whist, sometimes écarté (a two-person game) – always for money. He kept a note of what he lost or won, usually only relatively small amounts, up to £1 or so. However, 'young George Stephen' lost £18 at cards. He earned only five shillings a day, wrote Boyes – so lost 72 days' pay.

Boyes was a talented artist and enjoyed sketching; he played the violin for hours at a time, and he loved reading and going for walks. He also enjoyed – sometimes – going to parties and balls. 'Went to a party,

George Boyes often noted in his diary that he went for a walk and painted. Here is his 'View from the Domain looking N.W. across New Town Bay' (TA ALMFA SD_ILS:74235)

home by 12.30, 27 there, lost 9s [9 shillings] at whist. Severe headache next day.' Presumably Boyes' pleasures were typical for the educated classes: dining with friends, reading, walking in the bush, playing an instrument and singing to the extent of one's ability. Working in the bush, surveyor John Wedge was often invited to people's homes for dinner and a 'noisy rubber of whist' or a game of backgammon. His hosts often took him for a walk to some local beauty spot with a beautiful view.[34]

In his reminiscences about his boyhood, Hugh Hull described swimming in the river and shooting wattle birds with a single-barrelled flint gun. The garden contained a bower of roses and willows where his father played the flute and 'we used to sing our little songs'. He and his friends would go camping and enjoy a 'merry life', living in a tent, fishing, shooting birds and collecting oysters, mussels, cockles and shells.[35]

Charles Arthur was sixteen when he accompanied his uncle, the governor, to the colony in 1824. Four years later, in letters to a friend in Launceston, he described playing cards and billiards, flirting with pretty girls, and attending a party where guests drank wine, smoked cigars and played whist until 5 am, then found the street not wide enough when going home. Charles was living at Government House and his upright uncle strongly disapproved – 'a devil of a rumpus ensued'. But parties were rare. Charles once told a friend that 'Hobart Town is as dull and stupid as ever', and asked whether 'Launceston vilest of all places is dull or lively'.[36]

Sex was an enjoyable recreation for many: for single men there were brothels or, decreasingly through the 1820s, illicit affairs; for married people the marital bed. Charles was entertained by 'Old Kemp', whose wife 'shows symptoms of the old Boys salacious disposition – this will be, I believe, the 15th – Good heavens the old boy will never stop'.[37] (Anthony Kemp was 56 at the time. He and his wife Elizabeth, then 43, had eventually eighteen children.)

On the whole, colonists' recreations were the same as in Britain, though many enjoyed the novel scenery, for walking or just admiring. Some tried to tame native animals. James Ross had a tame kangaroo which he described as lapping tea out of a saucer and picking up a bone 'like a monkey'.[38]

13. COMMUNITY LIFE

The early phase of European settlement in Van Diemen's Land was summed up Wesleyan minister Benjamin Carvosso in 1820 as 'kindly, but dissolute'.[1] 'Kindly': the amazing flourishing of this benevolent attitude in such a barren soil.

Perhaps surprisingly, though many people wanted to make a fortune and return to Britain, others were happy in the raw little colony. Robert Knopwood's diary depicts a contented man, busy with his wide circle of friends, his garden and his duties as clergyman and magistrate. He seldom indicated his feelings, but showed no yearning for Home. Another contented group comprised those convicts, soldiers and free settlers who despite many problems managed to make a living from their land grants or businesses, often with more success than they could have expected in Britain. Ex-marine Daniel Stanfield and his extended family farmed successfully at Brighton. Ex-convict and farmer Andrew Whitehead, his relations ex-convicts William Stocker and wife Mary Hayes who ran a first-class hotel – this group made no trouble for the government, happily making a living and bringing up their families. Some, like Andrew, were involved in illegal activities but managed to avoid punishment via their contacts. These colonists supplied the 'kindly' section of Carvosso's society.

However, they managed this by themselves, without a great deal of encouragement. There was no one to enforce standards. Why did people in Jane Austen's novels generally obey the law and behave as the middle-class expected? Because they had little option: a strong middle class boosted by clergyman, lawyers, magistrates, police and many wives and mothers were powerful forces that encouraged, even forced, people to toe the line. Jane Austen did not write about city slums where law-breakers created their own society, and it was this which flourished in Van Diemen's Land – the government actually exported it there.

In the colony the middle class was weak, numerically and mentally. Many members, like Ingle and Lord, were as dishonest as any convict, and the one clergyman made no move to reform anyone. Nor did any of a series of governors. The police were mainly convicts themselves, and there were few women. Stuck on the other side of the world, people in Van Diemen's Land could behave as they wished, untrammelled by

British society's expectations. Not surprisingly, in a community where, in 1820, 93 per cent of the inhabitants were of convict origin. This is surely the highest figure of any society trying to pretend it was a normal civil British community, rather than one huge gaol.

Outsiders took it for granted that a convict colony was a dreadful place, the home of crime, by its very nature degraded and appalling. Newcomers expected the worst, 'a depraved society', as John Hudspeth described Hobart soon after arriving in 1822.[2] Colonists hated this reputation and from the beginning there was a united effort – never mentioned but strong – to downplay the presence of convicts. It was difficult, given that they were the vast majority of the population, but when people's own interests are at stake, they can make stupendous efforts. Reading newspapers of the time, one forms a picture of a little community with quite a deal of theft (as in Britain) but with plenty of the usual activities of a small British town – sport, social activities, subscriptions to the Bible Society. Convicts were mentioned as seldom as possible. 'Even in our small menage, our cook has committed murder, our footman burglary, and the housemaid bigamy!' wrote newcomer Augustus Prinsep in 1829. 'But these formidable truths are hushed up, or tried to be so.'[3]

The dreadful word 'convict' was avoided. It 'is seen by them as opprobrious and highly offensive', wrote a visitor, and 'is by all right-minded persons, carefully avoided'.[4] So right-minded people considered convict feelings – or was it their own feelings, not wanting to be associated with criminals? At any rate, they called convicts by other names: prisoners, servants of the crown, involuntary emigrants – when they had to be called anything. In his 1822 book about the colony, George Evans mentioned convicts only five times. An astonishing feat, considering the aim and makeup of colony. Right up to the 1960s, avoiding any mention of convicts remained typical of books about Tasmanians by Tasmanians (as opposed to, say, Marcus Clarke from Victoria, with his *For the term of his natural life*).

For outsiders, the stigma remained on convicts even after they were pardoned. In the colony, since no one wanted to admit that most people were in this group, those who behaved well and lived respectably were allowed (tacitly – nothing was ever said) to rejoin the community, especially in the first twenty years. Governors Collins, Lord, Davey and Sorell all had friends among them, as did Knopwood who was very happy to dine with his friends Andrew Whitehead (embezzling) and William (possessing forged notes) and Mary (theft) Stocker. Thomas Peters (theft) ran a pub in Hobart and entered his horse and boat in races.[5] As 'Mr Peters' he seemed accepted by gentlemen who owned other horses and boats. It's doubtful his horse would have been accepted at Ascot.

As in Britain, men's status was denoted by their title: John Smith Esquire for a gentleman, Mr Smith for a respectable man, plain John Smith for the rest. If the few gentlemen convicts behaved like gentlemen (not that the bar was very high in Van Diemen's Land), they could be accepted by the colony's little elite. Robert Lathrop Murray (bigamy – trigamy, in reality) arrived in Hobart in 1821. Claiming to be not just a gentleman but an aristocrat, and an old school-fellow of Governor Sorell, he was R.L. Murray Esq from the first.[6] He was a rogue, but this was commonplace among Van Diemen's Land's elite and did not affect his social standing.

Ex-convicts who did not behave respectably – who cheated, stole, drank, swore, fought, gambled, frequented low pubs and brothels and all the rest of it *in a rough manner* – were not accepted as respectable, but they were not in Britain either. They appeared to live happily enough in their own world, and if they wanted employment, it was there, since labourers were in short supply.

Commentators thought the working class better off than in Britain, with a more benign climate, abundant and cheap food, plentiful jobs and high wages. Many could not obtain a female partner owing to the shortage of women but, perhaps oddly, no one commented on this at the time – possibly because all commentators were members of the gentry who were less affected. Many of the upper class cheated, stole, drank, swore and gambled as well, as shown in chapter 4, but that was accepted as long as they did it in a suitably gentlemanly way. Manners and appearance counted for more than principles.

How bad, in reality, was the effect of having a convict-majority population? Petty theft was rampant, as seen in chapter 3, but it appeared bearable, not enough to drive people away. Serious crime was rarer – at least among ex-convicts. The rate of murders and violence seemed lowish, in that there were few complaints in newspapers. People seemed to cope with the convict presence with only a few grumbles – possibly because they knew they needed convicts for labour. Colonies such as Canada, with no convicts, suffered from a severe labour shortage which, coupled with cruel winters, made settlers' lives much more difficult than in Van Diemen's Land. Overall, convicts seemed a benefit to the colony, rather than a hindrance.

At the other end of the social spectrum, as shown in chapter 4, gentlemen hardly set an example of upright living, and 'ladies', as in female members of the gentry, were in short supply and could do little to uphold the standards that Jane Austen would have expected. George Harris bemoaned that fact that because most of his brother officers 'have female Companions' (not wives, implied), he and his wife could socialise only with her family and one lieutenant who was respectably married.[7] The governor's wife was expected to take the lead in social activities for ladies, but governors Collins and Sorell had mistresses; Mrs Murray's entertainments stopped when she left her husband and Mrs Geils gave no recorded entertainments. Only Mrs Davey gave balls which ladies could attend.

In 1814 Knopwood listed the 64 ladies and gentleman in Hobart: fifteen married couples, a widow, two single women, fourteen girls and eighteen boys. A quarter were of dubious 'gentility', with two confirmed drunkards, at least three rogues and reprobates, two ex-convicts, and eight children or grandchildren of convicts. But none of this group attended a ball at Government House held at the same time, so perhaps Knopwood's standard of gentility was lower than Margaret Davey's. Still, later that year, wrote Knopwood, 'all the ladies and gents' attended Edward and Maria Lord's 'great dinner, ball and supper ... the greatest dinner given in the colony'.[9] All of them, presumably including Margaret Davey, were happy to attend a ball held by Maria Lord, ex-convict, who had lived with Edward for years before their marriage.

The colonies were known as places of upward mobility, where people who took on the way of life and manners accepted by the gentry, and made enough money – or gained a job which gave gentry status – were accepted as ladies and gentlemen. Adolarius Humphrey, from a merely middle-class background, was pleased to tell his family to address his letters to 'A.W.H. Humphrey Esq. ... for they have told me that all officers in his Majesty's service have a right to it, and I shall appear less than they if my letters are not directed that way'. Henry and Sarah Hopkins, poor though respectable, arrived in the colony in 1822 with little more than two boxes of shoes for sale. They made plenty of money and by 1832 Henry was being addressed as H. Hopkins Esquire, the mark of a gentleman. Clearly, this was a more tolerant society than Britain's – it had to be, to remain coherent. Did people instinctively realise this? Or did they fraternise more freely because otherwise life would have been very boring?

The picture that emerges is that of a group of people co-operating reasonably well in setting up a new colony from scratch. Standards were not unreachably high, and they helped each other when necessary. When Benjamin Briscoe drowned, leaving a widow with five young children, friends organised a subscription to help him. They employed 'an elderly man', ex-convict Joseph Bennett, to collect the subscriptions but, 'destitute of all the feelings of humanity', he stole them. He was gaoled for six months for theft. The grieving widow opened her own subscription and gratefully acknowledged help from 37 people (names were published to encourage generosity).[10] This story, a mixture of generosity and theft, epitomizes Carvosso's description of a 'kindly, but dissolute' community.

There are relatively few documents to flesh out this picture, but from available sources such as Knopwood's diary and, from 1814, a newspaper, it seems the mass of people jogged along reasonably well, managing to appear like a relatively normal British community, a huge achievement considering their make-up. There was a strong undercurrent of crime, lawlessness, corruption and skullduggery, but it never became an 'overcurrent', never overwhelmed community life.

Standards hardened in the 1820s with the arrival of more gentry. In 1829 Michael Fenton, gentleman, advised his wife to see his (middle-class) agent and be courteous to him, but on no account to enter the agent's house, for 'merchants were not visited by the first class' and she would lose caste. Elizabeth Fenton did not need such advice. The daughter of a clergyman, herself a huge snob, she was prepared to find no society 'I could mingle in', and was surprised to meet several ladylike and gentlemanly people with taste and education (one fortunate woman was 'indisputably a lady'). This was rare. Elizabeth

The Fentons' home at Fenton Forest, some time after this period, but showing what a good view Elizabeth would have had of approaching visitors, giving her time to hide in the bush.
(TA ALMFA AUTAS001124074295)

refused to make the acquaintance of anyone in the hotel she stayed at, including a Mrs Roper who, though dressed in the latest French fashion, 'had the indefinable air of a second-rate actress', while her husband was 'not aristocratic or anything bordering on it'.[11] (He became a police magistrate but was dismissed for misconduct.)

The Fentons moved to their property at Plenty. On the way they sought shelter with the family of a merchant who had feathered his nest 'in the good old times': nouveaux riches. Elizabeth found the house dirty and her hostess ridiculous, keeping Elizabeth waiting while she changed into a beautiful French dress. Did the woman imagine Elizabeth would think it her normal attire? Elizabeth was not at all grateful for her help, complaining that the (expensive) pair of leather shoes her hostess gave her, hurt her feet. The Fentons' next stop for help was with a Scottish gentlewoman, well-educated and neat – though even she was not of high enough social status to become a friend. Elizabeth wrote that there was no one in the neighbourhood she would associate with – she preferred being alone, possibly lonely, to associating with people she thought inferior. There was a clique of good friends in the neighbourhood but Elizabeth refused to visit them. Once she saw a group approaching her house. In horror, she climbed out of a window and hid in the creek until they had left. She did not tell Michael, fearing a lecture on universal benevolence.[12]

I think with pleasure about the happy clique at Plenty, enjoying their socialising, probably relieved not to have Elizabeth Fenton looking down on them. They were probably feeling sorry for the poor, lonely woman and visited to cheer her up. You get the feeling that, while the elite might be looked up to in Britain, there was less of that in the colonies, where there were no traditions of squire-of-the-manor, no House of Lords, and everyone's money was as good as everyone else's. Elizabeth Fenton was an outlier, not a typical example.

By the 1820s, with children growing up and marrying, there were some large extended families, such as the Morrisbys. In 1826 George Morrisby, aged 31, dined with Knopwood. Later that night, drunk, he was driving home and when trying to overtake someone else, overturned his cart and was killed. Three days later, his relatives gathered at Knopwood's house and 'a very large number all in deep mourning attended the funeral'. Next Sunday Knopwood preached on the text, 'For the living know that they shall die'. George's family and friends all attended, Knopwood recorded, 'and scarce a dry eye in the church when I mentioned the dreadful accident and the uncertainty of human life'.[13] A mere two decades since a heterogeneous lot of people had been dumped at the Derwent, here was a large and close family.

However, this book is dotted with mentions of community rifts. The sailing regatta encouraged good feeling, otherwise described as wanting. At Clarence Plains, John Wedge found farmers 'most of them quarrelling with each other ... they are a rum set.'[14] George Boyes, perhaps lonely without his wife, went to a ball attended by both the elite and the middle-class and wrote of the

> impossibility of amalgamating two classes of Society – so very distinct in their habits and education – as even the upper and lower classes of Van Diemen's Land, without creating envy and

Such a respectable family, Captain Barclay with his wife and child – but Mary Barclay had been a convict (Tasmanian Museum and Art Gallery)

dislike on one side and contempt and disgust on the other. The distinction has been of course accidental, but it cannot be destroyed[.][15]

He possibly meant that some of the middle class had convict connections.

The poorer convicts were looked down on, and the always-free people had nothing to do with them socially; non-convicts did not want their children to go to school with convicts' children. But some convicts prospered, and in any case given the small number of women, they were always in demand. Ex-convict Maria Lord was the leading merchant in the colony; her daughter Caroline married an up-and-coming lawyer (who sadly turned out to be alcoholic). Lawyer William Williamson married the daughter of a convict, a shot-gun marriage but still a legal union. In Launceston Captain Andrew Barclay married his convict partner Mary Colquhoun, a year after the birth of their daughter. Eliza Eddington, illegitimate descendant of both a convict and Governor Collins, married leading landowner James Cox – and so on. By 1831 the community was riddled with such marriages and people were adept at hiding these connections. Certainly no one ever mentioned them.

Some ex-convicts felt no shame in their status, one commentator remarked. They were audacious, and knew their rights: 'It is no unusual thing to be told he is as free as you are.'[16]

And a generation was growing up, born in Van Diemen's Land and united strongly by that – they felt as superior to newcomers as Elizabeth Fenton did to any second-rate actress. In 1829, seventeen 'native-born' young men from the Brighton area asked Governor Arthur to help them preserve 'the Character of Britons' by setting up a racecourse. (No, Arthur replied. That was rather too British, encouraging gambling and drinking.)[17] The lads' parents were a mixture of convict and non-convict but the young people overlooked this.

George Boyes was impressed by these locally born:

> It is extraordinary the passionate love they have for the country of their birth ... There is a degree of liberty here which you can hardly imagine at your side of the Equator. The whole country round, Mountains and Vallies, Rocks Glens, Rivers and Brooks seem to be their own domain; they shoot, ride, fish, bathe, go bivouacking in the woods – hunt O'possim and Kangaroos, catch and train parrots, Wombats, Kangaroo Rats etc etc.

> A wonderful life, riding, picnicking, swimming...

> They are in short as free as the Birds of the Air and the Aboriginal Natives of the Forests. They are also connoisseurs in horses, Cattle, Sheep, Pigs, Wool Grain and leather – And they all understand before they can speak that two and two make four.[18]

Born and bred in the colony of whatever parentage, knowing nothing else, quick on the uptake, enjoying their lives: this was the Tasmania of the future.

14. A SMALL MINORITY: WOMEN

What would it have been like to be a British woman in early Van Diemen's Land? Above all, you would have been part of a small minority. Far fewer female convicts arrived than male, a ratio of 6:1 overall, mainly because women generally commit fewer crimes than men, and juries were less willing to convict women. The military and administrators also had a far higher percentage of men. In 1804, women formed 12 per cent of the adult white population; in 1820 this had risen to 20 per cent, only one in five. Even in 1830, by which time more women had arrived, they formed only 25 per cent of the population.[1] It was a tough, heavily masculine society. (Not that statistics of the time can be relied on, but they are all we have.)

Conditions in the colony were often hard for women. Woman's place was seen as in the home, and to maintain her there, she was meant to be cared for by a male relation: first a father then, after marriage, a husband – or, if necessary, a son, father, uncle, brother-in-law, cousin – any even vaguely related male (as in the story of Eliza Hammond pp. 121-2). But if the male deserted her or failed in any other way (such as sickness), the woman had to do as best she could, in a world not geared for it; women's wages were low, there was no social security and not much charity.

The expected career for women was marriage and with so many more women than men, almost every woman who wanted to marry could, no matter how plain, poor, drunk, rough or criminal she might be. Mary Lynch, transported for seven years for theft in 1820, was continually in trouble for assault, threatening the life of her master, being drunk and disorderly and causing a breach of the peace. Mary married twice.[3] Perhaps her illiterate convict husbands were no better.

Of 51 female convicts who arrived in 1820 on the *Morley* (the first shipload direct from Britain), 44 married in the colony. Three died soon after arriving and most of the others vanished, perhaps going to Sydney. Only one is known to have died unmarried in Tasmania: Mary Ann Ashton, a servant aged 65, an alcoholic.[4]

The Angel of the Hearth: a happy mother with her well-cared-for, adoring children, by Thomas Bock. But no one was painting her opposite, the drunken prostitute. (TA ALMFA SD_ILS: 90098)

The women's behaviour varied enormously. Eleven committed no offences as convicts and another sixteen committed only one or two, so 27, half, were well-behaved – though one of Elizabeth Meredith's two offences was harbouring a bushranger. A further quarter behaved moderately well, with between three and nine offences, and the last quarter were serial offenders. Mary James, a lifer, totted up 32 offences, endless 'drunk and disorderly', absconding, 'inveterate laziness'. She died aged about 44, still under sentence.

The other end of the behavioural (and age) spectrum was Sarah Webb, who was assigned to Governor Arthur. She committed no offences, married a publican and bore five sons. In 1840 she deserted her family, her husband describing her as aged 53, very thin, with black eyes and 'very dark hair on the upper lip'. She was wearing a black velvet bonnet, a dark blue gown 'with a light flower', and leather boots. At some stage she returned, for four decades later she died at Carlton aged 98 at the grandly named Rockford Hall, the residence of her son, Captain Copping. She retained her 'memory and senses up to the last'.[5]

Only eleven of the 51 women, under a quarter, are known to have borne children in the colony, a surprising figure given that most were married. However, the true figure was certainly higher (not all births were registered) and venereal disease could have caused infertility.

The authorities strongly encouraged marriage as 'unquestionably the most effectual method of domesticating' both men and woman, tying them down with responsibilities but also, with luck, providing the pleasures of children, companionship, a cosy home. In this charming scenario, women played the role of 'angel of the house.' The press represented women in the two traditional extremes, domestic angels and damned whores. The angels were described as respected and amiable, honest and industrious, fond mothers and affectionate wives. After describing a case of violence against such a woman, the *Hobart Town Gazette* exclaimed: 'He who lifts his arm against a woman is not a man, but a monster, and, as a monster, should be extirpated'.[6]

However, **domestic violence** seems to have been widespread in this rough, masculine environment. For example, in 1828 Elizabeth Prosser left her husband Thomas, then died. The cause was not stated. He married again; but this wife Mary left him shortly afterwards.[7] Two wives leaving, one dying suspiciously ...

In many such suspicious cases no actual evidence is discernible, but there was one way in which domestic violence was implied. Between 1816 and 1831, 96 husbands advertised they would not pay their wives' debts because these women had left them, usually adding 'with no provocation'. Eleven cases sound possibly amicable: eight were 'mutual separation', in two the husband paid the wife an allowance, and another sounds quite friendly: E. Pratt's wife Hannah had gone to live with her sister upcountry for her health and to be with her children. Others were not amicable: wives deserted 'a child scarcely weaned' and 'her five small children'; others took property with them or went off with other men.[8]

A telling example is Irish convict Jane Quinn. Arriving in 1814, almost at once she married convict constable Joseph Martin. They had no children, and in 1818 she 'absconded into the woods with Benjamin Gibbs'. She returned to Joseph but ten months later left again and 'has taken with a Fellow who looked after Cattle in the Neighbourhood of the Macquarie River', advertised Joseph. 'This is to give Notice, that I will not pay for bite or sup, or for any other thing she may contract on my Account to man or mortal': he would prosecute anyone harbouring Jane.

It's not clear where she was for the next few years, but in 1825 she was in Hobart, fined for being drunk and disorderly. Though Joseph's death was not recorded, in July 1827 Jane, calling herself a widow, married ex-convict butcher Samuel Pate. 'A very decent looking elderly man', he had a business in Bagdad. Only three months later Jane left him and in 1830 she tried to stab him, but was discharged from court. At the same sitting a man was convicted of trying to murder Samuel with an axe. Meanwhile, the authorities had long suspected Samuel of receiving stolen meat, and in 1833 he was caught and transported again. Jane herself was in strife for using obscene language and being drunk. She died in Hobart, in the bleak hospital, aged 41, an object of charity.[9] Why did she leave husbands three times? Was she flighty and promiscuous, or suffering domestic violence? Violence was obviously part of life for many ex-convicts who had no opportunity, no wish, or perhaps no idea of how, to reform and settle down as law-abiding citizens.

Some women were tough enough to stand up to husbands, though without necessarily stabbing them. James and Hannah Ballance had a mutual separation with James paying Hannah an allowance – as long as she remained 'morally good'. He suspected she did not and stopped the allowance. She sued him; but he won the case.[10]

Ex-convict John Duffield advertised that his wife Lucy had left him and he would not pay her debts. She advertised back that it was she who was not going to pay his debts. He already had a wife in England, she had discovered, 'and if he continues to molest either myself or those persons who humanely protect me against his brutal violence, I will prosecute him for Bigamy'.[11]

William Broadribb advertised in the usual way that he would give no credit to his wife Hannah. A newspaper commented that while it would be 'inconsistent' to interfere between man and wife, she was a sober and industrious woman compelled to return to her parents for succour, only nine months after the marriage.[12] Hannah and Lucy were fortunate to have family and friends to escape to. Many women, particularly convicts, had no family in the colony. If they wanted to escape domestic violence, finding another man to support them was about the only way they could help themselves.

Newspaper articles imply that some violence was taken for granted. Told as just another event was the story of a husband throwing a bottle of ginger beer at his wife and wounding her, because she did not find him a candle as quickly as he wished. When one husband murdered his wife, a neighbour heard her screams but did nothing, explaining to the court that the couple often quarrelled. Mary Ann Clark's husband was a sober gardener with a violent temper. She drank and he often beat her, witnesses claimed. When one beating ended in her death the court sympathised with the sober husband and brought in only a verdict of manslaughter.[13]

Men charged with assaulting their wives were ordered to keep the peace, or to make up their differences as there were faults on both sides. In only one (serious) case was the husband sentenced to exile at the penal station at Macquarie Harbour for three years. A convict tried for indecent assault on a woman was punished more severely: 100 lashes and sent to Macquarie Harbour.[14]

You can't but feel sorry for Catherine Hanigan. In the worst-case scenario, she was raped as a teenager then trapped in a violent marriage. Her background is unknown but, aged only nineteen, she married convict shopkeeper Mark Solomon in 1823. He had already been in trouble for assault. Their first child was born a month later, the second a few years afterwards.

How soon did his domestic violence start? In 1827 Catherine left her family. Three weeks later Mark found her 'lovingly in the arms' of his friend John James. Catherine and John attacked him, leaving his face 'all the colours of the rainbow'. It was the Female Factory for Catherine, her head shaved, a fortnight in a cell on bread and water. She was sent back to Mark, but in 1828 returned to John James. When she was discovered, she was returned to Mark and the girls. Mark showed his violent side, one evening found by police 'in a great rage, labouring under great excitement from the effects of liquor, cutting and slashing all before him'. How terrifying for a mother of two small girls. Mark had to pay a small fine.

In 1833 Mark was charged with most cruelly beating his wife, and ill-usage of her for a long time past. He pleaded her 'constant drunken habits' as extenuation, and was told to set her a good example and use other means to regulate her habits. Was the judge in fantasy land? Catherine died a month later, aged only 29. Did Mark kill her? It sounds likely, but no charges were laid. Three months later Mark remarried, in Hobart's first Jewish wedding – and turned respectable, running a pub and never in trouble. He died in 1839 aged 38, leaving yet another young widow with children.[15]

At least three men abused their wives by selling them openly for their value in sheep and rum. The stories were reported humorously by the masculine-run press. The prices were fifty ewes; £5 and a bottle of rum; and a gallon of rum (4.5l) and twenty ewes – although the woman was 'no way prepossessing in appearance', ran the article. 'From the variety of bidders, had there been any more in the market, the sale would have been very brisk!'[16] Selling a wife was presumably illegal but the authorities did nothing. While angels of the house were protected, lesser women were seen as bringing their fate on themselves, by drinking, deserting families or looking unprepossessing.

The accepted situation for a woman was to be a wife, supported by a husband, leading a domestic life, working only inside the home. But among the poorer classes in Britain, women had to work as hard as men, and similarly in a new colony it was all hands to the pump. Women found themselves working in many areas. Visiting the Hayes family on their farm in 1806, Joseph Holt found the womenfolk

A rare painting of a woman working, hanging out the washing, at a sawmill in Hobart, 1828, by Louis de Sainson (TA LPIC33/1/250)

plaiting straw, presumably to make hats, and Mary Hayes raising a litter of pups to sell.[17] Later she ran a pub, very competently.

Elizabeth Fenton, used to a household of servants in India, was appalled when she had to nail down her own matting, care for her own baby, and make butter and a sago pudding. People told her horror stories of the early days: Mrs Ashburner, a most accomplished woman and beautiful performer on the piano, had to sit up in bed immediately after giving birth and sew sacks to contain the wheat, which otherwise lay loose on the floor of her room![18]

Stories abound of capable, forceful women – like Maria Lord, businesswoman; Carrotty Kit (see chapter 12) or Catherine Kearney who ran a dairy. In the chaotic early days, opportunities were there for both men and woman with the drive to grasp them. However, life could be hard for widows, especially if they had young children to care for. Some women were fortunate enough to have families to help them. In 1813 Mary Sherbud married James Folley, a whaler. Five babies appeared in as many years and Mary was heavily pregnant with the sixth when James was knocked out of a boat by a whale. Though a good swimmer, he sank instantly. Mary must have been devastated. Fortunately her family helped her. Six years later she remarried, providing herself with a husband's support and her children with a stepfather.[19]

Harriet Lansdell's case illustrates the general attitude to women. Her husband John arrived in 1820 on his own as a respectable settler, and was granted 500 acres at Jericho – but in 1823 was sent to Macquarie Harbour for receiving stolen sheep. When 'highly respectable' Harriet arrived with their children, sympathetic Governor Arthur let John return. The family settled on the grant, but in 1829 John was convicted of stealing a bullock: 7 years' transportation. (Why would he throw everything away in this manner? Did people usually get away with it?) Presumably the government resumed the grant.

Harriet rented a farm, employed a ticket-of-leave manager and applied for assigned servants, saying she had not the slightest involvement with her husband's criminality but had always conducted herself 'as becomes a faithful and honest Wife, and a virtuous and anxious Mother' – appealing to men to support an ideal woman. Thomas Anstey, the leading local settler, advised the authorities that she could not maintain her family on her small farm; the assigned convicts would be their own masters, 'and she at their mercy'. (The ideal woman was not tough.)

Arthur told Harriet the children could be admitted to the Orphan School and he would try to find her employment, but she replied that she had started ploughing and sowing and wanted to keep going.[20] Then she vanished from the records. Let's hope this indomitable woman was able to take the children back to her family in Britain.

What employment was there for Harriet? A few such respectable, middle-class women staffed female factories and gaols, or opened schools, but women's main work was domestic service, badly-paid drudgery from dawn to dusk in someone else's house. Little was written about brothels but surely in such a society they did a roaring trade, providing alternative employment for women if they wanted it. Some evidence comes in convict records: Catherine Burns was reprimanded for being found in a disorderly house in Hobart; Ann Williams and Mary James were punished for living by prostitution; and Ann Harwood for being found in bed with Constable Peacock, though possibly she had no financial incentive.[21]

What about farming, as Harriet Lansdell tried? It was unusual for women to farm by themselves but, astonishingly, of the 2264 people granted land between 1804 and 1831, 93 (4 per cent) were women.

There were four smallish groups. Wives of convicts: in 1804 Collins and Paterson were keen to get people, anyone, on the land producing food, and (as we've seen) gave land to seven of the intrepid women who had accompanied their husbands into the unknown, such as Ann Dry and Ann Peters. Wives of officials: these men were not allowed to own land but, to get round this, grants were given to fourteen female relations, especially of governors, such as Elizabeth Paterson and Martha Hayes, mistress of John Bowen. Norfolk Islanders: they were brought to Van Diemen's Land with the promise that they would be given double the land they had owned. Fourteen women had owned land there, and they had to be recompensed. Young locally born: When Macquarie visited in 1811 he gave land to promising young people including four girls, such as John Fawkner's sister Elizabeth. Two women remain blanks. Who were Mary Ann Cleary (50 acres in 1823) and Mrs Rae (1200 acres in 1831)?

The largest group of female grantees were widows (37) and the occasional orphan (2). In Britain, charities or families cared for the destitute, but these were lacking in Van Diemen's Land. As one widow wrote, 'I am left unprovided for, in a country far removed from the assistance and solace of my friends'.[22] To avoid women having to turn to prostitution the government helped them, not with scarce money but with land, of which it had plenty. Such help was not automatic. Widows had to apply for it, which probably deterred the poor and illiterate.

Female grantees' success rate was similar to the general picture. Of the 82 who obtained grants, nearly half (47 per cent) did nothing to their grants, 29 percent did something and 24 per cent established viable farms.

Only a few of these women farmed the land themselves. Mostly, work was done by a male relative: husband, brother, son. Some women did physical farming, however, such as Mary Monaghan. Her husband Alexander was a soldier, who retired on a pension in 1814 and promptly deserted his family. Mary received a small grant near Launceston where she brought up her children 'with industry', as she told Governor Arthur in 1832. She was now, at 57, 'old and feeble and unable to do for myself'. Could she have an assigned convict servant? One hopes she did, but within three years she had died.[23]

Governor Sorell declined to give grants to single women on the grounds that they were incapable of cultivating land, but in 1821 London ruled that there was no reason why not, if they had the money.[24] Nevertheless, Arthur disapproved. There were some fascinating cases.

The widow of a Jamaican slave-owner, Eliza Badley arrived in 1825 with her daughter and son-in-law. She had money and applied for 2000 acres of land. Contrary to regulations, said Arthur. Undaunted, Eliza wrote to London, arguing that others had such grants and her son-in-law would supervise hers (bowing to masculine dominance). London agreed and Eliza gained her 2000 acres on the Blackman River. Whether she did any cultivation is unknown but she did build a handsome house, which burnt down. Eliza moved to Launceston.[25]

Others in the elite class could be just as demanding. Captain Moriarty emigrated to Van Diemen's Land in 1828 and obtained excellent grants. His sister Ellen followed – in 1832, when free grants had ended. Ellen insisted on gaining one, and her forceful appeals to London resulted in a medium grant at Westbury, despite her limited finances. She demanded the maximum grant and many letters were exchanged – 'I cannot please her!' wrote a despairing official – but Arthur refused to increase the grant.

Ellen did develop her land. Her brother was police magistrate at Westbury and locals complained that the family took up all police resources – the policemen were branding Miss Moriarty's cattle, instead of catching thieves. It is not surprising that this strong-minded woman remained single. I was startled to see her brother's *Australian Dictionary of Biography* entry claiming 'she was well known for her amiability of disposition'.[26]

A truly astonishing story starts in the colony in 1827, with the arrival of Captain and Mrs Henry Ramus. Henry, a junior army officer, eloped with Maria who was from a wealthy American family. As an officer, he obtained a land grant at Ouse but in 1829 Aboriginal warriors robbed his hut and speared an employee. Perhaps too shocked to stay, Henry and

Maria sailed for England but soon returned – and then Maria left her husband, claiming to have divorced him (impossible without an act of parliament, which was not passed).

Henry apparently died, intestate, and in 1832 Maria was running the Ouse property, Leintwardine, infuriating a neighbour by grazing sheep on his land. A Ramus relative tried to claim it and the local court was puzzled: could a divorced woman inherit her intestate ex-husband's estate? Maria retained Leintwardine.

She was obviously notorious, and in 1836 a newspaper which opposed Governor Arthur published a letter under Maria's name which insinuated a sexual liaison with upright, even prudish Arthur (paying 'extreme personal attentions …'). A universal burst of indignation greeted it, wrote an opposition paper. Then a notice in a Sydney paper purportedly by Henry Ramus disclaimed his wife: was he in fact dead?

Unperturbed, Maria continued at Leintwardine, employing staff and being assaulted by a neighbour when she, possibly accidentally but possibly not, touched his cart with her whip when passing him. An apparently successful woman farmer for perhaps eight years, in 1838 she married a Sydney surgeon, Thomas Fowler, and sold Leintwardine. In 1845 Fowler, living at Mudgee, disclaimed his wife. The authorities refused her a licence to run a pub in Melbourne. The only Maria Fowler I could find was a disreputable Melbourne lady of the night, often in court as a vagrant and streetwalker. In 1858 Thomas Fowler died and, once more Maria, though an estranged wife, claimed a husband's estate.[27]

This extraordinarily independent woman was atypical of the local ladies of Van Diemen's Land and it is doubtful if she had a wide circle of female friends, but she certainly provided material for much highly enjoyable gossip.

Another woman apparently good at seizing an opportunity was Frances Cawthorne. Her family arrived in 1818: married couple John and Maria, and Frances, 65, who was surely John's mother. John gained a grant at Macquarie Plains, though surveyor Evans thought he did little to it. (Later, asking for a second grant, John claimed as an asset the money already spent maintaining convicts. Arthur saw through this.) In 1821 three things happened. Governor and Mrs Macquarie visited the district and met the leading inhabitants; ten days later John and Maria's daughter was baptised Elizabeth Macquarie Cawthorne; shortly afterwards Frances gained a 200-acre grant.

Imagine the scenario. Greeting the great and good of New Norfolk, Elizabeth Macquarie meets a smiling, curtseying elderly lady, who gushes that her daughter-in-law has just given birth to a dear little baby girl. Could they have the huge honour of naming her after Her Excellency? Elizabeth Macquarie is enchanted and readily agrees. Telling her husband later, flattered, she wonders if something else can be done – land perhaps? Frances Cawthorne gains her grant.

But not at once. The clerk in Sydney makes it out to *Francis* Cawthorne and, as no one knows such a person, it sits in abeyance. Frances has to send in a request for her land before, with considerable embarrassment, the mistake is rectified. (Don't roll your eyes at the past. *Frances* Cawthorne's death notice is marked 'male' in the Tasmanian Archives today.)[28]

Rape of females was possibly widespread, but there is little information. Cases brought to court usually involved children. In 1807 Knopwood examined convict John Wilkinson for two hours about 'Lou's child of 5 years and 3 months old'. John was found guilty of assault and sentenced to one hour in the pillory: 500 lashes for stealing, an hour in the pillory for rape. A free settler from Port Dalrymple, accused of assaulting a six-year-old girl, was bound over to keep the peace.[29]

In 1820 ex-convict James Rochford, whose wife had left him, was accused of abusing ten-year-old Sarah O'Brian. He lodged with a neighbour, Mrs Madden. Sarah's mother was out and the child was washing her face when Rochford entered her home. He asked her for a coal from the fire to light his pipe. She bent over to get one and he seized her, tied a handkerchief round her face, tied her hands, put her on the bed, unbuttoned his trousers 'and hurt me'. Then he untied her hands, told her not to tell her mother, and ran away. Sarah told Mrs Madden that a shocking thing had happened: Rochford gave her some beads and 'put his hand up her Peticoats'. She did not tell that Rochford 'had laid upon me, I forgot that part of it before I got there'. Mrs Madden examined her and said Rochford had tried to rape her. Sarah was also examined by her mother and a doctor. No one could say rape had actually taken place, though there were 'evident marks of violence ... the [private] parts were much inflamed and swollen'. Rochford was committed for trial, found guilty and sent to the penal settlement at Newcastle for twelve months.[31]

Some rapes caused more outrage. In 1827 James Conhope, a 'dissipated' carpenter who 'had a singular practice of decking himself out in women's clothes in visiting his favourite haunts', was hanged for a brutal assault on a six-year-old child. Another tragic little girl was Julia Anstey, born in 1824, daughter of Thomas and Mary of Anstey Barton, a large property near Oatlands. In 1830 three convicts were found guilty of her rape. They could expect no mercy, said the judge; they had committed a vile and atrocious crime 'of the very blackest die'. Two men were executed (it is not clear what happened to the third).[32] When Julia was seventeen she married the Oatlands doctor, aged 35, and they had three children. Let's hope she enjoyed marriage and motherhood, briefly; she died aged 25 of tuberculosis.[33]

Something that outrages people today but did not always then was much older men taking teenage girls as partners; with so few women, this was relatively common. David Collins aged fifty had a child with fifteen-year-old Margaret Eddington, and in 1818 Alexander McKenzie, aged 48, married fourteen-year-old Elizabeth Murphy. The journalist did record this marriage with exclamation marks.[34]

Information about convict women is vague at this period, as so few records were kept. Between 1804 and 1819, a total of 470 arrived, both convicts and ex-convicts. These included 70 Norfolk Islanders, their sentences long since served.

Convict women were seen mainly as sexual objects or, more politely, as partners. As already stated, there was no institution for them. Some were assigned as domestic servants but most were left to look after themselves, which usually meant living with a man. There was plenty of scope for them, with so few women, and some could find a reasonably well-off partner and live in comfort. But life could be difficult. Many had been vagrants, or lived a hand-to-mouth existence in the London slums, and it must have been difficult to settle down as suitable wives or domestic servants, both of which meant long hours of domestic work, cleaning, sweeping, cooking, sewing and so on.

Women convicts were widely regarded as immoral drunken whores.

Perhaps the red hair denotes a feisty character? An unknown girl, by Thomas Bock
(TA ALMFA AUTAS 00113182215)

The difference between their reputation and reality is shown in this story, told to John West for his 1852 *History of Tasmania*, about events in 1814:

> Two hundred female prisoners were brought down from Sydney, in the brig *Kangaroo*: proclamation was made, and the settlers were invited to receive them. There was little delicacy of choice: they landed, and vanished; and some carried into the bush,

changed their destination before they reached their homes. Yet such is the power of social affections, several of these unions yielded all the ordinary consolations of domestic life![35]

The *Kangaroo* did arrive in 1814 with female prisoners (52, not 200). The vast majority, 80 per cent, committed no offences while under sentence – though perhaps, having 'landed, and vanished', they were out of range of the authorities. Two-thirds married respectably; several are known to have had de facto relationships, though probably more did so. A third are known to have borne children, though again probably more did so. Women were more likely to commit offences once they were free, perhaps because the punishment was milder. One-third were in strife, with Mary Carter committing twenty offences (after none under sentence). But overall, the statistics show a much more law-abiding group – mostly married, committing few if any offences – than tradition tells.

Mary Carter was the exception: the average number of offences these women committed, before and after sentence, was only two, and they were mainly 'drunk & disorderly'. A typical convict, Ann Baker, wife of William, was told to behave herself after threatening another woman. Next year she was given a month's hard labour in the gaol for receiving stolen sugar, then a fine for being drunk and disorderly.[36] Hardly a model citizen, but nothing very serious.

Two women offended employers, which was seen as serious. Jane Murray insulted her master and refused to return to his employment (punishment: hard labour), and Ann Smith was found guilty of robbery (to wear an iron collar for a week) then neglecting her duty and being drunk and insolent to her mistress (the iron collar again).[37]

The son of a superintendent of female convicts described the iron collar as an instrument of torture: a band of iron about an inch and a half deep, opened by a hinge at the back, with four long spikes projecting outwards, tapering to sharp points. His father, a kindly man, provided padding under it, and let women take it off at night.[38] Alice Blackstone's inhumane treatment with the iron collar was described in chapter 8. Soon it was decided that this punishment was too cruel. In the first few years a couple of women had been flogged, but soon that too was discarded. So how did you punish women? Admonishing, fining, time in the stocks, time in prison sometimes with hard labour, which usually meant washing.

One of the *Kangaroo* women was the only female convict transported to Tasmania to gain a land grant. Bridget Judge went to live with ex-convict Patrick Langton, who farmed at Paterson's Plains in the north. Children began to arrive in 1816, and they married three years later, when a priest was available. In 1823 Patrick died, aged 53, shortly after being accused of cattle theft. A widow in an advanced state of pregnancy with three infant children, Bridget asked for government help and was granted 90 acres. She moved in with another convict, Daniel Leary. They had two children, but in 1829 Daniel was executed for stealing a steer.

Meanwhile Daniel, Bridget or a tenant cleared Bridget's grant and planted crops, but she had financial problems and in 1832 was threatened with a sheriff's sale. By now she was an alcoholic. She was living with a third ex-convict, William Rodd, and their five children made a total of eleven for Bridget. In 1838 she and William were tried for setting fire to a barn and destroying wheat. The charges appear to have been dropped. In 1846 the family moved to Victoria, and both Bridget and William died in the Portland Benevolent Asylum, Bridget aged about 64.[39]

While some women prospered, for many life in the new colony was not easy.

PART 3
TOWARDS A MODEL COLONY, 1820 TO 1831

15. FREE SETTLERS ARRIVE

On 27 November 1820 two ships sailed up the Derwent. On one, entrepreneur Edward Lord brought fourteen passengers: his friends and relations and eight others, including rascally William Williamson (if you have forgotten his iniquities, look back at the Introduction). This was a traditional cargo of a few, varied passengers. The other ship was the *Skelton* from Leith in Scotland, with fifty to sixty emigrants including eight families. They were the new type of emigrant, mostly hard-working and upright. 'By the capital which they invested, and the habits of decency and enterprise they exhibited, they gave a new tone to the colony', wrote John West[1]– well, perhaps not all of them, but enough.

A few days later a third ship disembarked 156 men, part of the other flood of newcomers: convicts.[2] They provided both a labour force and welcome funding, their costs in the colony which the British government had to pay.

These newcomers were two prongs of the four forces for change about to transform the colony: free settlers, far more convicts, churches and Governor Arthur. The fifth force was already established: the rough-and-ready but functioning white community that had grown up in Tasmania, largely made up of convicts, soldiers, marines and, importantly, their children. They had lived largely in the background until now, but with encouragement could come into the open as law-abiding citizens providing Arthur with support. He could not have achieved all he did had he come to the chaos Bigge described.

Free settlers were induced to come from Britain by the promise of free land. This was vividly publicised in three influential books about the colony. William Wentworth's ... *Description of the Colony of New South Wales and ... Van Diemen's Land* (1819) gave moderate praise: 'large tracts of land perfectly free from timber or underwood, and covered with the most luxuriant herbage, are to be found in all directions'.[3] Much more gushing were Charles Jeffreys (*Geographic and Descriptive Delineations of the Island of Van Diemen's Land*, 1820) and George Evans (*A Geographical, Historical and Topographical Description of Van Diemen's Land*, 1822). We've already met them as a smuggler and a surveyor who took bribes. They extolled the island as heaven on earth: 'one of the finest dependencies of the British crown', extremely beautiful, its climate 'perhaps the most salubrious of any on the globe for an European'. There were fertile plains, delightful tracts of land; trade was extensive, and bushranging, though appalling, was now 'purely historical' as it had been put down. Cattle and sheep flourished; emigrants were bound to do well.[4] The Aboriginal inhabitants had been brutally treated by stockkeepers and sealers but that was in the past, and a friendly intercourse with these 'apparently harmless people' would develop. Although Van Diemen's Land was a convict colony, Jeffreys and Evans largely ignored this, mentioning convicts rarely and then positively, for example as providing labour.[5]

This praise was echoed in paintings by Joseph Lycett, published in London in 1824. They show a pretty, controlled landscape of hills, plains and respectable people. Nothing negative at all – no crime, no obvious convicts, but smiling, picturesque scenes.

A hint of reality appeared in Evans' foreword. He was 'rather provoked' when on a trip in Lieutenant Jeffreys' ship, his manuscript disappeared temporarily – and Jeffreys brought out his book, word for word with Evans in places, two years before Evans could.[6] So this was the sort of antic that occurred in the colony! Evans had the last laugh, however, for immigrants blamed Jeffreys for encouraging them to come to Tasmania under false pretences. As early as 1821 a young man took only 34 days in Hobart to write back to England advising people not to believe a word Jeffreys wrote, except for his praise of Pittwater.[7]

The reason emigrants were encouraged and given free land was so they could turn this virgin soil into farms, to employ convicts and create a flourishing economy. This would be an enormous advantage in the battle to transform a 'land of rogues and scoundrels' into a stable, law-abiding community. Not that the old scoundrel type of immigrant was entirely gone – Peter Harrisson recalled that as his ship was about to sail from London in 1822, creditors came aboard, seized a passenger who was trying to leave with goods he had not paid for, and put him in gaol: 'many who go to our settlements are not more honest than those who are found out in their iniquity, and transported'. But there were more upright citizens among the newcomers than in the previous ragbag collection. They came, said Harrisson, 'full of hope and expectation', seeking their earthly paradise.[8]

From 1820 they arrived in their thousands, and the number of land grants rose:

Land grants

	1804-19	1820-31
Free settlers	34%	95%
Ex-convicts	53%	3%
Families of convicts	11%	1%
Civil status unknown	2%	1%
Total grantees	1155	1113
Average grants per year	72	93
Average size grant (acres)	312 (126ha)	1079 (437ha)
Total acreage granted	358,598 (145,119ha)	1,199,303 (485,702ha)

In the years before 1820, when the need for farmers was acute and virtually anyone gained a grant, many ex-convicts profited:

Grants given 1804 to 1819: total 1147

	Nothing	Partial	Viable farm	Average size
Free settlers	31%	46%	23%	591a
Ex-convicts	31%	42%	27%	191a
Families of convicts	19%	44%	37%	403a
All grantees	30%	44%	26%	312a

The figures for ex-convicts and free settlers were roughly similar, though ex-convicts were slightly more successful at establishing viable farms. The most successful were convicts' families, mostly sons, with over a third successful. However, this still meant nearly two-thirds were not.

After 1820 many more free settlers arrived and applied for grants.

The authorities preferred them as farmers, thinking them more upright and industrious. As well, grantees were expected to have enough capital to develop their grants, which from 1825 were a minimum of 320 acres. This was a good deal of land to give an ex-convict and the authorities were hesitant. It helps explain why grants were so much larger, on average well over double, after 1820.

Grants given 1820–1831

	Nothing	Partial	Viable farm	Average size
Free settlers	38 %	39%	23%	1125a
Ex-convicts	70%	21%	9%	188a
Families of convicts	25%	42%	33%	933a

The few ex-convicts struggled; so did most free settlers; and as in the earlier period, the most successful were the few relations of convicts. Overall, 22 per cent of grantees in the later period established viable farms, considerably fewer than in the earlier period.

Why was this? Earlier grantees had land nearer towns and could grow wheat, the most successful crop, and there were few Aboriginal attacks. Later grantees had to have enough capital to develop their land (in theory, at least). Were they people with no farming experience, possibly no experience at all of manual labour, who found the problems overwhelming? Or avaricious people who gained a grant by chicanery, only to sell it at once?

One sad reason for failure is that most emigrants left Britain because they could not succeed there. Convicts were the not-so-bright or unlucky ones who were caught; many free settlers had failed in business or were caught up in debt, scandal or family problems – or lack of opportunity. Failure was not always their fault, but many brought to the colony the traits that had led to their problems in Britain – indolence, incompetence, lack of intelligence or common sense, hot temper, alcoholism – and many could not succeed in the colony either.

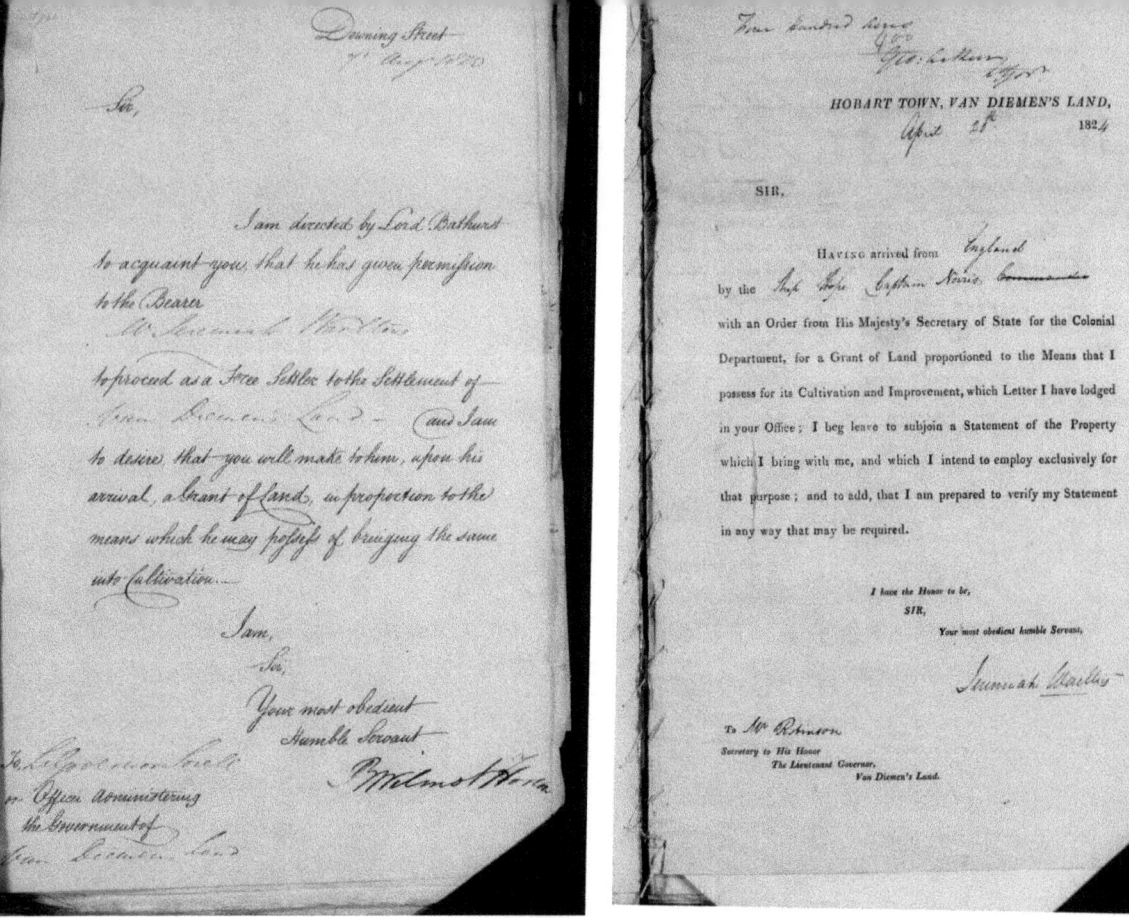

Jeremiah Walters' permission letter from Lord Bathurst and application for grant, 1824. He was granted 400 acres on the Clyde but did little if anything to it, moving to New South Wales in 1825 (TA CSO1/1/208 file 4934)

As we have seen, early governors gave land grants more or less to anyone they liked. People were meant to live on their grants and cultivate them, and not sell them within five years. These rules were widely ignored (for example, Peter Harrisson sold his at once, buying better land – the government took no notice[9]).

Probably due to Bigge's advice, in 1822 the British government ruled that those wanting grants must apply in writing to the secretary of state in London, with two references from 'respectable persons' as to their good character and capital (minimum £500, a large sum).[10] But too many respectable people came out without permission from the secretary of state, and it was hard for governors to turn them away. From 1825 people wanting grants had to apply only to the governor in the colonies, and list their assets. The smallest grant was 320 acres, the largest 2500 acres. They could not receive an additional grant until they had improved their first.[11] (It is impossible to give figures but I do feel from my research that men who called themselves Esquire, that is, part of the ruling class, received grants more readily than others.)

The next year, 1826 saw a more streamlined system. Applicants filled in a form, and if the governor was satisfied with their respectability, the Land Board of three surveyors assessed their capital and their capability for improving the land, and estimated how much land they could improve to a maximum of 2560 acres. If the governor approved, applicants moved on to the surveyor, chose their land and gained possession. They MUST, live on their land or employ a free overseer, and make improvements.[12] But no matter how often the government repeated this, abuses continued: it was impossible to police people on their scattered grants.

John Hudspeth's experiences show the problems a farmer could face.[13] Son of a schoolmaster, solidly middle-class, he was born in Northumberland in 1792. He trained as a doctor and began to practice, but it cannot have been too lucrative as he and his wife Mary decided to emigrate. Convinced by the books they read, they chose Van Diemen's Land. John bought goods as a speculation and September 1822 found him, Mary and their baby daughter Alice sailing up the Derwent to the 'Land of Hope'. Alice was thriving, John wrote to a friend, 'and will be a great amusement to us in that wilderness'. It was exciting to see a crop of fine wheat on Bruny Island, to view Hobart: they expected a miserable hamlet but it turned out to be 'one of the prettiest towns in the world'.[14]

Once on land, things deteriorated. John tried to sell his goods, but many had been damaged or stolen, and he made a loss. He visited Governor Sorell, listed his assets to show he had capital to develop a grant, and gained 600 acres. Major Bell, the inspector of roads and bridges, kindly took him upcountry to inspect possible sites. Everything was already granted as far as Jericho, but there John saw fine land. How to choose? he wrote. One place was well-watered but distant from the road; another was too thickly wooded; a third was thinly wooded but lacked water. He selected Lemon Springs. 'This delightful spot I resolved should be mine, and I returned to a Dinner of Kangaroo well satisfied.' They went on to the Salt Pan Plains (Tunbridge): 'Here Thousands of Acres are crying "Come and possess me"', wrote John: no mention of the Aboriginal owners.

The plains of Jericho, where John Hudspeth and Peter Harrisson started their farms. A beautiful painting by Joseph Lycett – implying nothing of the hard work of farming (SLV, ID50629006)

Back in Hobart, surveyor Evans told him Lemon Springs had been already granted. John was disillusioned by the corruption in this office. He selected another site near Jericho and began to organise the trip there, but ran into problem after problem. Workmen would not be hurried: 'no ones word is to be depended upon in this country ... it is hardly possible to get anything done'. The cart had to have a licence, he had trouble getting hold of his bullocks, there was endless waiting around: 'I began to despair of getting out of that vile town'. But on 18 October the family left with two convict servants. The bullocks could manage only 16 miles (26km) a day, and they camped at night by the cart, or sought shelter at a nearby house.

On the third day they struggled up Constitution Hill. At the end of the day, while the men had dinner and fed the bullocks, the family walked on and found a party of convicts, building the road. The overseer gave them a hearty dinner of kangaroo steak, while 'Alice was very happy in the arms of some of the felons', a charming picture. Later someone tried to rob the carts, and John spent the night sitting on a chest with his gun ('very uncomfortable').

They had already met Thomas Gregson, a fellow Northumbrian who had land at Jericho. He lent them a hut. They inspected the land John had chosen but 'Mary decidedly against it', and they fixed on land near Gregson, calling it Bowsden after John's home in Northumbria. Soon John and the convicts were busy digging up the ground near their hut. He planted potatoes, 300 young cabbage plants and seeds he had brought from England; but hardly any seeds sprouted, and any young plants were trampled by cattle or eaten by grasshoppers and caterpillars. But the potatoes grew and John enjoyed a dish of new potatoes. Let's hope Mary did too – John hardly mentions her.

Once they gained approval to settle at Bowsden, work started there: digging a garden, felling and burning trees to clear land for wheat, choosing a site for the house and building a preliminary hut of sods, thatched with grass. John was a capable man who could turn his hand to almost any task: making handles for tools, building a hut, felling trees. But progress was slow, as convicts were idle. 'It requires great patience to bear with these creatures', wrote John; 'most of them neither can nor will do any thing right and their whole study is to get their time doled away as easily as possible. What else can be expected of London pickpockets or Edinburgh thieves?' And later, 'their procrastination and idleness almost drive me mad, but what can I do? ... Unless I urge on the men they will do little or nothing'. John, an energetic man of thirty, hated 'trifling away my time'.

His convicts seem to have behaved well enough, mostly, but one was grossly rude to Mary while John was absent – punishment, 100 lashes and sent to the grim penal settlement of Macquarie Harbour. Another, Ned, was a grumbler. 'Ned wishing to have his own way with it as with every thing else he does, was impertinent and refractory', wrote John. He was a tough taskmaster, expecting everyone, including himself, to work seven days a week. One Sunday Ned went off somewhere, telling John he worked six days for him and was going to have the seventh to himself. John hauled him in front of the magistrate, but Ned begged pardon and was discharged with a reprimand. He seems to have been a reasonable worker. One evening at ten John set off for Hobart, telling Ned to drive the cart. Ned refused, but 'after a little scolding and coaxing' agreed. At other times he seems busy enough – 'Ned making a ladder', 'Ned began breaking up the ground'.

Ned, transported for highway robbery, had no special skills, but John had to make more allowances with Tom, a brickmaker, because he was indispensable. Tom dug clay for bricks and made them, but when John asked him to cut saplings for the house he refused, threatening to have nothing to do with the bricks. 'I was obliged to yield to the rascal.' John's own convicts did not steal from him but others did: 'nothing escapes their rapacity'. Once a man took his handkerchief from his pocket. 'I seized the thief & searched him but he was too expert for me.'

John had other problems. Bullocks strayed; a family of 'bad characters', notorious sheep-stealers, lived nearby, though this was not a worry as John had no sheep yet. He had several horrendous trips to and from Hobart: getting lost, accidents to carts, bullocks unable to pull loads uphill, incessant rain … His land proved too stony to plough, and sometimes in summer it was so hot that meat went off rapidly. One evening they slaughtered a cow. Next day they cut it up and Mary salted it, but overnight much had become flyblown with enormous maggots.

The Gregsons were good if sometimes irritating neighbours. John thought Thomas too inclined to trifle time away, but Thomas obtained two paid jobs for him: medical attendant to government labourers, and chief district constable. He once superintended punishment (50 lashes), and held Sunday musters of convicts as Governor Sorell ordered, but few attended and John had no way of making them. He was also asked to deliver summonses. With no horse, he had to walk, sometimes long distances.

John seldom mentioned recreation. He hunted kangaroos and possums for food, and once he brought home a baby possum to tame, surely as a pet for Alice. On New Year's Eve he went to Gregson's to pick up letters from England, and he and Mary spent the evening happily reading them. It was not a night for drinking. John did not drink heavily; only once in six months did alcohol prove 'too powerful for my weak head', when he overindulged at the York Hotel at Jericho and on the away home lost his shoe in a quagmire.

Aboriginal people seldom rated a mention. Occasionally the Hudspeths saw smoke from fires to the west, where 'the natives' had lit the grass. 'They have been troublesome in some places to settlers, killed one man and wounded 2 with spears', wrote John. On one trip to Hobart he ran into a group who could speak a little English and asked for bread. They were called the tame mob, wrote John. He had no special sympathy with Aboriginal people and his diary gives no sense that whites were taking their land.

Altogether, wrote John to a friend in England, the colony was not the paradise described by Jeffreys, who was 'an Author of lies'. But after the first difficult years – there was a terrifying episode in 1825 when armed robbers burst into the house, ransacked it and threatened lives – John proved a successful farmer, known for breeding fine-woolled sheep and stud horses. He and Mary had three more children and John took a prominent part in district affairs. However, in 1834 he was pronounced mad, a lunatic. Bowsden was sold. John died in 1837, aged 45; in 1853 Mary and one son died, and the rest of the family returned to England.[15]

John Hudspeth was well placed to succeed. He was young, sober and energetic, able to tackle manual jobs like making a dovecot and felling trees. He had a practical and hard-working wife. Yet even so, he made no profit on his first six months and produced little beyond those potatoes. Without his two paying jobs, life would have proved difficult. How did other settlers cope? Many immigrants had done no manual work in their lives. Hudspeth was a doctor, other immigrants were businessmen or military officers. How did they know where to start, faced with 1000 acres of wilderness and only the help of sometimes unwilling convicts and womenfolk equally unused to labour?

Grantees had to be prepared to work hard. In Britain landowners could leave everything to managers, but Hudspeth's diary shows that in Van Diemen's Land you had to do or at least superintend everything yourself, and work alongside the men. People unused to hard work, unwilling to dirty their hands, were more likely to be cheated by subordinates and fail. Convict labourers might be lazy and unreliable – understandably, as they were not paid and gained no benefit from working – but they were all there was. Even tough John Hudspeth had to overlook faults and coax his men, jollying them along. Then there were losses from sheepstealers, attacks by bushrangers and Aboriginal people, and the possibility of accidents and disease. Pioneering was hard and, at least at first, unprofitable. It is not surprising that the majority of people did not stay on their farms.

Edward Curr, trying to give possible emigrants a picture of the reality facing them, wrote of the solitude of the bush, the 'stern realities of hard labour by day, watchfulness by night, seditious, unruly, unwilling servants, and the thousand trials of patience'. Van Diemen's Land was not terrestrial paradise.[16]

Making a profit from the land was, as seen above, a major problem for grantees. The main saleable crop was wheat, and wheatgrowers near Hobart and Launceston could make a living. At first they had no tools but spades and hoes, and had to dig the ground manually, but by 1817 ploughs had superseded hoes. Then threshing machines arrived: men on top of a stack of reaped wheat forked it down into the machine's rotating drum, where ears of wheat were stripped from the stalks. Plodding horses provided power. Such machines were expensive and only repaid the cost on large estates. Winnowing machines were simpler and cheaper, separating wheat from chaff using a rotary fan. No horses were involved and perhaps the operator turned a handle, as with chaff cutters.[17]

These machines meant somewhat less manual labour but were not earth-shattering, just moderately helpful. Accidents happened too: in 1829 at Norfolk Plains a labourer fell from the stack into Mr Lyttleton's threshing machine and was badly mangled. Bystanders pulled him out but had to make 'the greatest exertions ... to prevent the poor lad from being torn to pieces'. He had to have his leg amputated – without anaesthetic.[18]

However, though wheat yielded a 'tolerable' price, in 1831 it was noted that 'those who desire to become rich' were producing wool.[19] This had not happened at once. For new grantees, mostly with land far from towns, up through the Midlands or around Bothwell, grazing sheep and cattle was the only possibility. They could be sold to the commissariat for meat, or to newcomers looking to build up their stock, but both these options were limited. Sheep were coarse-haired and there was no market for wool. It was thrown away or burnt.

From 1820 people tried to export wool, and in 1822 experienced Henry Hopkins arrived and set up as an agent but, even so, the first wool was too coarse, only gradually improved as merino and other fine-woolled sheep were imported.[20] Besides, farmers did not know how to present it. Letter after letter came from London advising more care. As well, wool prices were volatile. However, many farmers (like John Hudspeth) improved their herds by breeding their ewes with fine-woolled rams, and learned about washing, shearing and packing wool. Hopkins and others set up a system of exporting wool and selling it in London, so when fine wool was properly packed, from the later 1820s it fetched high prices. Light, imperishable, needing relatively little labour to produce, easily transported, with the textile mills of the Industrial Revolution providing an inexhaustible market, it was an ideal export.[21]

James Sutherland kept a diary of his work on his 1000-acre property of Rothbury, near Campbell Town. His first wool was dirty and had to be thrown away, but he improved his flock with merino rams, and in 1825 washed his sheep before shearing and dried the wool on the joist of the new hen house. He sold 660lb wool in Hobart for £20 in goods – not a vast sum. By 1829 he was earning £84, still not enough and still paid in goods. But like farmers around him who had persevered, he was about to become much wealthier as the wool industry really took off from 1830, with excellent prices in London.[22] Until then, however, it was hard for farmers to support their families. To make ends meet, many (like Hudspeth) took government jobs: constable, poundkeeper (impounding straying animals) or, for the better-qualified, higher-ranking jobs.

For the first few years after Arthur arrived, he told London that farmers were struggling, in 'real distress': old hands were needy and unproductive, and recent settlers were generally in straitened circumstances, their money exhausted by setting up their farms. By the end of the decade, however, he was much more positive, talking of growing prosperity rather than distress.[23]

How did this all work out in practice? Here are stories of grantees in the three main categories: those who did nothing, those who did something, and those who established a farm.

Some applicants made extravagant promises about cultivating their grants which they had no intention of keeping. Captain Lister sailed his barque from London in 1830. He spent three months in the colony and applied for a grant, promising to leave money with an agent to invest in stock and implements. He was granted 1000 acres and sailed away, and there is no indication that he or his agent did anything to his land.²⁴ There are many similar stories. Joseph Reichenberg, a music teacher, based his application for land on his long army service as bandmaster. He gained 200 acres but continued to teach music and did nothing to his land. Such men saw a land grant as a reward for service, not a possible farm. Others worked in Hobart or Launceston and ignored their land. James Thomson ran his boarding school and did nothing to his grant, which was grazed on by a neighbour's cattle.²⁵

Some grantees did not appear at all. William Effingham Lawrence arrived in 1823 with instructions from London to grant him and his brother Edward 2000 acres each. This was done: but Edward never arrived and William kept his land.²⁶ Governor Murray's son Charles was seven when he left the island in 1813, having been granted 600 acres. He never returned, and did nothing to the land; he joined the army and died in Sierra Leone aged 27. Nathaniel Mockeridge was a sailor whose ship called at Hobart in 1821. He was discharged due to illness and received a 30-acre grant at Launceston, but no more was heard of him.²⁷

In 1824 Joseph Dixon, described as a well-respected gentleman, was found guilty of trying to provoke a man into fighting a duel. He does not seem to have been punished. The son of a wealthy Scottish manufacturer, he had qualified as a lawyer but spent his time in foreign travel, arriving in Hobart in 1823 aged 21. He was granted 1760 acres at Kingston but shortly after the duel affair he returned to Britain, and was elected to parliament. Reporting this surprising event, a Hobart newspaper reminded readers that he had been 'a settler at Brown's River'.²⁸

Other people appeared, gained a grant and vanished. Matthew Keane, an ex-convict, worked as a plasterer in Sydney, then moved to Van Diemen's Land and in 1823 was granted 30 acres at Launceston. There is no evidence that he did anything to it; he worked as a plasterer in Launceston and disappeared in about 1826. Others sold their grants. Thomas Young gained an order for a land grant in 1821 and sold it, first to a man named Quinton then to James Hinchy, leaving them to fight it out – with a third man who also claimed the land.²⁹

Edward Lord, great friend of Sorell, managed to get grants for his friends and relations, deserving or not: in his shipload of 1820, all his male passengers as well as the captain received grants. Two farmed in the north, with William Talbot developing the large and successful property of Malahide; but the captain and William Williamson almost certainly did nothing, and a lawyer and a doctor practised in Hobart with farms not mentioned. The seventh man might have done something, but in 1825 his land reverted to the crown after he was convicted of stealing four cattle.[30]

Some people were granted infertile land. Robert Neil received 200 acres, but took a job in the commissariat. Later he applied for another grant, claiming Macquarie had promised him one if he worked in the commissariat for seven years. Arthur asked what improvements he had made on his grant. None, replied Neil. It was small and useless so he sold it. He received no second grant.[31] Nicholas Gribble selected his 500 acres on Mangalore Tier but found there was no water. Could he move it to the land granted to Dixon, who left the island and sold his land to Patterson, who sold to Atkinson, and the grant had lately been cancelled because of non-performance with the conditions? No answer to Gribble was recorded.[32]

Some people started to farm, but left their land or sold it after only a few years or even months. They could, like William Sams who had been a page to the Duke of Kent, realise they were 'not cut out for a successful bush colonist'; he moved to an office job. Thefts could dishearten or even ruin farmers. Captain and Mrs Sockett arrived in 1822 and gained a grant on the Clyde. They had hardly arrived when their shepherd stole their sheep, with another theft the next year. Dispirited, they left the colony in 1825.[33]

In 1820 William Chambers, a former soldier, gained a grant at Bagdad and settled there with his family. He sold meat to the government, but lost three oxen, 'strayed' (often a euphemism for 'stolen'). Then in 1821 thieves broke into his sheep yard and drove off his sheep. He left the colony soon afterwards.[34] William Millikin Esquire arrived in 1823 with his family and gained an excellent 1500-acre grant at Ross, but left the next year, abandoning his farm.[35] Was the hard physical labour too much for this gentleman, or the primitive life overwhelming for his family?

Hugh Hull found the physical labour too hard. A slight thirteen-year-old, on his father's farm he took the sheep out to feed all day, bringing them home at night. He also helped with general work, digging, ploughing and fencing. 'I did not like farm life', Hugh wrote. 'Being physically weak the duties were too hard; digging tired me.' He was relieved when, three years later, he gained an office job as a clerk.[36] How many others must have been similarly relieved when they could exchange the hard, endless toil of farming for an easier life.

It was hard to make ends meet in the 1820s; even William Talbot found running his magnificent property of Malahide barely covered expenses. People had to diversify. The Stodart family arrived in 1822, gained a grant and in 1823, when their baby son died, were farming at Broadmarsh. However, by 1824 Robert was running a hotel in Hobart. What happened to the land is not clear but it was obviously not the family's main interest. Other settlers opened shops, and one lived on the profit of shoes made by a convict servant.[37]

Others turned to crime to get by. John Stirling and his family arrived in 1823. Armed with his recommendation from the secretary of state and claiming a good sum in cash, he was granted 1500 acres on the Macquarie River. In 1825 he sold his land (too early) and returned to England – perhaps to escape justice, for he was said to be a notorious receiver of stolen sheep. Another settler kept a sly grog shop on the side.[38]

Ex-convict Lachlan White applied for land in 1825, saying he was married, working as an overseer and well acquainted with agriculture, and had oxen and implements to enable him to farm. Sounding an ideal grantee, he gained 50 acres near Launceston. In 1828 he requested a second grant as he needed more room for his cattle. H. Simpson supported his claim. Did White reside on this grant and was he of respectable habits? Arthur asked the Launceston magistrate. The answer: White resided 'but is a disorderly & dissolute Person'. Furious, Arthur refused the extra grant and told Simpson to check his facts in future.[39]

In 1829 White was charged with stealing a bull. Evidence depicted notorious bushranger Bevan visiting White's farm and helping an employee, a convict runaway, bring cattle from the bush. Probably stolen, they were slaughtered at once and White sold the meat. White and Bevan suspected the runaway of betraying them, so one night dragged him from his bed, thrust hot cinders in his mouth and tried to cut his throat. He threw himself out of the window and ran naked to a farm two miles away. More evidence told of drunken quarrels, and a witness knew Bevan was dead 'because I shot him myself'. Despite protesting his innocence, White was sentenced to seven more years' transportation and had to give up his farm.[40] This grant cannot be classed as fulfilling the British government's hopes.

The inn at Spring Hill – such small inns were the downfall of many a settler, like Arthur Buist (TA ALMFA, AUTAS001144582780)

George Lloyd, who worked with his uncle Charles Jeffreys on his grant at Sorell, recalled Uncle Charles' enormous pride at his first crop of waving golden corn. But after four years of hard work, Charles realised that growing crops was never going to pay and was a challenging life for men like him, used to the army and navy. Where one man succeeded in farming, considered George, fifty did not. In spite of rigid economy, slavish work and the help of convicts they could not keep their heads above water. Wiser men concentrated on rearing horses and cattle and producing wool, but even these were of little value in the early 1820s.[41]

Captain William Holdship was possibly in this category. Arriving in 1823 with his son and daughter, he gained an 800-acre grant and chose a 'delightful situation' on the sea shore at Northwest Bay. He soon

A typical home of a successful farmer: the McCra family's Selma at Bothwell (TA ALMFA AUTAS001131820649)

realised it was barren. The government refused to let him change it, so he set about making the best of it, spreading 'marle' washed up by the sea (presumably seaweed) as manure. However, wheat and barley crops failed, and bushrangers tied him up, pointed a loaded musket at his head and stole his guns. Shortly after this he died and his children sold the property, describing it as a fine dairy farm with the most excellent feed for horned cattle, and 'part of a house'.[42]

Far less deserving was Arthur Buist, who arrived in 1823 with the correct documents and gained a grant at Campbell Town. He 'ran away' with Christian Taylor – with her consent or not isn't clear, but their daughter was born before they married. They settled down on his grant and Arthur did some work, but Christian realised that he was an alcoholic. When he applied for a second grant, the local police magistrate reported that he was 'a most drunken disorderly character'. Buist spent all his cash on rum at John Headlam's pub, swimming across if the river was too high to ford. Or he sold goods: a bag of sugar for four bottles of rum, a dish of carrots for a pint. Once he pulled off his trousers and sold them for half a pint of rum, then his jacket and waistcoat for another half. At last Christian, 'almost broken hearted', took her children to her father's house. By 1830 Arthur was in financial difficulties. More and more of his goods were sold to pay debts, and in 1836 he committed suicide.[43]

Other people established long-term farms, and this list includes the well-known dynasties who flourished in the colony: the Archers, Gibsons, Burburys, Bisdees, O'Connors, Leakes and other families who seem to embody the idea of 'pioneer'. They managed to establish profitable farms and keep them in the family for generations. But it was not necessarily easy.

James Sutherland recorded daily work on his property near Campbell Town. Within two months of arriving in 1823, he and his men built a house, dug a garden, ploughed land and planted wheat, barley and potatoes, and Sutherland bought sheep from neighbours. This was his pattern of work for years, growing crops and raising sheep. There were endless problems, Bullocks strayed and were only found after days of searching. Convicts usually worked well but sometimes did not, and had to be replaced. Crops failed. Thomas Gregson cheated him over selling sheep. The sheep developed scab and had to be treated, and in the absence of fences were prone to stray. Farmers spent a good deal of time returning sheep which had become mixed with theirs, telling them apart by their brands – Sutherland's had ICS pitchbranded on their left ribs with one slit in the right ear and two in the left, and a head brand of two parallel lines between the eyes, which was difficult for sheepstealers to eradicate. (The pitch was made of tar and grease.) All these improvements meant Sutherland qualified for a second grant of 500 acres. He was made a magistrate.

Two major facts are clear from the diary. One is that despite being a 'gentleman', Sutherland did much manual labour: 'preparing ground for potatoes by breaking sods with hoes', 'Colin and I shingling', 'I shore Six of the longest woolled sheep – and they were pretty well done for a first attempt'. The second is the difficulty of making money. Sutherland did not mention selling wheat or meat, and only once sold stock. As seen above, he made something from selling wool, but his income as a magistrate must have been very useful.[44]

In his description of the colony in 1827 (see chapter 16), Roderic O'Connor praised those who did well due to hard work. The Amoses were a large and industrious family who had come out as employees and by hard work and frugality were prospering. At Kempton, ex-convict Joseph Johnson, 'a fine, sensible old Man, of great integrity', had built a two-storey house, fenced many acres and ran 1200 sheep. Further north, the Archers cultivated their land, had large flocks of improved sheep, and employed many men, showing what could be done in Van Diemen's Land if people worked hard. Not everyone who succeeded was British: Rum John Con, an Indian, gained a grant in 1818. He bought more land and by 1827 ran a large flock of sheep.[45]

Men who accompanied employers from Britain as overseers or others who had similar experience often did well once they had their own land. Many industrious ex-convicts were doing well. John Bell was a shepherd for Governor Sorell, and afterwards rented land and ran sheep. He received a grant of 50 acres and later asked for a second. He lived on his land with his wife and five children and had fenced and cultivated it, most praiseworthy; he received 100 acres more. Similarly, Edward Chaplin asked for land: he was free by servitude, had conducted himself well and wanted to devote himself to farming. He rented a farm, and had bullocks, a cart and some wheat, all gained by honest industry. He had references from five employers. This model ex-convict was awarded 320 acres. He married, fathered a string of daughters and died in 1874, still a farmer at Broadmarsh.[46]

Not quite such a model ex-convict was James Ratcliffe, a short, possibly malnourished chimneysweep from Manchester. He worked his whole sentence, six years, 'with perfect propriety' for one employer; married Sarah (also a convict) and they had seven children. James applied for a grant and gained 50 acres on Ralph's Bay, though no second grant as the gentlemen of the Land Board thought his character 'not such as to receive' it: he was suspected of selling spirits without a licence, and spent some time in gaol for stealing sheep. But when not in gaol he worked his land, and died a farmer aged 41.[47] Not exactly what the British government hoped for in granting land, but considering his background, a fair outcome.

Carmino Reago was a Spaniard, tried in Sicily in 1808 when the area was briefly under British command. Transported for life, he served his sentence with one minor offence – missing at muster – and then farmed a grant at Green Point. Fluent in English and clearly well-educated, he wrote a stinging letter to the press criticising corruption in the Survey Department.[48]

Governor Arthur tended to be more generous to deserving ex-convicts than the upper-class gentlemen of the Land Board. Ex-convict William Waterson applied for a second grant, saying he had cultivated the first and needed more pasturage for his stock. The Land Board thought he did not have enough capital to develop it, but Arthur said he was an industrious man who deserved more land, and authorised 170 acres.

William Atkins had served out his term working for Mr Harris at Clarence Plains (working for only one employer showed stability and was a good sign). He was now free with a family: could he have a grant? Again, the Land Board thought he did not have enough capital. The colonial secretary thought he could get a job instead, for it was undesirable to give land to such people – 'it is labourers not landowners the Colony wants'. Arthur agreed but two years later changed his mind. 'As [Atkins] is very industrious, & has 5 children, I approve of 50 acres being located to him.' Arthur even gave a small grant to ex-convict John Johnson, who had committed no misdemeanours and had three good references, but admitted to a paralytic infirmity which meant all he could do was tend sheep.[49]

Many men unable to make their land yield a profit moved to other activities. Very popular was a government job, either local – constable, poundkeeper, magistrate – or in Hobart, in one of the government offices. Both the Parramore and Leake families, farming at Campbell Town, had one member working in Hobart, and Roderic O'Connor took on the job of land commissioner and later inspector of roads and bridges. Other people let their farms and moved to Hobart to a job with a regular salary, or set up their own businesses as, for example, tallow chandler, teacher or auctioneer.[50]

Shopkeeping offered promise: people had to buy goods. At first the only serious merchant was Maria Lord, Edward's ex-convict wife, who ran the best shop in town. In the 1820s she was joined by other successful merchants. Henry and Sarah Hopkins arrived in 1822 and did not apply for a grant, as Henry aimed to set up an industry selling wool. To start with, he and Sarah had brought two boxes of shoes. Renting a small house of two rooms and a skilling (a lean-to at the back), they slept in one room and divided the other into a living area and the shop. Henry sold any goods he could obtain, walking every morning to the harbour to see if any new vessels had arrived with goods for sale. Satirist Henry Savery described him as mean, refusing to give his customers bags for their goods. 'A spare thin man, of a very vinegar aspect', he said profits would not allow it. Savery continued:

> Presently a fat middle-aged female in great dishabille, approached the shop from a neighbouring public-house, and entering with a semivole [flourish], and, throwing some money on the counter, said, in a tone and style which could only have been acquired by a long acquaintance with Billingsgate [a rough area of London], "Give me some tea and sugar."
> "What have you to put them in, my good woman?"
> "None of your good woman for me, d– your eyes." at the same moment stooping to draw off a dirty stocking from a dirtier foot, "here's a leg'll bear looking at and here's something'll hold the tea and sugar," handing over the stocking, into which the sugar was first placed, and then tying it in the middle with the woman's garter, so as to form a division for the sugar, she received her change and left the shop.[51]

Others praised Henry's 'careful attention to business and his unswerving rectitude', his 'enterprise, industry and integrity': an active man, hard-working, careful of every penny. It worked. In 1828, Henry and Sarah wrote that 'the God of providence has made our cup to run over with temporal supplies': they were doing very well indeed.[52]

The Robertson brothers did equally well. Poor tenant farmers in Scotland, they gained land grants and developed them, but decided to sell (early), making a good profit, six times what they had arrived with four years earlier. They set up shops and businesses in Hobart and Launceston and flourished, so much so that when the *All-Time Australian 200 Rich List* was published in 2004, William and Daniel Robertson were ranked numbers 141 and 75.[53] Not all shopkeepers did as well – as with farming, success needed hard work and acumen – but many people earned a living by selling goods.

Henry Hopkins supporting the new Bank of Van Diemen's Land by buying a share
(TA AUTAS001125643171)

A great advance occurred partly due to these newcomers. In 1823 a group of merchants decided to set up the badly needed Bank of Van Diemen's Land. At first the currency had mainly consisted of commissary receipts and promissory notes put out by merchants – or even rum – as well as any coins and notes people happened to have, from pounds sterling to Spanish and American dollars. There were numerous problems, so Hobart's merchants held a public meeting and the Bank opened in March 1824. It could issue bank notes, a far more stable currency.[54] This was a huge advantage for businesses.

Running a pub was often lucrative in this hard-drinking colony, and this was a popular activity – as Robert Stodart found (see above). In the early 1820s the British government lifted restrictions on whaling and more local men entered this industry, the majority as sailors and a handful as owners and entrepreneurs, notably Captain Kelly. The small community supported little manufacturing industry. But employers mentioned above needed labour. Those who did not want to, or did not have the ability, confidence or finance to start a business, could work for employers for good wages, higher than in Britain.[55]

Not everyone prospered, however. Through abuse of alcohol, or lack of ability, ambition, competence, or luck, some people could not start a successful new life in the colony. Many left, either returning to Britain or seeking other opportunities in Sydney or elsewhere. Overall statistics are difficult to obtain but of people who gained land grants, as far as can be ascertained 43 per cent left the colony and 57 per cent remained, their deaths recorded.

Was West correct in saying that free immigrants who arrived from 1820 changed society, with their capital and their more upright behaviour? There were rogues among them, or at least those prepared to bend the law to advance their interests, such as claiming more in their schedules than they actually possessed. However, on the whole, enough of these emigrants had the requisite virtues of the day – honesty, sobriety, industriousness – that they did make a difference. They set standards that gradually became the norm; the more upright and capable were more successful in positions of responsibility than most previous officeholders; and, generally, they supported two major influences in reforming the colony: Governor Arthur and churches.

FLIGHT OF FANCY: ADVICE ON A VOYAGE

Scene: The mess in a passenger ship to Van Diemen's Land, 1824
An old hand returning to the colony explains the ropes to new passengers

Old Hand: I went out in 1820 and got a good grant, but then went home for a cargo of goods to sell. But I know all about getting a land grant. Oh yes, I do!

New passengers gather round keenly

Old Hand: When you arrive, you go and see the governor, and you show him your letter from the secretary of state, authorising you to get a land grant.

Innocent Young Man: What letter?

Old Hand (*smiles patronisingly*): You meant you don't have one? Oh dear! Well, you can plead with the governor, say you hadn't intended to settle but now you see how wonderful the place it, you want to. Something like that.

IYM: But that would be lying!

Old Hand (*bursts into laughter*): If you don't like lying, you're going to the wrong place! Everything everyone says in Van Diemen's Land is a pack of lies!

IYM looks horrified, as do several other passengers

Old Hand (*enjoying himself immensely*): You tell the governor how much money you have to develop the grant. Well, how much you'd like to have. There's ways – oh yes, there's ways.

Enthusiast: What do you do?

Old Hand: Well, you can get some friends and pool your money, then take it in turns to show it to the governor. Money all looks the same, doesn't it? He can't tell he's seen it already.

IYM looks appalled; Enthusiast looks thrilled

Old Hand: Or you go to a bank, get them to write a cheque, show it to the governor, and give it back to the bank – for a consideration, of course.

IYM: How can bankers lend themselves to such deception?

Old Hand: They're doing it all the time! I tell you, if you're looking for an honest man in Van Diemen's Land you've got your work cut out! Anyone like to top up my glass? This is helpful information I'm giving you.

Enthusiast produces a bottle and pours.

You add in the value of everything you've got with you. Estimated value, that it (*taps his nose*). Your estimate. Include everything – kitchen stuff, the fares out, the lot. How's the governor to know how much you're worth?

Enthusiast: They base the land grant just on what you say?

Old Hand: What else can they do? They can't check everything. So you get your two thousand acres, whatever, depending on how persuasive you are. Then you have to brave the surveyor (*rolls his eyes*). First expense – bribing him to give you a good grant.

IYM: A civil servant, taking bribes! How dishonest! Dreadful!

Old Hand: Yes, it is dreadful, a terrible expense, and he doesn't always give you a better grant anyway. Law unto himself. But like I tell you, everyone in Van Diemen's Land's on the take. How else are they to make a go of living there?

IYM: By farming? Growing wheat, raising cattle?

Old Hand: Lad, you're got a tough time ahead of you. Let me tell you ...

16. THE LAND COMMISSIONERS: FARMING IN 1826–1827

In 1825 the British government decided its Australian colonies needed to be thoroughly surveyed, to ascertain what arable land had been granted or sold and what remained. Each colony had three commissioners: a surveyor who remained in town and two others who travelled all over the colony and reported back.

Among the settlers arriving in Van Diemen's Land in 1824 was Roderic O'Connor, a middle-aged Irish landed gentleman whose family had run out of money. Competent and strong-minded, he was determined to make a new life with his two illegitimate sons and (never mentioned but almost certainly present) their mother Catherine. Despite Arthur urging morality on the population, O'Connor never married her, for a Protestant gentleman could never wed the daughter of a poor Catholic tenant. Nevertheless, O'Connor became a close friend of Governor Arthur. He was good at getting his own way.

O'Connor gained a grant and settled on a location, but the Survey Office cheated him, trying to extract a bribe. He was having none of this, and pursued the matter for years until he won. The Survey Office was a sink of corruption, he declared.[1] He settled on his grant at the Lake River but like others could make no actual profit. Meanwhile, Arthur was impressed with this capable, honest, fearless man and selected him as a land commissioner. The others were young surveyor Edward Dumaresq and Peter Murdoch, an ex-army officer who had been commandant at the Maria Island penal station.[2] It would have taken a tough man to stand up to O'Connor, and he dominated the others.

While Dumaresq stayed in the Hobart office, O'Connor and Murdoch travelled over the settled districts, their report commenting not only on vacant land and its quality, but occupied or at least granted land. Since it is in O'Connor's handwriting and Murdoch seemed to have just agreed with him, I'll call it his.

O'Connor mentioned almost all the colony's farms and their owners, often giving a potted history: the succession of owners, the present man or occasionally woman, successes and failures. Here is O'Connor's neighbour, Thomas Fletcher:

> August 7th [1826] rode thro' Fenton's farm formerly occupied by Fletcher the District Constable, he after having spent all the Capital he brought out, was obliged to quit in consequence of its not yielding any return, it is bad land, only fit for Sheep, Fletcher was no farmer, Curling, who is since dead, had taken a very fine farm at the other side of the River, and having no Neighbour, prevailed upon Fletcher to pitch his Tent opposite to him, he did so, and lost both his time and Money.³

Two men who failed, through death and, apparently, lack of knowledge. It is not surprising that O'Connor knew the details about a neighbour, but wherever the commissioners went they picked up information:

'Hilly and indifferent, very little fit for Sheep', wrote the Land Commissioners about New Norfolk. Painting by John Ommanney (TA ALMFA AUTAS001124072901)

2nd [March 1827] Strike our Tents & proceed to the Banks of the Derwent. thro' Spodes grant sold to Wells, fine pasture, consists of 700 [acres], thence thro' 700 acres to Haywood he has built an excellent Barn & outhouses, & commenced a dwelling House – excellent stone, he has fenced a very large Paddock.[4]

One grant sold, one developed successfully. Haywood was one of the minority of settlers O'Connor praised: those who worked hard, built neat houses, cleared land and improved their farms, and were 'steady', 'industrious', 'decent' and 'respectable'. There was the industrious, practical Gatenby family, not too proud or lazy to work. The women milked cows and made butter and cheese; the sons ploughed, sowed seed and sawed timber; and the family was becoming wealthy, comfortable and independent, a delightful change after being tenant farmers in Scotland, where they worked merely to benefit others.[5] (The Gatenbys actually came from Yorkshire: O'Connor was not always correct.) Another excellent farmer was Mrs Humphrey. Her husband was the chief police magistrate in Hobart, and she ran their property very competently. It was one of the most gratifying sights in the colony, said O'Connor, with highly improved sheep, a beautiful bull, a fine garden and an excellent pig yard.[6] There was no mention of the embarrassingly lowly social origins of Mrs Humphrey, or that she and her husband had lived together for years before marrying – Roderic O'Connor was hardly in a position to criticise. Neither did he show surprise that a woman was such a competent farmer, for O'Connor praised achievement, especially in those of (now) high social status.

But settlers praised by O'Connor were in the minority. He had nothing but contempt for lazy, drunk, slovenly settlers, foolish and improvident, who did not improve their grants, or farmed badly and overstocked their land, with farms where 'every thing wears the aspect of distress and mismanagement, the Wool of five hundred sheep lying rotten about the Stock yard'. One man 'spends more Money in Rum, than in improvements'; three brothers 'might have succeeded had they not been foolish and improvident'; and the Von Bibra family 'are a lazy, indolent, good for nothing set, and how they contrive to live, is a mystery'. 'Never did a Man come to this Colony who has shewn himself so completely ignorant of its capabilities as Mr Oakes, or who has spent so much Money to such little purpose': Oakes abandoned his farm.[7]

So did many others. 'Allen, Holmes, Newton and Young have left their farms', wrote O'Connor of one district.[8] Some people abandoned farms for reasons not their fault – losing eyesight, illness, death, being murdered, or in Major Bell's case, being transferred to New South Wales – but O'Connor showed little sympathy. Nor did he when people left because they were tired of farming, or fled after Aboriginal attacks or losses of stock to theft or wild animals. Some men could not get their land measured by the surveyors so abandoned it. Weaklings! Everyone should pull their weight. O'Connor scorned women who did no work but 'spend half their time papering and curling their hair, playing the Piano, reading Romances and Novels'.[9] They should be making butter like the Gatenbys.

O'Connor barely mentioned smaller farmers who were doing well, such as ex marine Daniel Stanfield, let alone ex-convicts (he did not go to remote Kitty's Corner to see my ancestor James Pillinger struggling). It was the larger, more respectable farmers who interested him, and he seemed to see people with smaller properties as a nuisance, typically running stock everywhere, including on their neighbours' properties, stealing stock and ignoring the law. He thought poorly of most convicts:

> a life of idleness in a Stock Hut is the summit of a Ticket of Leave Man's ambition, there he lies, taking a view of his Sheep perhaps once a day, never moving to any other occasion except from the Bed to the Frying Pan, or when a Party is made to rob some unfortunate Settler of his sheep, then he is all alacrity, nothing can withstand his dexterity and eagerness in the Pursuit, like a Boa Constrictor he makes a huge Prey, then coils himself up until a fresh opportunity occurs of devouring another Victim[.][10]

There were many non-respectable people:

> we saw a Hut, no one within, a person in the neighbourhood informed us, it was occupied by four men and a woman who had no occupation or ostensible mode of support, we met one of its Inhabitants returning from Kangarooing in a state of

nudity ... this Parish is infested with Huts of the description of the one alluded to above ... it abounds with licentious characters & it was asserted by respectable settlers that the perpetrators of the most serious crimes were openly at large defying justice[11]

At the other end of the social spectrum, O'Connor detested four men who tied up huge tracts of land: Edward Lord, David Lord, George Meredith and William Field, all free arrivals. David Lord cherry-picked huge areas, buying small areas of land with a water supply or good soil; no one wanted the rest so he took it. By grants and purchases he acquired a huge area on which he grazed cattle and sheep, and made no improvements except a log hut. He employed the minimum of men to care for the sheep, while cattle were allowed to roam at will, only mustered once a year to brand calves and send some off for sale. They often trespassed on others' property, destroying crops, mixing herds. But David's father James, a convict, had amassed wealth by breaking the law, continued O'Connor, selling spirits without a licence, then buying land for a bottle of rum per acre. What could you expect? And it was an atrocious example. People said, if the Lords can do it, why can't I?[12]

Edward Lord (no relation of David) and Field did the same, while Meredith gained an enormous amount of land through chicanery (claiming a grant for his nephew, for example, and keeping it). And these and similar men, wrote O'Connor bitterly, 'reside in Hobart at their ease drinking their Champagne, and Brandy and Water, while their Hordes of wild Cattle are destroying the Crops of the industrious Settlers with impunity'. They could get vicious: ex-convicts James Stynes and Richard Troy, smaller villains, possessed a vast herd of cattle 'nor dare a Settler approach their Territory, he would be eaten up in a Week'.[13] How could the colony prosper? asked O'Connor.

O'Connor described a huge amount of dishonesty. It started when newly arrived settlers fudged their schedules of assets to gain larger grants:

A Settler arrives with a very triffling Sum as Capital, he finds on landing, that it will entitle him only to a minimum grant, whereas he is determined if possible to obtain a maximum.

Among the Passengers, one or other of them discovers the proper method of deceiving the Government go to an obliging merchant who, for a percentage, gave the settler a cheque on a bank, but warned the bank's cashier not to cash the cheque.[14]

The settler showed the governor the cheque and obtained a large grant, then the cheque was destroyed. This, said O'Connor, occurred daily. Page, who had a good farm at Lemon Springs, came out without a shilling. When asked how he obtained so much land, he said that when he was asked to swear (on the bible, then presumably kissing it) to his schedule of assets, 'I kissed my thumb'. Historian John Beattie wrote of fellow-passengers pooling their money and taking it in turns to present the same amount to the governor as their own. Much land 'was parcelled out among several settlers, in virtue of a single bag of dollars, hired for the purpose'.[15]

These stories were all hearsay, but two such activities were documented. Governor Arthur found Norman McDonald borrowed money from three people, showed it as his assets, gained a grant of 1200 acres, returned the money and sold the land. The government resumed it. A similar rogue was John Newton, given 50 acres in 1823. Arthur found his statement of property 'perfectly false'. Moreover, he was trying to leave the colony under 'very suspicious, if not fraudulent circumstances'. The grant was cancelled.[16] Sponsors could make fictitious claims: William Williamson presented a letter from Sir John Owen, MP (Edward Lord's brother) describing him as a very respectable man with over £8000 capital, though he told his sister he had only £15 in the world – but this was before Arthur's stricter regime, and Williamson gained a large grant.[17]

Schedules show people claiming all sorts of improbable sources of finance: fares out (already paid), kitchen utensils, household furniture and linen, debts due from Britain … Values were also exorbitantly exaggerated, and suspiciously round figures presented.[18] 'In no Country in the World is circumspection and a little knowledge of the World more requisite than in this', wrote O'Connor. 'It has been the Asylum of Sharpers, Swindlers and Blacklegs.' One apparent gentleman 'fell into all the Vices of the Colony, such as drinking Rum to excess and branding Cattle that did not belong to him'. Settlers stole stock ('the old and profitable trade of Sheep and Cattle stealing'), sold their grants

Panshanger, owned by Joseph Archer. 'He has built a newt Brick House, in a pleasant situation, commanding a delightful prospect of the surrounding Country', wrote the Land Commissioners. 'He cultivates largely, and has fine flocks of highly improved Sheep.' Painted by William Lyttleton in 1835, nine years after this comment (TA ALMFA AUTAS001122921521)

several times over, bribed the commissary to accept their wheat and meat ('Corruption was the order of the day'), sold grants as soon as they received them instead of waiting five years to sell, then returned to Britain, taking money out of the colony.[19]

O'Connor did realise that farmers faced problems – surely he did so himself. Much of the island was unsuitable for cropping, because of poor soil or lack of rain. Land could be mountainous, hilly, stony, barren, dry, sandy, with poor soil, marshy, inaccessible except to goats, marshy, heavily timbered, nothing but a succession of gullies and bad land and, possibly the most gloomy of all, 'frightful Glens, with perpendicular sides of huge Rocks, totally impassable and little or no herbage'.[20] Neighbours encroached on property; thylacines, Tasmanian devils and native dogs attacked stock; frost killed wheat; people cheated settlers, or set fire to their wheat or their barns; houses burnt down; wives died; husbands died too, or became ill, indebted, blind, bankrupt or mad. They drowned, they ruined themselves by speculation. Some were murdered. A number committed suicide, and more gave up and returned to Britain.

Some were cheated by large landowners or merchants intent on enriching themselves – for O'Connor, among the worst villains of all. He described how it was done. An improvident settler asked a merchant for supplies – tea, sugar and rum – and provided a warrant of attorney for the farm as payment. 'The foolish fellow takes these goods on a credit of at least three hundred per cent, he goes home quite happy, is drunk as long as the Rum lasts, no farm can pay for these excesses, the farm is soon siezed and sold.'[21] (Frankly, this seems the settler's fault rather than the merchant's.)

How was a settler to succeed in Van Diemen's Land? To ensure success, the government should make sensible regulations and enforce them, declared O'Connor. It should grant land more carefully, and strictly scrutinise people's claims to assets. The laws about impounding straying stock 'appear to have been framed by large Stock owners' for their own benefit. They should be made fairer. Settlers should be obliged to fence their land. Overall, the government should protect the 'resident improving settler'. It must stop abuses for 'How is it possible that a Colony can prosper while such practises are allowed and sanctioned?'[22] These were all sensible recommendations, but O'Connor also disapproved of small grants. They encouraged sheep stealing and the independence of poor men, who would otherwise be available to work for wages for landowners like himself.

Settlers should know something of agriculture. 'No matter what the line of life a Man has followed at home [Britain], he imagines that he can farm to advantage in Van Diemen's Land'; 'who would have thought of a Pickle Merchant turning Farmer'. Men who had farming experience in Britain were more likely to be successful although, strangely, 'Men who were scientific Farmers at home, often make the worst selections of land here'.[23] Capital was helpful but not the deciding factor: 'industry and a knowledge of agricultural affairs goes much farther towards ensuring prosperity than any amount of capital in the hands of inexperienced persons'. It helped a man to be married; too often a young, single man had no one to manage his domestic affairs, found he could not bear 'the solitude of the Bush', and fled to Hobart and disaster: he 'falls into company similarly situated as himself, to drown care they have recourse to the Brandy Bottle, and the inevitable consequence is, total loss of property'.[24]

To succeed at farming, claimed O'Connor, a man 'must have a mind fitted for solitude, as if he wishes to prosper, he must remain eternally on his farm. To quit it for the delights of Hobart, is certain ruin'. He must work hard:

> fence your land, rouze yourself from your drunken Couch, send no more for Rum, attend to your Men, instead of dosing away your existence in so brutal a manner, get up early, look after your affairs, if you cannot cultivate largely, clear, fence, and cultivate as least as much as will supply your family ...[25]

Overall, despite the difficulties of pioneering, O'Connor felt that men failed because of their own ignorance, idleness or imprudence:

> Few Men will allow that they have been the cause of their destruction, they blame all but themselves ... We are in the daily habit of hearing abuse upon abuse vented on the Colony, and the Ruin that it has entailed on many. We say that in no one instance has any Man been reduced to Poverty but by his own misconduct or imprudence.[26]

In fact, continued O'Connor, the emigrant 'cannot pitch upon any part of the Globe, so perfectly fit for his purpose as this Colony'. Other places had disadvantages such as dreadful climates and endemic disease, but

> Here, the advantages are innumerable, the Soil is in a great measure prepared for him, the grass feeds his Sheep and Cattle the year thro', without having the expence and trouble of providing food for the winter for them, he obtains the land free of all cost, and he generally finds as much clear as suffices for all the present purposes of agriculture. Under such flattering circumstances with a fine healthy climate, provided a Man goes on slowly and steadily he must succeed.[27]

The picture O'Connor painted of the colony was grim: a place where honest, hard-working people could succeed, but with dishonest people breaking the law and cheating their fellows, and incompetent, drunken people failing. How accurate was it? O'Connor was prone to exaggeration, and like Bigge he largely ignored the success of working-class settlers, ex-convicts, their children and the military, but after twenty years when corruption raged virtually unchecked and the forces of law and order were weak, his picture is probably substantially correct. His journals certainly gave Arthur a frank picture of the colony, and advice on how to improve matters.

O'Connor took his own advice. He worked extremely hard on his property, made sure he oversaw everything, spent very little time in Hobart, drank alcohol moderately – and made a fortune with wool, becoming one of the most successful graziers in the colony.[28]

FLIGHT OF FANCY: ISABELLA LEWIS TRIES TO HIDE THE PAST

Isabella McKellar, sister of Lilias, married Hobart merchant Richard Lewis. By 1824 she's settled in Hobart society. Richard has become friendly with a newcomer, Mr Smithers, and has asked him and his wife to dinner. Mrs Smithers has heard enticing gossip ...

Mrs Smithers: How kind of you to invite us! And how long have you lived here, Mrs Lewis?

Isabella: I arrived nine years ago, in 1815. It was a small town then! But so prettily situated, don't you think?

Mrs Smithers: How brave of you! You must have been very young! Were you by yourself?

Isabella (*carefully offhand*): I came with my sister and her husband. But I married Richard the next year, and dear little Jane was born a year later, so I had no time to be lonely ...

Mrs Smithers: And how are your sister and brother-in-law?

Isabella: They returned to England, but we stayed here. So many business opportunities, as you'll find. Your husband ...

Mrs Smithers: Why did they return? Such a long voyage!

Isabella: Life here isn't for everyone, you know. And I have two sons, David and Neil. Neil is such a promising boy – do you have children, Mrs Smithers?

Mrs Smithers: Not yet. I believe you have one sister still here?

Isabella: Yes, she's happily married, living in a beautiful property at Tea Tree. Are you going to take up land?

Mrs Smithers: Oh yes, my husband is applying for a grant. I'm fascinated by all your convicts. What happens after these criminals are freed?

Isabella: Like offenders in Britain, they return to the general community. Why not? (*gives Mrs Smithers a Look*)

Mrs Smithers: I suppose this place is a hotbed of gossip?

Isabella (*coldly*): Some people enjoy gossip. It isn't to my taste. I think the servants are about to serve dinner. Shall we move to the dining-room?

Mrs Smithers, finally vanquished, follows her meekly.

(*Isabella's grandson, convict descendant Sir Neil Elliott Lewis, became a lawyer. Three times premier of Tasmania, he was instrumental in bringing about Australian federation.*)

17. CHURCHES BRING NEW OPPORTUNITIES

In 1822 Robert Mather arrived in the colony. Like others, he was influenced by Wentworth's and Jeffreys' accounts, but also by letters from the Wesleyan minister in Hobart, seeking to entice industrious and god-fearing men to the colony.[1]

Mather was a draper, the sort of man coming to the fore by the 1820s: middle-class with no pretensions, upright, hard-working, a devout Christian. It was such newcomers who helped establish the second force for change: churches, especially evangelical churches with their emphasis on upright behaviour. The growth of these churches was a reaction to the established Church of England, as the colony's only clergyman Knopwood understood it: the church as a branch of the state, undertaking and recording baptisms, marriages and deaths, and holding services according to the prayer book. Nothing extempore, nothing heartfelt.

John Wesley and others preached a more personal religion of faith in an almighty God, and new churches formed or were re-invigorated. As part of their aim to preach the Gospel world-wide, they sent ministers to Tasmania. There, as well as offering salvation, they provided a warm welcome and acceptance of everyone – they were keen to increase numbers and every sinner was a potential soul saved. The government paid for ministers' salaries and (at least partly) church buildings – it was only too keen to encourage any way of reforming the largely convict population. It was an uphill battle, for many such people had never entered a church in their lives. They despised its teachings and had no intention of changing their lives for any puritanical minister. Churches in England sent missionaries to the colony, as to a pagan land.

First to arrive was a Wesleyan Methodist minister, Benjamin Carvosso, who visited Hobart in 1820, preaching open-air sermons, but then moved to Sydney.[2] The following year William Horton arrived as resident minister. Aged only 21, he was determined and energetic, holding services and public prayer meetings, starting a Sunday School open to all for free lessons in reading and writing (and religion). Horton

A fond painting of Robert Knopwood on horseback by his friend Thomas Gregson. He has his white pony, his dog Pincher – and a bottle of liquor in his back pocket (TA NS0103/1/1820)

enticed godly emigrants like Mather by writing to London, and requested subscriptions to build not just a chapel in Hobart but small chapels around the colony. From the long list of donations he was well supported, but in 1823 he too moved to Sydney.[3]

In 1825 Carvosso returned. Over the next five years he worked untiringly with the general public, and also convicts and seamen. He built chapels in Hobart and Launceston and, with assistance from devoted followers like Mather, established societies: the Wesleyan Missionary Society, the Tract Society, a library. He also set up the Seamen's Friend and Bethel Union, which preached on ships and distributed tracts and bibles – six thousand tracts on 68 ships in its first year alone.[4] Active, dynamic, going into the community to spread the message, working with the more unpromising sections of the community – this was Christianity undreamed-of by Knopwood. Many people were attracted, and Wesleyan congregations grew.

Arthur, an evangelical Anglican himself, strongly supported this church, which was prepared to work with convicts. Not everyone could face trying to convert convicts, to preach the Gospel to those who seemed all too likely to scorn it, and one can only admire these brave men. They had some success. A former convict told Quaker visitor James Backhouse that he blessed God day and night for having caused him to be sent to the colony, where Carvosso had reformed him.[5]

Meanwhile, those Scottish settlers on the *Skelton*, and many others who followed, wanted their own Presbyterian church. They asked the Scottish kirk for a minister, and Archibald Macarthur arrived in 1822. He too built up a congregation, and St Andrew's church was opened in Hobart 1824. Many Scots settled around Bothwell and Campbell Town, which soon had their own churches and ministers – extraordinary growth in only a decade. This church too had its Sunday School, Missionary Society and Tract Society, and Macarthur preached to female convicts.[6]

Henry and Sarah Hopkins, devout Congregationalists, arrived in 1822 on the same ship as Robert Mather. At first they worshipped with the Methodists, with Henry teaching in the Sunday School and distributing tracts to sailors. Later, admiring Macarthur's preaching, they moved to the Presbyterians, but they missed their own church.

Henry was an astute businessman, and by 1828 had made enough money to feel able – with Sarah – to ask the parent Congregational church in London for a minister, whom they would support. (The Congregational or Independent church remained independent of government aid.) The Anglican church was tolerably well attended, they wrote, and there were Wesleyan, Presbyterian and Catholic chapels; but 'the people, in general, have so little concern for their souls that they would not walk any distance to hear a preached gospel ... and for the most part live in total neglect of the Sabbath'.[7] Clearly, though all churches had some enthusiastic adherents, converting the heathen – especially those 'free by servitude', as the Hopkins put it – was a struggle.

This plea attracted an ardent young Calvinist minister, Frederick Miller. He arrived in 1830, full of zeal to 'proclaim salvation by Christ to the people in this land of darkness and wilful ignorance', where the minister must 'grapple at the very gates of hell, if he would rescue a soul'.[8] Within a few weeks Miller was attracting two hundred people to his services, and a Congregational chapel was opened in 1831. However, though the Congregationalists welcomed everyone, the chapel was in a poor area. Miller preached both there and in a room in central Hobart for his more respectable adherents – they did not wish to mix with the non-respectable poor, who were almost all of convict origin.[9] Meanwhile, Baptists, Quakers and Jews all had individual members in the colony but did not have yet any organised body.

The first Catholic priest, Philip Conolly, arrived in 1821 and established this church, which largely comprised convicts and ex-convicts. A witty man, 'full of dry humour', Conolly was popular. He was a great friend of Knopwood, and often after a convivial evening they would stroll through the town arm in arm. Conolly worked for fourteen years among 'a wicked and perverse generation', travelling widely around the colony, and was well-known for his kindness, lack of reverence and love of creature comforts. Arthur thought highly of him and tried to gain him an increased salary, without success.[10]

Some decades later, chatty historian James Beattie told an entertaining story which occurred later than the period this book covers, but illustrates Conolly's style. Archbishop Polding of Sydney paid an unexpected visit to Hobart. As he approached the presbytery, he was surprised to hear sounds of revelry, with Conolly leading the singing of 'For he's a jolly good fellow'. Polding knocked on the door but no one inside could hear, and the tune changed to 'We won't go home till morning'. At a pause in the singing, someone did hear the knocking and opened the door, 'unsteadily holding a candle to face the dignified and stately prelate'. This story should be taken with a grain of salt, advised Beattie, but it was typical of Hobart's social life.[11]

From 1823 the Anglican church in the colony was transformed. Knopwood, now sixty, retired. His replacement was William Bedford, another zealous evangelical who preached to convicts as well as the usual congregation. Arthur praised him for his sincerity and devotion. Bedford was determined to attack 'immorality' – couples living together unmarried. In Knopwood's day many couples did this and no one seemed too concerned. But Bedford was different, searching out sinners and trying to reform them.

Phillis Johns, ticket of leave, was charged with immorality for cohabiting with John Woodrow. Many respectable people employed her as a nurse and she and John had tried to marry, but Bedford heard she had a husband in England and refused permission. Then John tried to shoot Phillis, and was bound over to keep the peace. She left him but Bedford pursued the case, and in court the magistrate said he had no choice but to remove her ticket of leave for living in sin. Dr Scott said firmly that interfering in these cases did more harm than good and a newspaper correspondent agreed: 'is it not much more injurious to disturb them than to leave them together, whilst they behave well?'[12]

Young and enthusiastic Bedford sent a list of offending parties to the governor of the day, continued Beattie. Sorell, who should have been on the list himself, took no notice, but Arthur agreed with Bedford, and a government order instructed all government employees to marry the women they lived with. The offending officials were terror-struck (wrote Beattie) but their pleas to escape the order were unavailing. They turned on Bedford, but he was made of stern stuff and stood his ground. 'The worst evil was broken, and social regeneration started' (Beattie was writing in the Victorian era).[13]

Some officials did marry their mistresses, but various female convicts were sent back to the Female Factory, vowing vengeance. Bedford visited the Factory to preach to the women, but was attacked by

Church with fence by Thomas Lempriere, about 1828. It is not clear which church this is, but it is symbolic: a small church, redolent of Britain and British values, sitting in the wilderness
(TA ALMFA AUTAS001136186657)

a mob and suffered 'outrageous personal insult'. Sure enough, in October 1825 Ann Livingstone and Johanna Leahy were punished for abusing and being insolent to Mr Bedford in the Factory.[14] Whatever 'outrageous personal insult' did they commit? Hit him, spit at him, remove his trousers?

Bedford was also active in promoting new Anglican congregations, assisted by more priests: Bigge had urged the need for more clergy, and by 1831 there were five Anglican churches and eight clergymen, their salaries paid by the government. Morning Prayer was the most usual Sunday service, and by 1831 hundreds of Anglicans heard the opening biblical quotation: 'When the wicked man turneth away from his wickedness that he hath committed, and doeth that which is lawful and right, he shall save his soul alive'. This was the message churches were bringing to many people – in 1829, a visitor described 'overflowing congregations'.[15]

All churches ran into problems. Most ministers volunteering to come to a distant colony were young men inspired by a mission. Some were not capable of filling such a challenging role, while their parishioners were extremely human. There were bound to be disagreements. As we've seen, some thought Bedford too zealous. There was also division among the Congregationalists, with Henry and Sarah Hopkins leading a group who thought Miller too harsh on sinners. The Presbyterians also saw strife, with Macarthur in trouble (though after the closing date for this book).

In 1824 a second Catholic priest arrived, Samuel Coote, claiming to have authority to supersede Conolly – who fought back. He complained that Coote's 'low habits' were beneath the dignity of a priest, that he was illiterate, blundering through Mass, singing in taverns with the lowest class of convicts. Conolly exiled him to the country at Richmond – where 169 free Catholic settlers asked for Coote to stay, praising his 'conciliatory and pious manner' and 'unremitting endeavours' in teaching their children. However, Arthur supported Conolly, the established priest, and Coote returned to England in 1825.[16]

What was the result of this religious activity? The churches presented the path to salvation and, to obtain this, urged another way of life, respectable and law-abiding. Churches formed communities and, as well as religious benefits, provided companionship and support, particularly helpful to those without family in the new land. Going to church on Sunday meant not just worshipping God but meeting friends and acquaintances and (hopefully) being greeted warmly, feeling a valued part of a community. People wishing to better the lives of themselves and their children were offered not just salvation but also acceptance by the respectable class with its increased comfort and stability.

Many new settlers went to church as a matter of course and some inhabitants were converted or, now there was the opportunity, reverted to former church-going habits. It is impossible to estimate numbers, but Miller's congregation of two hundred is impressive. Some people, distant from a church building, read the service on Sunday, to themselves or to their families and servants. Surveyor John Wedge, for example, camping out in the field, regularly 'Read prayers to the men in the Tent'.[17]

Perhaps respectability and the churches grew together, each encouraging the other. But the result was that respectability – decency, honesty, upright living – became more valued, with society divided not only into the elite and others, but the respectable and the not respectable. The 'not respectable' included the thieves, drinkers, fighters of the pubs and brothels. Attending church showed you were respectable, and the churches, with their energetic (for the most part) ministers, were successful in encouraging not just the worship of God but respectable living. Overall, they had a noticeable effect in improving the morality and stability of the community generally.

18. GOVERNOR ARTHUR

It's clear already that the final force in bringing change to Van Diemen's Land was Lieutenant-Governor George Arthur, in charge from 1824 until 1836. When Commissioner Bigge reported to London he was discreet, not saying directly that he thought Van Diemen's Land a pit of corruption, immorality and crime, but giving enough hints to indicate it.[1] And who knows what he might have told those in authority over a few convivial dinners.

To establish law and order, Van Diemen's Land needed an experienced and capable governor rather than, as so often, the needy hanger-on of a patron. The authorities appointed George Arthur, who had competently governed the smaller colony of British Honduras (now Belize).

Born in 1784, George Arthur had risen through the army to become a major – and his wife Eliza was the daughter of a general, so they were an army family, used to obeying orders and, in Arthur's case, giving them and having them obeyed. When the Napoleonic War ended, so did most active soldiering, and Arthur moved to the civil service. In Belize he showed his qualities: administrative vigour, a passion for reform, high ideals (he tried to improve conditions for enslaved people) and genuine interest in the colony's welfare – but also a dislike of criticism. He arrived in Hobart in 1824 with his wife and family (eventually twelve children, almost the only way in which he was similar to Sorell). Such was Arthur's effect on the colony that 1824 became known as 'Governor Arthur's year'.[2]

Unlike Davey and Sorell, Arthur had no powerful patron, and could not, like them, thumb his nose at London. He had to please his bosses by obeying their commands – often not practical for the colony, not what colonists wanted, or both. He walked a perpetual tightrope between London's orders and colonial life. But London came first: Arthur's job was to obey London and his career depended on it. The Colonial Office in London was in charge of promotion, not Hobart.

Arthur inherited a mess. Sorell had improved administration, but Arthur found much to horrify him: rampant crime, scheming and cheating as regards land grants, an inadequate police force, churches

Governor George Arthur (TA SD_ILS:167409)

still in their infancy, couples living together unmarried, a disorganised convict system and a public service riddled with incompetence and corruption. The report of the Land Commissioners showed the size of the job Arthur had to tackle.

Sorell wrote him a report which was, of course, as positive as possible; but reading between the lines, the situation was pretty grim. He had to some extent put down bushranging and smuggling, and tried to encourage churches and schools, but could not claim much actual success. The colony was suffering a depression, with revenue down and unlikely to improve. Sorell admitted that the convict police force was defective and that he had no way of restraining convicts, though his punishment settlement at Macquarie Harbour was dreaded. He would have done more, he wrote, but for his feeble powers and scanty means.

With more convicts arriving, crime was bound to increase.[3] Nothing was actually going well.

It sounds extremely daunting, but Arthur was made of stern stuff and got to work. He had some excellent advantages:

- Personally, he was intelligent, competent, hard-working, honest, upright, an excellent administrator.
- The first Tasmanian governor about whom no social scandal circulated, he had a supportive wife and close family.
- He was supported by churches and a growing number of settlers and colonists who appreciated the benefits he brought to the colony, especially law and order, and respectable living.
- In 1825 Tasmania became independent of New South Wales, so Arthur had a freer hand.
- Tasmania also gained its own court system.
- Many more convicts arrived, which brought much more British funding to pay for them, and a larger labour force
- There were more free settlers, and the economy gradually improved

Arthur was assisted by many respectable immigrants. As there was no large wharf they were rowed ashore from their ships to Hunter's wharf. Hobart Town by George Frankland, about 1827 (TA ALMFA AUTAS001139593552)

But Arthur also had disadvantages:

- As he himself said, it was difficult to rule a colony which was both penal and free.
- He had to balance obeying London's micromanagement with ruling to benefit the colony.
- Unlike Davey and Sorell, Arthur was not affable. Stiff and formal, he was not generally popular.
- He inherited a public service with far too much corruption and had to cope with a succession of incompetent and drunken officials sent from England.
- As the Land Commissioners' report showed, there was huge corruption over land grants and far too many land grants were not cultivated.
- Some settlers who had prospered under Sorell's lax regime hated Arthur's strict rule and set up newspapers that attacked him endlessly.

In 1820, William Williamson had described the colony as the 'land of rogues and scoundrels'. Astonishingly, only nine years later new arrival Augustus Prinsep wrote Home:

> I daresay you have never dreamt of Van Diemen's Land as of any thing else than a kind of wilderness; an appropriate insular prison for the vagabonds who are sent to it yearly from England. You have never supposed that it has a beautiful harbour, a fine metropolis, with towns, streets, shops, and pretty shopkeepers ... Englishmen have here successfully shown what industry can do in seven-and-twenty years.[4]

A society founded on the 'dregs from England'! How had this transformation happened?

For the British government and therefore for Arthur, Tasmania was primarily a convict colony. Its purpose, as an under-secretary of state reminded Arthur after he asked for more mechanics among convicts, was not providing labour for settlers but 'the saving of expence to the [British] Public' by absorbing British criminals.[5] Arthur's main task was to set up a proper system under which convicts were controlled and punished, though he himself thought it equally important that they were reformed.

Maria Island penal station: artists usually made even these institutions look peaceful. Perhaps the man fishing is a convict (TA ALMFA AUTAS001127111482w800)

Under his system, some male convicts were put to work for the government, and at night slept in barracks so they were under control, instead of having to find their own lodgings and spending the evenings drinking, carousing and robbing. However, most convicts, male or female, were assigned to settlers, who were part of Arthur's machinery. He felt convicts were more likely to be reformed if they worked in the countryside, under a civilian master instead of a gaoler, away from the temptations of town and gangs of other convicts. The settlers' task, in return for convict labour, was to reform their assigned convicts by setting them a good example, treating them fairly, encouraging good behaviour and not providing rum. Arthur appointed police magistrates throughout the settled districts to keep an eye on everyone. Employers who failed had their convicts removed. This happened rarely, but the victims bitterly resented it.

Convicts who behaved well could apply for a ticket of leave part way through their sentences, and then an early pardon. Those who committed offences – slight ones sometimes, neglecting work or missing church, but including serious robbery and murder – were punished with increasing severity, by time in prison, flogging, working in a road gang, working in chains then, if these had no effect, a period at the penal stations: Maria Island (for lesser offenders) and harsh, grim Port Arthur (which had replaced Macquarie Harbour, for the worst). Meanwhile, female prisoners were assigned as domestic servants under the same system: rewards for good behaviour, punishment (hard labour, solitary confinement) for those who committed offences. Female factories housed those pregnant, waiting assignment or being punished.

The system was not perfect but it ran reasonably well, much better than the almost complete lack of control of earlier years. It benefited most the perhaps two-thirds of convicts who were well-behaved or reasonably so, providing a pathway out of their cycle of poverty and crime. Arthur thought real reformation was rare but, with convicts under more restraint, at least they were behaving better and there was less drunkenness.[6] In 1833 he told London that most convicts, instead of being the plagues of their fellow creatures, and useless and miserable themselves, were now useful to society, contributing to the wealth of the Empire – an exaggeration to his bosses but doubtless partly true.[7] (I hoped he was going to say convicts were happier, but perhaps that was implied.)

Also vital was improving the police: 'everything in this colony depends on an efficient police force'. There were still only convicts and ex-convicts available, but Arthur organised them better. To control bushranging, he set up the field police, chosen from the best-conducted convicts, promising mitigation of their sentences for good work. Allied to the system of police magistrates, the interior was brought under far more control than previously. So were towns, with less crime and less disorder on the streets. 'It is strange to be in a country of thieves at all, but still stranger to be there without any fear of having your pocket picked!' wrote Prinsep. 'Such is the admirable arrangement of the present governor.'[8]

The Survey Department was corrupt. When Arthur arrived he was flooded with complaints about it: the surveyor only acted if he was bribed, land jobbing (doing deals) was common, 'fraud and robbery so extensively prevail', sheep-stealing was rife and many settlers were struggling.[9] Samuel Hood, a great friend of Sorell and Lord, asked Arthur if it were true that London had instructed him to resume land grants

Schedule of Property belonging to
Mr John Bisdee — Passenger per
Ship Westmoreland

	£	s	d
Specie	200	0	0
Ironmongery & Nails	20	0	0
Saddlery	35	0	0
China & Earthenware	42	0	0
Glass	10	0	0
Piano Forte	53	10	0
Cloth	33	0	0
Carpenter's & Joiner's Tools	25	0	0
Stationary	30	0	0
Implements of Husbandry	80	0	0
Plate	85	0	0
Medicines	10	0	0
Fowling Pieces	40	0	0
Household Furniture	36	0	0
	£694	10	0
50 p. cent	347	5	—
	1041	15	0

700 acres —

Personals in addition
300 £

John Bisdee's schedule of his goods. To gain a larger land second grant, he claims goods he is never going to sell or use to develop the land at what seem like exaggerated values, such as silver plate, a piano and household furniture – then, without explaining why, inflates the total by 50 per cent. Arthur approved a small extra grant. (TA CSO1/1/91 file 1019) when grantees did not fulfil the conditions. Yes, replied Arthur. Do you intend to act on those instructions? Certainly, replied Arthur, doubtless startled at the idea that a governor would not obey London. Hood told Arthur, rudely, that he would ruin the colony. Arthur realised that Sorell, protected by the prince regent, had felt little need to obey London. He wondered (he told Bathurst) how Sorell had conducted matters apparently so smoothly, while he himself found so many problems. No man can do his duty to the crown in this colony and be popular, he answered: that is, Sorell had not done his duty to the crown.[10]

Arthur was determined to do his. Though the conditions for land grants were clearly laid out no one had attempted to enforce them, as indicated in evidence given to Bigge. Arthur did, resuming grants sold too early. In 1827 Alexander Paterson protested to London against having land resumed. Since the colony was established, he told London, the five-year condition had been 'altogether disregarded' by everyone. When he bought land before the grantee's five years were up, 'I did no more than had been done in innumerable instances by others'.[11] He did not regain the land.

Although Arthur had no way of checking whether people's claimed assets existed, lists of assets were scrutinised, and claims such as 'Investments expected from England £1000' did not impress.[12] Arthur thought claimants should have their money in hand. Granting of land was more strictly controlled, and people could not gain a second grant unless they had resided on and improved their first. Those who sold their first were not allowed a second.

People tried all sorts of stratagems to get more land. John Hammond Esq. complained to London that the government had resumed his grant unfairly. Arthur said Hammond had not complied with the conditions and was guilty of 'much cunning and prevarication'. Arriving in 1824, he gained a grant of 2000 acres, sold it far too early and returned to England. The government resumed the land. Hammond returned with a cargo of goods and created a storm at seeing his land resumed, while the purchaser sued him, usefully proving Hammond had sold it. Another complainant was Alfred Luttrell, who said Arthur had refused unfairly to give him a land grant, claiming he had never received one. He had, replied Arthur: 300 acres which he sold illegally.[13]

Arthur found great difficulty satisfying the 'craving desire for land' and 'unwarrantable expectations of Settlers'. People tried to get land for sons who turned out to be aged five, claimed to have made improvements they had in fact not, omitted to state they had been convicts, made false claims to have assets ... the attempted scams were endless. One impressive-sounding application for a second grant was annotated, 'This Man has sold the Farm he has the audacity to state is in his possession, & is one of the worst of the Emancipists'.[14] Another, also impressive, actually came from 'a very drunken old man ... his means small and wasting by excess'. Two convicts called Joseph Roberts arrived in the same ship. One was steady and respectable. After he was killed by a falling tree, the other Joseph Roberts, not so respectable, applied for land in his name. Arthur was horrified.[15]

Hammond and Luttrell were examples of upper-class settlers who did not believe rules applied to them. So was Lieutenant Thomas de Burgh, from an elite Anglo-Irish family. He was appalled at the colony's lack of esteem for the socially superior. Very well, he had not presented a letter of introduction from the secretary of state, as he was meant to do, 'but my name has been a passport to me in every part of the habitable globe', except the purgatory of Van Diemen's Land, where convicts and vagabonds received equal treatment with gentlemen. He finally received a 2000-acre grant, but only after a long wait, and returned to Britain in disgust.[16] Unlike previous governors, Arthur made everyone play by the rules.

In 1831 the British government suddenly ended free land grants. Arthur said he would never have made such a sudden change – he had to cope with new settlers expecting grants now disallowed – but there were so many abuses under the old system 'that I must say I do most heartily rejoice that it has been put a stop to'.[17]

Arthur also tried to raise moral standards. He did not give positions to those he considered badly behaved, refusing a job to settler Walter Bethune, for example, because of 'circumstances connected with his manner of life' (what these were, I can't discover). In 1828 Thomas Hammant, former commander of a ship, applied for the position of division constable and poundkeeper at Norfolk Plains. The magistrate, Malcolm Smith, could not recommend the application as he was 'an habitual tippler and frequently intoxicated for several days'. Hammant was not appointed.[18] And, as seen in chapter 17, Arthur supported the Rev. Bedford in his efforts to stamp out couples living together unmarried.

The churches and many newcomers such as the Hudspeths and the Hopkins supported Arthur's ideas, and the number of loose-living hedonists so strongly encouraged by the likes of Davey gradually dwindled. By 1830 Arthur could report to England that the 'better classes' showed 'a very gratifying improvement in morals', excellent not just in itself, but because one could hardly expect convicts to reform if the families they were assigned to were 'immoral and vicious'.[19]

Is a community happier, more cohesive, if its members are made to obey the law? I can find no research on this, but surely many of its members are. The unhappy ones would be those trying to gain unfair advantage by breaking the law, and many respectable people are only too happy to see these people reined in. Surely, as well, the mass of the people would have been pleased to see entitled gentlemen like de Burgh having to toe the line like everyone else.

The change in attitudes, at least among the upper class, is shown starkly in a diary entry by George Boyes in 1826. Ten years earlier, men and women living together unmarried was taken for granted. Boyes' wife was in England while he was earning their living in Tasmania. Clearly the Hobart gossips were at work for, wrote Boyes:

> In this moral country if a man holds any communication with a woman except indirectly through his wife – his character is gone irretrievably. I had a great deal of trouble selecting a *washerwoman* whose attributes might shield me from scandal. By persevering I was at last successful ... she is certainly as plain and ancient as the [illegible] and when in the same room with me I always out of delicacy, look at anything but her.[20]

Arthur's achievements were all the more amazing considering the impediments in his way. To begin with, just after he arrived a dozen convicts headed by Matthew Brady stole a boat at Macquarie Harbour, sailed round to the east and terrorised the population, plundering goods and murdering people – including Thomas Keston or Kenton, whose diary has been so helpful in describing the early years. Arthur found much of 1825 taken up with subduing these bushrangers, assisted by energetic Colonel Balfour, commandant in Launceston. Finally, after huge exertions, all the bushrangers were captured and executed, to the community's enormous relief. Arthur could turn his interests to running the rest of the colony.

One problem was a lack of skilled administrative staff, especially an engineer. There was none in the island, and Arthur was expected to build roads, bridges and public buildings. Lack of knowledge meant that, for example, after he finished the half-built Richmond bridge, repairs were necessary at once as the piers had sunk. London sent architect John Lee Archer as civil engineer and architect; but he knew nothing about engineering. Arthur put Roderic O'Connor in charge of roads and bridges; he too knew nothing about engineering but was at least practical and competent. A qualified engineer did not arrive until 1836.[21]

At least Archer was a competent architect. There were other excellent public servants, like George Hull the commissary and Arthur's two nephews-by-marriage, all very capable. (This was Arthur being nepotistic, but at least his relations were competent.) O'Connor did a good job and some London appointments were excellent, such as George Frankland (see below). But London sent out far too many inadequate men. The public service grew enormously from 1825 when Tasmania became independent, with its senior members mostly appointed from London. There, influential people leant on officials to give jobs to problem relatives, with no thought of whether they would be any good. Some knew nothing of office procedure – John Burnett, as colonial secretary the top public servant, had led a life of leisure and was wholly unprepared for daily toil in an office, while Rolla O'Ferrall, naval officer, thought this meant dashing around in a boat chasing smugglers, not sitting in an office supervising the collection of customs dues. Both proved inadequate, O'Ferrall dependent on his clerks, Burnett incompetent, anxious, working into the night to try and keep up. Thomas McCleland, attorney general, went insane on the voyage out as he desperately read law books, and soon returned to England.[22] A new judge was 'a very convivial Character', meaning an alcoholic, but as he was also insolvent Arthur could dismiss him.[23]

The most extreme case of incompetence was Roger Woods, sent as superintendent of convicts to replace a competent local appointment.

Arthur was told he drank heavily on the voyage out and offered him another job, but Woods insisted and, as London's appointee, had to be inducted. Arthur wrote urgently to London: could he suspend Woods? As well as his 'habitual intemperance', he mismanaged the Convict Department appallingly, creating confusion and irregularity, convicting people wrongly, abusing magistrates publicly ... Arthur suspended Woods, who fortunately returned Home to state his case (but got nowhere). He left his family behind; his wife, who had complained of his outrageous conduct to her, eloped to Sydney with an overseer, and the four children were put in the Orphan School, which Arthur had recently opened to care mainly for convicts' children.[24] A shocking story, the elite behaving as badly as any thieving convict. And Woods complained there was a prejudice in the colony against London appointments!

Just as badly behaved were five senior public servants dismissed for fraud. The most dramatic case was Dr Edward Bromley, colonial treasurer. Sorell praised him highly, but Arthur found, to his horror, that 'there is no check whatever upon the accounts of this officer, and his receipts were never examined or audited'. When Arthur queried Bromley's delay in presenting quarterly accounts, Bromley told him he had been busy investigating a robbery from Treasury of £275. Arthur set up a board of enquiry which found over £8000 missing. Bromley and his convict clerk Bartholomew Broughton were the obvious culprits, though it was difficult to work out what had happened as no accounts had been kept. Bromley pleaded ignorance: he was unconscious of any deficiency as he had never counted the money. He was dismissed and his property sold to make up the deficiency. Broughton lived in suspicious luxury, but little could be done to him as Sorell had given him a pardon just before Arthur arrived.[25]

Joseph Gellibrand, former attorney-general, told Arthur that Sorell was involved. He was sure there was a much larger deficit even than £8000, and that Sorell knew about it. George Hull confirmed this strong suspicion. There was no proof – there wouldn't be – though there was a story of wool the government sold to Sydney, whose commissary was asked to write out the cheque in favour of Edward Lord. No one actually accused Sorell of embezzling government money, but they certainly believed Bromley, Broughton, Evans and Lord did.[26]

As soon as Arthur arrived, he heard complaints about the Survey

Office, particularly its head, George Evans, who demanded bribes (as noted by O'Connor, Hudspeth and many others). O'Connor's story showed clearly what was wrong, Evans stating to him that Sorell let him do what he liked and his word about surveys was law. Now Evans, in poor health, asked to resign. To avoid open scandal and because, as Arthur said, he had done valuable work in New South Wales, this was permitted.[27] George Frankland was the new, competent head of the Survey Office. A man after Arthur's own heart, he checked everything carefully. For example, he found people had been granted additional land after claiming improvements they had not made. Now these were verified.[28] And no longer did settlers wait months, even years, in frustration because the Survey Office lost their documents.[29]

Gellibrand himself was a problem: a good lawyer, but far too friendly with Arthur's enemies. He behaved unprofessionally, representing both sides in a court case, for example. Arthur found him 'most trying', not a gentleman, acting in bad faith, his behaviour 'inconsistent with the duties and dignity of high office'. Arthur suspended him, and Gellibrand complained to London endlessly.[30] London supported Arthur – but there was always the worry, wrote Arthur, that Lord Bathurst would believe what his, Arthur's, enemies wrote in their newspapers and complaining letters. He was really anxious at first – 'no officer can administer the affairs of this colony [without] the entire confidence of his Majesty's Government'[31] – but as his success in turning the colony round became obvious, the worry ebbed. Soothingly, in 1830 the under-secretary of state wrote that he granted Arthur permission (to dismiss Woods) 'which I am quite sure you will exercise, as you always do, in the best manner'. After reading such praise, one hopes Arthur forgave him for complaining that the ink he had used was too pale.[32]

Arthur's achievements made him enemies. Gellibrand, Gregson, Kemp, people who had their convicts taken away, those who failed to gain land by fibbing, and others who felt badly treated by Arthur disliked him. The leaders attacking him viciously, complaining endlessly to London and starting opposition newspapers in Hobart (Gellibrand edited the *Tasmanian* which detested Arthur[33]). It was quite easy to hire a journalist, pay a printer and publish a four-page weekly newspaper, helped by paid advertisements. Arthur was naturally upset:

reading these articles today, some attacks seem justified but others not. His attackers supported, for example, outright liars and cheats such as Woods, Hammond and Bromley.

'It is not very usual I find for the Settlers to represent things exactly as they are', wrote Arthur to London; 'you can form no idea of the manner in which I have been beset ... the Governor of a Colony is in matters of personal attack almost defenceless'.[34] He accused Kemp and others of being troublemakers: 'the question was agitated mainly for the purpose of embarrassing the Government ... Mr. Bethune has stated just as much as would suit his case, and suppressed all such facts as were calculated to make an impression against it'.[35] 'It is perfectly absurd to place the least credence in any of these reports', wrote Arthur's nephew Charles about one rumour. 'I really believe they are all inventions of the damned old fool Kemp.'[36] However, it was rare for London to believe these enemies as Arthur's defence was always watertight.

Arthur's opponents can seem manic. When asked why he criticised the government sometimes undeservedly in his newspaper, hothead (and not very bright) Thomas Gregson replied, 'Everything they do deserves lashing'. He fought a duel with one friend of Arthur, and horsewhipped Arthur's nephew Henry 'like a convict at his hated master's bullock'.[37] But personal dislike, and hating having to obey the law, were hardly motives that could be advertised. The protesters claimed they wanted – or really did want – the rights of Englishmen, chiefly trial by jury and an elected legislature, which the government thought they forfeited, coming knowingly to a convict colony and accepting the benefits of free land and cheap labour.

In 1831 Gellibrand chaired a public meeting gathered to congratulate King William IV on his accession (which sounded good) and discuss local grievances: taxation, tenure or lands, the administration of justice, the Survey Department and so on. Arthur was not criticised personally. At the end of the long, vociferous meeting (which actually forgot to congratulate the king), Kemp – a veteran republican who called his house Mount Vernon after George Washington's home – demanded trial by jury and representative government. Someone flew the tricolour, the flag of revolution, though afterwards the organisers denied that the meeting was revolutionary.[38] This meeting was remembered as the 'glorious 23rd of May', the first step towards Tasmanian independence, though a faltering one.

How unpopular was Arthur? Were Kemp, Gregson et al a few empty vessels making the most noise? Were they merely 'monopolists, usurers, grog-sellers' unprepared to consider the public good, as an Arthur supporter claimed? Or did they have widespread support? Arthur suffered from following two popular governors, Davey and Sorell, both affable and approachable, which he was not. John Burnett thought there was chilling formality at Government House; the Arthurs had 'no want of good intention to do what was civil and agreeable and make themselves popular' but 'they had not the tact and could not understand it'. Arthur was a different man when it was just the two of them, added Burnett. They sat one night after a council meeting till midnight and finished two bottles of port.[39]

However, relatively few people went to Government House or had personal dealings with Arthur, let alone sharing bottles of port. What most people want from a government is stability and the rule of law, so they can lead their lives in security, and this Arthur brought them. The Rev. James Garrett reported that 'our good and beloved Governor [was] hissed and insulted when passing the race-course the other week': so gambling race-goers disliked him, but to Garrett and his correspondent he was good and beloved. Henry and Sarah Hopkins approved of him so much they named a son after him.[40] Arthur's supporters thought most people approved of his rule, one claiming that by 1827, when he had 'finally placed the colony on a respectable footing [and] we sleep in peace and safety in our beds', that he had obtained the 'respect and popularity which he deserves'; but his detractors claimed most people hated him.[41] In the absence of opinion polls it is difficult to say one way or the other.

As far as Arthur's career went, his popularity or lack of it in Van Diemen's Land did not matter. His results satisfied London. 'Of all the Governors which my department has employed in my time, you have enjoyed the most uninterrupted reputation for all the qualities which a Governor ought to possess and the strongest hold upon the favourable opinion of your official superiors', James Stephen, a senior official in the Colonial Office, wrote to him in 1835.[42] Compared with this, Kemp's invective was nothing.

Arthur was helped enormously in Tasmania by an improving economy. In 1824 colonists had few ways to make money; in 1831 Arthur described the colony as 'exceedingly prosperous'. A visitor commented that it contained valuable property – he bought land for ten times its price six years earlier – and had many sources of wealth, security, health. Everything in fact but ready money, which gave a very profitable return, with banks paying dividends of 16 per cent.[43]

In 1831 the population was about 24,000, over four times what it had been in 1820. Convicts were kept under 'perfect control'; the growth in the wool trade excited general admiration and meant sheepowners could make a good living at last; whaling was expanding, making money for shipowners and employing locals, and helping Hobart's economy via its visiting ships. Arthur reported that less drunkenness was visible and the crime rate had fallen, though crimes were still 'not infrequent', inseparable from a convict colony. There was 'much general harmony and good feeling' in the community and 'a good moral, and, I hope, religious, feeling growing up'.[44] As early as 1827 Arthur had commented that he saw no reason to change his general policy, which 'has led to such results as the most sanguine friends of the Government could scarcely have anticipated'.[45] The great drawback was the Aboriginal war, admitted Arthur but, he wrote chillingly in 1833, the pacification of the island was now complete, with Aboriginal people and bushrangers no longer a threat.

Such was Arthur's report to his bosses, naturally drawing a rosy picture. Many problems continued, particularly drunkenness. Petty theft also continued a problem until the end of the convict period, though it was more under control.

However, the now all-white colony had passed its difficult early years and could forge ahead, a successful British colony. Its worst transgressions were in the past and, implied, to be forgotten.

FLIGHT OF FANCY: AN EVENING AT GOVERNMENT HOUSE

The dining room at Government House, early one evening. Eliza Arthur is sitting sewing by the fire, about to exert her wifely charm in soothing George, as she does every night. She's good at it by now.
　George stomps exhaustedly into the room.

Eliza: Here you are, dear! Come and sit by the fire, and have a sip of sherry. Had a hard day? (*It's a rhetorical question. George has always had a hard day.*)

George: That stupid old fool Kemp! He's actually defending Woods, the superintendent of convicts! In his editorial, says the man's able and indefatigable! Indefatigable in drinking perhaps – of all the incompetent half-wits the Colonial Office has foisted on me, he's the worst!

Eliza: I've met his wife. She seems pleasant.

George: Poor woman! The man's an idiot! Cursed and swore at the magistrate in court, with heaven knows whose ears flapping. What sort of an example is that for the lower orders?

Eliza: Can you get rid of him?

George: I've written to London but it's tricky. The man has impressive patrons. Surely they knew he's a drunkard. Really, I sometimes think the Colonial Office has no morals whatever! They don't care what happens here as long as they can please some influential nincompoop trying to get rid of an embarrassing relation.

Eliza: If he does something utterly unforgiveable, could you suspend him?

George (*brightening*): Yes, and I'm sure the Executive Council will back me. They're as shocked as I am. Though not surprised – the stories some of the old hands tell! Apparently that man Hogan could drink anyone under the table.:

Eliza: The one we see in church? Good heavens!

George: Same one. Oh well, at least he seems reformed. I'd rather a reformed convict, to show my plan is working, but anyone reformed is good news.

Eliza: Well, dear, the servants are about to bring in dinner, which I'm sure you need. Afterwards the girls would like to play you their new duet.

George (*happily*): Ah, how charming!

They enjoy roast mutton and apple pie, love hearing their daughters play the pianoforte – then:

George: Thank you, girls, you played very nicely. You're obviously practising hard – well done! But now I must get back to work.

19. THE BLACK WAR WITH THE ABORIGINAL PEOPLE

A truth behind many warlike situations, writes Nicholas Clements in his authoritative *The Black War*, is that almost everyone involved believes they're a good person, their actions justified. They're caught up in extraordinary circumstances not of their making, and moral judgements are unhelpful. But the extraordinary circumstances in Tasmania in the period 1824 to 1831 produced horrific violence.[1] This chapter is unashamedly taken largely from Clements' book; he knows far more about the topic than I do.

The Tasmanian Aboriginal people had lived in the island for tens of thousands of years and, like the British in Britain, believed it was theirs. From 1804 the British arrived. Some were settlers who had often invested everything in starting a new life in Tasmania. Most were convicts, generally ordinary working-class people, but all too often brutalised by squalor and violence. Others were soldiers from much the same background. Convicts and soldiers were not in Tasmania by choice and had little interest in Aboriginal welfare, at worst seeing them as savages to be hunted.[2]

As shown in chapter 7, until 1820 the Aboriginal people and the invaders co-existed with little outward violence. In 1824 the *Hobart Town Gazette* assured its readers that 'the sable natives of this Colony are the most peaceable creatures in the universe'.[3] But in the background the Aboriginal people felt intense and growing resentment. Stockkeepers and shepherds were abusing them, in particular abducting and raping scores of Aboriginal woman and girls.

As white settlement expanded into the midlands from 1820, the invaders took over Aboriginal hunting grounds and, in retaliation and as resistance, Aboriginal attacks started in earnest. By 1828 the whites realised they were fighting a war, against an unusual enemy. The Aboriginal people had no home base or command structure. No one knew how to find them, much less negotiate with them. Even if they did, the government had no power to redress their grievances. With every colonist who disembarked, with every new farm, war was less and less avoidable.[4]

Colonists had three options:

- Move the Aboriginal people to a distant home, such as an island: favoured by the press.
- Try to conciliate them so the two races could live together: government policy, even after it had become unrealistic owing to actual war.
- Exterminate them. This was popular on the frontier where white lives were in danger.[5]

Tension grew between pragmatic white settlers on the frontier and more humanitarian townsfolk. In January 1830 George Frankland, surveyor general, told the Van Diemen's Land Society that the European discovery of Van Diemen's Land

> heaped ruin and destruction upon those children of misfortune, the Aboriginal owners of the soil – a people naturally amiable and intelligent, who with better treatment on the part of those who have come in contact with them, might have been rendered valuable friends, and have continued a happy nation!

An Aboriginal corroboree, sketched by William Ashburner, who farmed near Meander from 1827 and presumably saw this scene (TA ALMFA SD_ILS:74247)

He proposed that the Society should acquire more intimate acquaintance with 'this much wronged people', to ameliorate their condition and save them 'from being extirpated from the face of that earth on which the Almighty had placed them!'[6]

But no action was taken. That month, the Aboriginal Committee, set up to discuss the problem, urged no wanton aggression against 'our wretched fellow creatures', but instead kindness and good faith. It suggested no actual moves to implement this policy.[7] 'God help us!' wrote a settler from Bothwell:

> What do they know about it? By the time the Committee is arguing, debating, bandying letters about from place to place, the white inhabitants are murdered, dwellings burned to the ground and terror and consternation spread over the country. The settlers in the country take quite a different view of the matter to what do [sic] the Gentlemen at Hobarton.[8]

As attacks multiplied, the government sent pursuit parties and roving parties to find and capture Aboriginal people, but they had little success. The native people knew the land and were expert at evading such parties, while their white would-be captors were dispirited by bickering, poor discipline and the physical difficulties of trudging through the bush for days at a time.[9]

Aboriginal attacks continued to increase and urban sympathy waned. On the frontier there was more violence by whites, seeking revenge and trying to suppress the threat. Some even saw killing them as a valuable public service. Some whites were psychopathologic in their behaviour. Was what happened to the Aboriginal people genocide? Clements decided that it depends on the definition. Aboriginal people were not killed because of politics, race or religion, and were not helpless; this was a war between white colonists and a 'capable, terrifying enemy'. Henry Reynolds thought 'ethnic cleansing' a more accurate term.[10]

Tasmania's white gender imbalance created a voracious demand for native women and was a trigger for the war,[11] but the basic cause was whites stealing land. Aboriginal people fought to expel the invaders, and when that became hopeless, kept fighting out of hatred and revenge – not the only ones in history to maintain desperately a lost cause. George

Augustus Robinson cited their love of liberty, and they often shouted at whites, 'Go away! Go away!' It was revenge for having their country stolen, for being cruelly abused and killed, for the violation and abduction of their wives and daughters. In 1829 Robinson wrote:

> It is very usual for a number of aborigines, when assembled by their fireside under the open canopy of heaven, to recount the sufferings of their ancestors, to dilate upon their present afflictions and to consult upon the best means of being released from their cruel and bloodthirsty foes.[12]

Aboriginal resistance against a technologically and numerically superior enemy was extraordinary. They speedily adapted their warrior culture to fight whites. The main weapons were spears, which they could throw with great accuracy, and shorter waddies, used as clubs or throwing sticks.[13] Their tactics were to exploit white weaknesses, to attack isolated outposts. Capable leadership, reconnaissance and planning were vital. They waited till the whites were at a disadvantage, and swiftly attacked. Hit-and-run ambushes were the safest and most efficient, and their resistance was protracted and efficient in the face of tremendous odds. But they never attacked at night or in the rain, and while they killed some stock and burned some crops and houses, they could have done this on a far larger scale. Why did they not do this? It could have been disastrous for the whites.[14]

Altogether, Aboriginal warriors killed 219 whites. Three-quarters were male convicts or ex-convicts without families, but the rest included women and children. These deaths triggered powerful emotions among whites, enraging them to boiling point. By 1828 the most harmless people in the world had become the most bloodthirsty enemies.[15]

Whites were afraid of economic ruin through loss of property, but most of all they were afraid for their lives, and those of loved ones. 'Death, by the hands of a savage, is indeed invested with the darkest terrors', wrote John West in his *History of Tasmania*. My own great-great-great-aunt, Ann Peters aged fourteen, was standing with her sister feeding a pet bird at the back of their house in Bagdad, when she was fatally speared through the chest. She was an innocent child – but an invader. The Aboriginal man who speared her was a murderer – but defending his property, his country.[16]

By this date, to the Aboriginal people the war must have seemed hopeless. They were so harried and hunted that mere existence had become a trial of hunger and cold, but they had no choice but to go on, to deal with the dead and wounded, 'the ever-present trauma of loss and fear'. During the day they were less vulnerable, but at night hundreds were caught because of the need to light campfires. One chief told Robinson he was with his people at Den Hill, near Bothwell, when whites attacked them:

> There were men cutting wood. The men were frightened and run away. As night they came back with plenty of white men (it was moonlight), and they looked and saw our fires. Then they shot at us, shot my arm, killed two men and three women. The women they beat on the head and killed them; they then burnt them in the fire.[17]

A solution was to have no fire, no warmth at night, no cooked food, but this was not practicable. People could have small fires, or camp in discreet places, or light decoy fires. Their dogs often barked at intruders, giving precious seconds to escape. By 1829, however, the interior of the island was crawling with armed white parties. The Aboriginal people retreated to the Central Plateau, a sanctuary – though a cold, bleak one.[18]

Robinson admired the Aboriginal people's 'sincere and warm affection'. To see friends and family killed and wounded was devastating, and led to feelings of overwhelming loss and powerlessness. As the war dragged on, Aboriginal numbers plummeted, while the white population was increasing through immigration. The Aboriginal inhabitants were being overwhelmed on all sides, hunted relentlessly by armed parties. 'In the end, the cost of fighting a guerrilla was against unsurmountable odds was more than they could bear.'[19]

By the spring of 1830, Aboriginal warriors had killed or wounded at least 417 colonists, and white demands for 'decisive action' were increasing. Arthur had resisted using force, both because of his sympathy for the 'natives' and because he feared rebuke from London. In April 1830 he sent London extensive evidence about the war and asked for advice, saying he was bound to protect settlers but also bound to treat Aborigines 'with the greatest forbearance ... I am most exceedingly desirous of doing

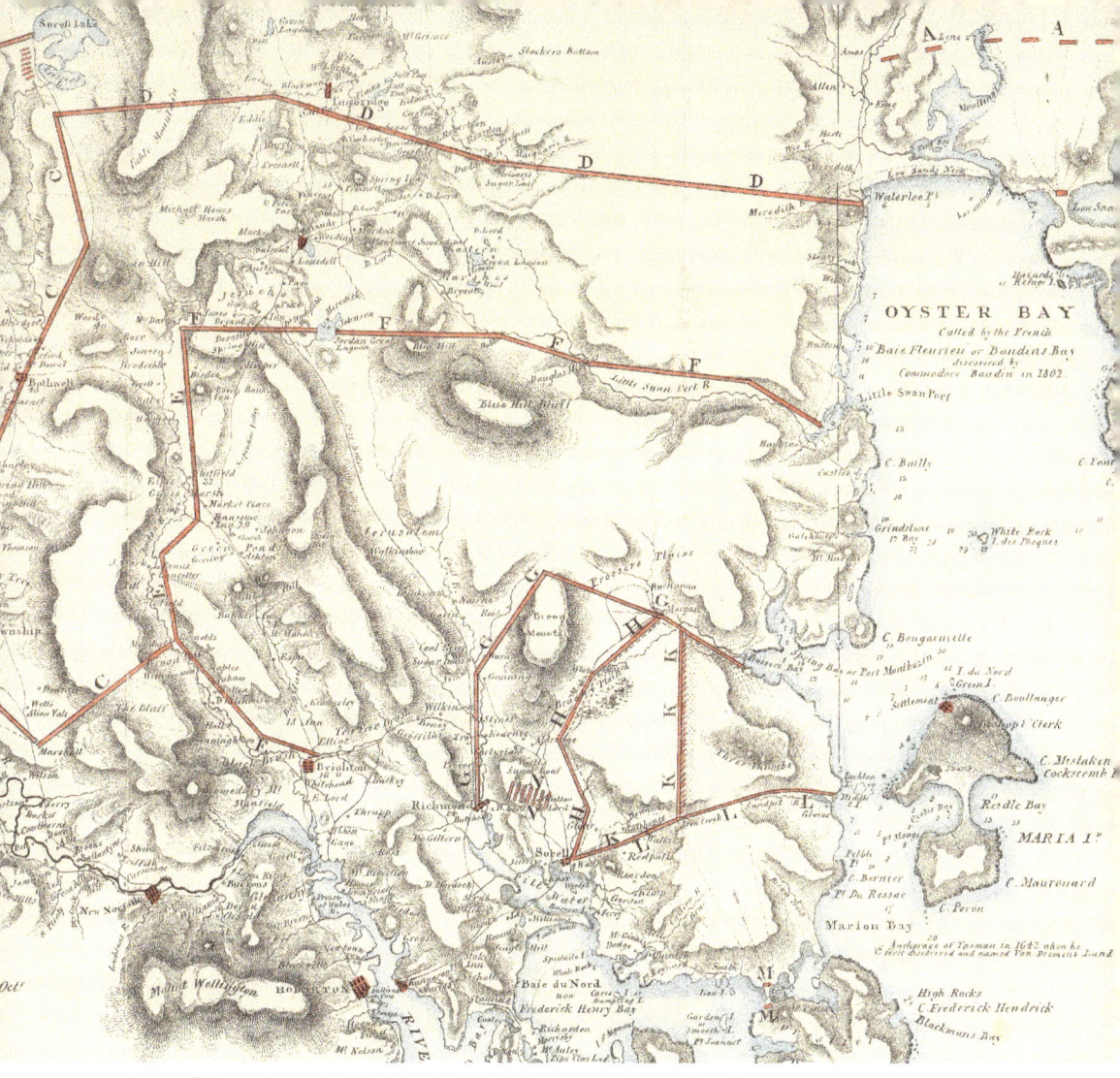

A map of the major part of the intended Black Line, converging on Dunalley
(TA W.L. Crowther Library AUTAS001139593537)

what is right, and of leaving no stain upon my Administration in this most perplexing subject'.[20]

In reply, the secretary of state sent completely impractical suggestions – for example, urging settlers not to irritate the natives. He worried that 'the whole race of these people may, at no distant period, become extinct', a result difficult to reconcile with feelings of 'humanity, justice and sound Policy', as 'the extinction of the Native-race, could not fail to leave an indelible stain upon the Character of the British Government'.[21] Arthur received this in May 1831, by which time it was irrelevant.

In September 1830 **Arthur capitulated** to public pressure, and organised an immense operation to subdue the Aboriginal people: the Black Line. This comprised some 2200 men in parties, stretched across the settled districts from St Patrick's Head on the norther-east coast, to Norfolk Plains, then down to the Central Plateau and New Norfolk. Men would gradually move south-eastwards to trap Aboriginal people at modern Dunalley, from where they could be moved somewhere safe. Despite the operation's complexity, the organisers were given only one month to plan it, not enough time.[22]

Men were called up: 550 soldiers, 440 free men and 1200 convicts. The Black Line started out as 'quite the party', greeted with enormous excitement, but from the start it was chaotic. Parties had inadequate food, clothes and shoes, and often no shelter. They got lost. The weather was appalling. Though it was October, it was often freezing, with squalls of wind, rain and hail. By November, men were sick from poor food, frozen from wind and rain, bored with endless patrolling. They were scared of Aboriginal attacks, with dozens of reported sightings. Most white participants were not interested in capturing Aboriginal people, only in killing them, but the victims were expert in eluding them. Killings seem to have happened rarely (or were not admitted).[23]

To make things even worse, no one knew what the plan was. Arthur developed his strategy according to incoming intelligence, but it was difficult to get information to the troops on the ground. In mid-November Robert Lawrence, who led one party, reached breaking-point:

> I am now quite tired of this business; there is very little chance apparently of success, and a report has just arrived up the Line, which if correct will make it useless to proceed further, viz. that the Natives have been traced through the Line in two different places. Hard work, without hope is distressing. The men are all disgusted, and grumbling; they have become so ill tempered that it is almost impossible to manage them except by compulsion. I do not wish to punish, for allowances must be made for the long succession of hard privations which they have endured.[24]

Men started to desert, and on 17 November Arthur ordered a final push towards Dunalley, over extremely difficult terrain. The Line fell apart through apathy and disorgansation, but there were no official rebukes. It resulted in the capture of just two Aboriginal people: a disastrous, expensive failure.[25]

Most Aboriginal people found it easy enough to escape through the Line, and in its rear they were safer than usual. But by now, years of warfare had drastically reduced their strength. In 1831 they made fewer than one third of the attacks of the previous year. However, even those terrified whites. More parties were sent out after them, and the government offered a reward for every person captured.[26]

The only hope for a non-violent solution was George Augustus Robinson's idea of a 'friendly mission', persuading Aboriginal people to give themselves up. Many people thought it would never work but Arthur supported Robinson. Accompanied by a group of Aboriginal people he travelled the island, seeking people who by now were exhausted:

> Incessantly harried by dozens of armed parties, the wounded had no time to recuperate, and the strong were sometimes obliged to abandon them, along with infants and the elderly. These crushing expedients, together with the constant loss

Aborigines in mournful exile on Flinders Island, by John Skinner Prout (TA ALMFA AUTAS001124065012w800)

of kinsfolk in campfire ambushes, caused a great cloud of sadness, anger and despair to descend on the survivors. From the perspectives of the [Aboriginal] Tasmanians, the Black War was a war of attrition, or trying to run, fight and survive as their society collapsed around them. Not surprisingly, [Robinson's] offer to relieve them of this hellish existence was readily accepted.[27]

On New Year's Eve 1831, the once powerful Mairremmener people surrendered: sixteen men, nine women and one child. Seven days later they walked into Hobart. Its citizens crowded the streets to watch this most infamous of the 'savage tribes' walk down Elizabeth Street, amazed that the people they had feared so much were so few in number.[28]

There was a little more violence in the north-west, but essentially, the Black War was over. The survivors were taken to various Bass Strait islands where, shattered by the experience of war and by being removed from their country, they pined away or died of disease.

Arthur and many others recognised that the Tasmanian Aboriginal people had been unfairly treated. In 1832 he wrote: 'it was a fatal error in the first settlement of Van Diemen's Land that a treaty was not entered into'.[29] A growing number of people have agreed with him ever since.

CONCLUSION

What does this story tell us about Van Diemen's Land/Tasmania, about British colonies, about the making of the British Empire?

For a start, it seems an amazingly haphazard venture: sending hundreds of people, mainly criminals, to a completely new country with little support, and expecting them to form a viable colony. Still, the British government stated, several times, that their main aim was to rid Britain of criminals, and this occurred. Over fifty years they exiled 72,000 people – men, women, even children – to Van Diemen's Land, and few returned to Britain. So that aim was achieved (though the greater aim, ridding Britain of crime, was not).

From this, we have to conclude that the British government was not particularly concerned with these convicts' welfare, or the welfare of the colony as a whole. It was far more worried about the war with Napoleon and conditions in Britain. Besides, Van Diemen's Land was only one of many colonies, and was far away on the other side of the world. Out of sight, out of mind.

The British Empire was run by an elite, which ruled its colonies by sending its members to govern them. If these men themselves broke the law, the Empire could not have them shown up in public. It protected them, with their mistakes and crimes glossed over. The patronage system resulted in some grossly incompetent misfits being sent to administer colonies. Away from Britain and its control mechanisms – families, the press, public opinion – most did not behave in the respectable way expected of them. Did the system infantilise them by removing their sense of responsibility, or any fear of retribution? The colony they set up was an inversion of the model British colony, with crime, fraud and brutality to the Aboriginal population rampant. Lacking effective law and order, Tasmania became a kleptocracy, with rulers who exploited the people to extend their own wealth.

It was only when the situation got completely out of hand, as in New South Wales in 1808 and (in Bigge's opinion) in Van Diemen's Land in 1820, that the British government sent out competent rulers (Macquarie and Arthur) to introduce law and order. If anyone threatened the Empire, the British Government was ruthless in suppressing them – Aboriginal people, bushrangers and rogue convicts.

In the history of Tasmania as a society, these early misfit rulers are entertaining enough, but a sideline. They came, created havoc and went. Those who stayed in the first twenty years were mainly the working class, convicts and soldiers. Such people varied from innate rogues to once-off petty thieves, but in the main were ordinary working-class people. Without powerful patrons or social standing to protect them, they were on their own. They supported each other through networks: among gaol mates, shipmates, convicts from the same cities and countries, soldiers from the same regiment, neighbours, business colleagues. growing families. Some took to crime to get by; many drowned their sorrows in drink; but enough took the opportunities the new land offered them, of free land, better-paid jobs, comfort and security, in return for accepting – perhaps only on the surface but even that was better than lawlessness – a certain amount of respectability, with its values of honesty, relative sobriety and industry.

And, importantly, these people raised a second generation who, brought up in prosperity, had no need to steal. They became hard-working, law-abiding citizens, praised as a great improvement on their parents. They were the vital basis of the respectable, stable, more-or-less law-abiding community that Arthur was able to establish by 1831, assisted by an influx of (largely) honest and industrious free settlers, Christian missionaries – and, tragically, by the near-extinction of the Aboriginal owners. Tasmania evolved into a community, strong enough to integrate and tame waves of convicts until transportation ceased in 1853.

Aiming just to get rid of thieves, the British government had, unintentionally, established a giant sociological experiment. What happens when you exile criminals to a new colony? Yes, some initial mayhem: but once people prosper and have no need to commit crimes, they go straight. The experiment proved that crime is not inherited but a product of poverty and oppression.

Tasmania suffered a stigma, largely coming from British assumptions of how diabolical a convict society must be; but in reality it became a relatively ordinary British colony. The indelible stain on it does not come from the convict presence, as colonists feared. That stain is the catastrophe of the fate of the Aboriginal population. In 1804 a viable and generally peaceful country was invaded, its people abused and killed, and the survivors exiled from their homeland. The stain continues.

ACKNOWLEDGEMENTS

Like all authors, I could not have written this book by myself. Many people helped me and I am most grateful for their ideas, suggestions and other assistance.

I would like to thank in particular John Dent, who generously shared his knowledge of the history of northern Tasmania; Nicholas Clements for his excellent book *The Black War*, which I quote from extensively; Jim Everett-puralia meenamatta for his advice about the Aboriginal sections; Ros Escott, for our frequent discussions about the book during our daily walks; and Susan Geason for her extremely helpful ideas about the conclusion. I gave a class at U3A about this book and members were extremely helpful, with (as usual) penetrating questions and observations. Thanks to Eddy Steenbergen for providing the excellent map.

Other helpful people have been: John Blackwood, for asking 'How did people live then?'; Dr Clare Smith and Dr Philip Thomson for advice on health; Colette McAlpine and all involved with the Female Convicts Research Centre database of female convicts; the staff of the Tasmanian Archives, particularly Janine Tan and Chris Pearce; the staff of the Army Museum at Anglesea Barracks, particularly Major Christopher Talbot; Rob Blakers, photographer; the Cremorne Ocean Dippers for suggestions made during our morning swims; Ann Ricketts for information about Thomas Keston; the audience at the talk I gave to the Tasmanian Historical Research Association. For answering specific questions, thanks to Steve Allen and Mary Harwood. Thanks to Andrew Chapman for his excellent design.

I'd also like to thank fellow historians Kevin Green, Hamish Maxwell-Stewart, Henry Reynolds, Michael Roe, Malcolm Ward; excellent proof readers and editors Susan Gleason, Marian May, Michael Sprod and Sheelagh Wegman; and the publishers John and Leigh Spiers who have been exciting to work with.

Alison Alexander

ENDNOTES

Abbreviations

ADB   *Australian Dictionary of Biography* (see website for biographies)
CT   *Colonial Times*
HRA   *Historical Records of Australia*
HTC   *Hobart Town Courier*
HTG   *Hobart Town Gazette*
LA   *Launceston Advertiser*
ML   *Mitchell Library*
SG   *Sydney Gazette*
TA   *Tasmanian Archives*

Introduction

[1] TA NS14/1/1, NS14/2/1.
[2] TA RGD36/1/1 575; RGD32/1/1 1551; HTG 26/4/1823; LA 28/6/1830; *Independent* 22/2/1834.

Part 1: 1804 to 1820
1. The newcomers

[1] Figures from Hobart Town First Settlers website https://htfs.org.au/settlers1804.php viewed 24/9/2024, and Vandemonian Royalty https://vandemonian.info/settlement–1804–north viewed 24/9/2024.
[2] Tipping, p.290.
[3] John Bigge, *Third report*, p.80, https://digital.sl.nsw.gov.au/delivery/DeliveryManagerServlet?embedded=true&toolbar=false&dps_pid=IE3732195 viewed 6/10/2024.
[4] Hamilton-Arnold, p.86.
[5] Peter Walker, p.139.
[6] HRA 3, 2, p.24.
[7] G. H. Stancombe, 'Youl, John', *ADB*.
[8] Hamilton-Arnold, pp.72, 137, 147–8.

2. Making an honest living

[1] HRA 1, 1, p.14, 124.
[2] The most similar was Russia, but Russian criminals went to already-settled areas and formed a small minority in the population They were not given land.
[3] TA NS395/1/1, pp.110–13.
[4] TA LSD354/1/2 p.240.
[5] HRA 3, 2, pp.17–18.
[6] TA NS395/1/1, pp.113–15.
[7] Fawkner, p.40.
[8] Holt, chapter 12, 23/12/1805 (no page numbers in online version), http://www.gutenberg.net.au/ebooks22/2200621h.html#ch12, viewed 11/5/2024.
[9] Tipping, pp.249–326.
[10] West, vol.1, p.37.
[11] Fawkner, p.41.
[12] *HTG* 19/12/1818.
[13] Curr, p.14.
[14] Colonial Secretary's Papers (NSW), James Frost, 15/5/1817.
[15] TA NS381, Samuel Guy to his brother 23/8/1825, page beginning 'to run Wild'.
[16] HRA 3, 2, pp.191–2.
[17] Harrisson, pp.25–6.
[18] Harrisson, pp.42–3.

3. Making a dishonest living: convicts

[1] Old Bailey online, ref t18391216-294, Mary Welch.
[2] Arulappu, p.36.
[3] Humphrey, p.89.
[4] https://www.mayoclinic.org/diseases-conditions/antisocial-personality-disorder/symptoms-causes/syc-20353928 viewed 21/9/2024.
[5] HRA 3, 2, p.282.
[6] Knopwood, pp.78–9; Hamilton-Arnold, p.73.
[7] Knopwood, p.82.
[8] Knopwood, pp.131–2, 135.
[9] *HTG* 7/2/1818, 27/6/1818, 29/8/1818, 14/11/1818.
[10] *HTG* 29/8/1818, 14/11/1818, 20/12/1817.
[11] *SG* 2/2/1806, 16/2/1806; Knopwood p.105; HRA 3, 1, pp.356–7.
[12] Fawkner, p.54; *HTG* 20/12/1817.
[13] HRA 3, 2, p.282.
[14] HRA 3, 2, p.294; *HTG* 10/5/1817, 21/6/1817, 20/9/1817, 17/1/1818, 19/12/1818; *SG*

1/11/1817, 22/11/1817.

[15] *HTG* 25/12/1819; Hudspeth 23/12/1822.

[16] Widowson, pp.96, 115.

[17] Lloyd, p.16.

[18] Bonwick, pp.43–4.

[19] Fawkner, pp.37–8.

[20] *HTG* 6/7/1816, 3/8/1816, 1/3/817.

[21] *HTG* 4/2/27, 19/4/1817, 1/6/1816; Backhouse, *Narrative*, Appendix E, p.lxii; O'Keefe et al, *Labour History* 127, November 2024.

[22] *HTG* 23/5/1818; Fawkner p.53.

[23] *HTG* 28/12/1816, 6/2/1819.

[24] *HTG*, 14/1/1825.

[25] *CT* 17/2/1826, 22/9/1826, 17/11/1826, 6/4/1827.

[26] *HTC* 20/10/1827.

[27] Knopwood, p.77; *HTG* 10/1/1818.

[28] Knopwood, p.83.

[29] *VDL Gazette* 4, 18/6/1814; *SG* 12/2/1814, 4/6/1814, 3/2/1816; HRA 3, 2, p.63.

[30] Knopwood pp.121–2.

[31] HRA 3, 1, pp.685–6; Cox, pp.11–26.

[32] HRA 3, 1, pp.466, 483, 537–8, 559.

[33] Fawkner, p.30; Bonwick, p.89.

[34] HRA 3, 2, pp.75–9.

[35] HRA 3, 2, pp.80–5.

[36] Sprod, passim.

4. Making a dishonest living: officials

[1] TA395/1/1 pp.124–5.

[2] TA395/1/1 pp.126–7.

[3] Earnshaw, p.38; Hamilton-Arnold, p.86.

[4] Hamilton-Arnold, p.95, Knopwood p.124.

[5] Knopwood, p.63.

[6] TA NS395/1/1, pp.119–20.

[7] HRA 1, 7, pp.468–74.

[8] HRA 3, 1, pp.439–50 especially 446.

[9] ML, NRS936, 4/3490A, 178–80, Macquarie to Murray, 1/4/1811.

[10] 'Bate, Samuel (1776–1849)', *ADB*.

[11] TA NS395/1/1 pp.137, 134.

[12] TA NS395/1/1 pp.143–34, 150; ML, DLADD 282/6; TA NS395/1/1 p.150.

[13] HRA 1, 8, p.243.
[14] HRA 1, 8, pp.238–9.
[15] HRA 3, 2, pp.44, 46, 52–54; 1, 8, p.460.
[16] 'Brabyn, John', *ADB*.
[17] Browne, pp.87–9; HRA 1, 7, pp.588, 682.
[18] Information from John Dent; TA395/1/1 p.151.
[19] HRA, 1, 7, p.585; 3, 1, 717–8.
[20] HRA 1, 7, p.589; 1, 8, p.250, 264; 'Mills, Peter', *ADB*.
[21] Richards, p.6; Isabella Mead, 'Mountgarrett, Jacob', *ADB*; HRA 1, 9, pp.67, 74, 204, 716.
[22] HRA 3, 1, p.451; 1, 7, p.291.

5. The nadir of governance: Thomas Davey

[1] Knopwood, pp.194, 203 also pp.166, 168, 173, 175, 191, 193.
[2] HRA 1, 7, 262.
[3] TA CO201/65/126.
[4] HRA 1, 7, p.790; 3, 2, pp.23–4; West, vol.1, p.50.
[5] Beattie, p.23; West, vol.1, pp.49–50; *Fitzroy City Press* 31/8/1912; *Critic* 11/5/1923.
[6] HRA 3, 4, 706.
[7] TA NS395/1/1, pp.147–8.
[8] HRA 3, 2, pp.566, 574; Fawkner, p.85.
[9] Beattie, p.23; [Abbott], p.152. 'Heeltap' is liquor left in a glass after drinking.
[10] Latrobe Library, 3661.1, vol 2, p.85.
[11] West, vol. 1, pp.51–2, 357.
[12] West, vol. 1, p.50; Scott Polar Research Institute MS248,48/86, Jane Franklin diary, 1/6/1839.
[13] HRA 1, 8, pp.242, 458–9, 556; Melville, p.112.
[14] HRA 3, 3, p.273
[15] HRA 3, 2, pp.643–4; K.R. Von Stieglitz, 'Howe, Michael', *ADB*.
[17] HRA 3, 2, pp.61, 436.
[18] HRA 3, 2, p.631.
[19] HRA 1, 8, pp.458, 472–3; 1, 9, pp.113–4, 338, 347; 1, 9, 113, 338.
[21] HRA 3, 2, pp.344–5, 419.
[22] HRA 3, 2, pp.41, 115; 3, 3, p.226; 1, 9, p.249.
[23] HRA 3, 2, pp.598, 625.
[24] HRA 3, 3, pp.474, 608–9; 3, 2, pp.592, 150.
[25] HRA 3, 2, pp.154, 156, 160, 169, 196, 604 612, 627; 3, 3, pp.479–80; *HTG*, 27/7/1816, 28/9/1816.

27 HRA 3, 2, p.154; Vivienne Parsons, 'Broughton, William', *ADB*.
28 HRA 3, 2, pp.591–5, 169.
29 HRA 1, 9, pp.762–4, 768–71.
30 HRA 1, 9, pp.762–3, 768–70; 3, 3, p.313.
31 West, vol.1, p.57.
32 HRA 3, 2, pp.455, 451, 461, 463–4, 467; 3, 3, 701.
33 HRA, 3, 2, pp.244, 340–1, 476–8.

6. Slight improvement: Governor Sorell

1 John Reynolds, 'Sorell, William', *ADB*; Sorell, p.88.
2 *The Times*, 7/7/1817.
3 Sorell p.88.
4 HRA 1, 9, p.347; 3, 3, p.230; TA NS395/1/1 p.153.
5 HRA 3, 2, pp.338, 376; TA NS395/1/1 p.171.
6 Macquarie, https://www.mq.edu.au/macquarie-archive/lema/1821/1821may.html viewed 4/7/2024.
7 HRA 1, 13, p.190.
8 TA NS/1/1/395 p.170.
9 Hudspeth, 14/10/1822.
10 TA CSO1/1/52/995, p.75; McKay, p.4.
12 HRA 1, 9, pp.61, 359, 398, 428–9; 3, 2, 199, 202–3, 208, 215–37, 631.
13 HRA 3, 2, pp.215–9, 629–31.
14 HRA 1, 9, p.558–9, 835; 3, 2, pp.271, 293–4, 631.
15 HRA 3, 2, p.751.
16 HRA 3, 3, p.844.
17 HRA 3, 4, p.691; **3, 3, p.21–3**; thanks to John Dent for his assistance.
18 HRA 3, 3, p.93; 'Cimitiere, Gilbert', *ADB*.
19 HRA 3, 3, p.709; *SG* 29/9/1821; TA NS395/1/1 p.171.
20 HRA 3, 2, pp.684, 686; 3, 4, p.8.
21 TA NS395/1/1, p.124.
22 *HTG* 9/4/1824, 25/3/1825.
23 Lloyd, p.280; Jack Cato, *I can take it*, Melbourne, 1947, pp.2–3.
24 *Tasmanian* 25/10/1827.
25 Sorell p.88.

7. Aboriginal Tasmanians

1 West, vol.2, p.1.

[2] West, vol.2, p.7.
[3] Humphrey pp.59–60; HRA 3, 1, pp.606–7.
[4] HRA 3, 1, p.281.
[5] HRA 3, 2, pp.284, 474, 741, 748, 750.
[6] HRA 3, 4, pp.134–54.
[7] West, vol.2, pp.7–8; Backhouse, p.212.
[8] Lloyd, pp.45–53.
[9] HRA 3, 1, p.529; West, vol.2, p.9.
[10] West, vol.2, p.8.
[11] HRA 3, 1, p.769.
[12] HRA 3, 2, p.576.
[13] HRA 3, 1, p.643.
[14] Von Stieglitz, p.7; West, vol.2, p.11.
[15] Reynolds and Clements, *passim*.

8. The Bigge Report: Van Diemen's Land in 1820

[1] J.M. Bennett, 'Bigge, John Thomas', *ADB*; 'Bathurst, Henry', *ADB*. Ritchie, pp.2, 29, 53.
[2] Bennett; Ritchie passim.
[3] *HTG* 19/2/1820, 27/5/1820.
[4] Knopwood, pp.325–6; HRA 3, 4, p.683–4.
[5] Knopwood, pp.325–6, 328, 331; HRA 3, 3, pp.363–8.
[6] Andell, p.7.
[7] HRA 3, 3, pp.399, 492.
[8] HRA 3, 3, pp.418–21, 429, 430, 452–3, 490, 215.
[9] HRA, 3, 3, pp.215–30.
[10] Bigge, 'Third report', p.80.
[11] HRA, 3, 3, pp.230–45.
[12] HRA 3, 3, pp.330, 414, 314–5.
[13] HRA 3, 3, p.384.
[14] HRA 3, 3, pp.407, 384, 448, 451, 486.
[15] HRA 3, 3, pp.493, 381, 224, 330, 334–5.
[16] HRA 3, 3, pp.362–3.
[17] HRA 3, 3, pp.279, 249, 365, 285, 442.
[18] HRA, 3, 3, pp.284, 460, 239.
[19] HRA 3, 3, pp.401, 407, 467.
[20] HRA 3, 3, pp.877–8, 853–65.
[21] HRA 3, 3, pp.264, 366.

22 HRA 1, 8, p.135; 3, 4, p.634.
23 HRA 3, 3, pp.315, 275, 449–51, 219, 282, 285.
24 HRA 3, 3, pp.32, 97, 127, 374–6.
25 R.L. Wettenhall, 'Hogan, Patrick Gould', *ADB*; HRA 3, 3, pp, 474–6; L.L. Robson, 'Maum, William James', *ADB* ; HRA 3, 3, pp.472, 374, 399. 475.
26 HRA 3, 3, pp.363–7, 442– 72, 285, 365.
27 HRA, 3, 3, pp.311–2.
28 HRA 3, 3, pp.355–6, 461–2, 353, 372.
29 HRA, 3, 3, pp.298, 351, 223.
30 HRA 3, 3, pp.283, 290, 351.
31 HRA 3, 3, pp.450–1, 384.
32 HRA 3, 3, pp.336–7.
33 HRA 3, 3, pp.223, 340, 335–41.
34 HRA 3, 3, pp.220–1, 228–9, 365.
35 HRA 3, 3, pp.318–22, 359, 310, 258, 367.
36 HRA 3, 3, pp.318–22, 359, 309–10, 258, 219,
37 *HTG* 12/4/1817; HRA 3, 3, pp.321–2.
38 HRA 3, 3, p.495.
39 HRA 3, 3, pp.251, 316, 361, 380–1, 461.
40 HRA 3, 3, pp.299, 486–7.
41 Bigge, 'Third Report', 1823, pp.24–30, 32, 47–9, 68–9, 76–8, 80, 83, 94.
42 Ritchie, p.227.
43 TA CON31/1/1 p.132; Clements, pp.51–52.
44 *Launceston Examiner*, 7/3/1884.
45 *HTG* 15/5/1819; Robson, 'Maum, William James'.

Part 2 Living in Van Diemen's Land
9. Food, clothes and homes

1 Knopwood, pp.63, 66–8, 76, 86, 90, 102, 104, 107, 120, 98.
2 Knopwood, p. 63.
3 Ross, p.86.
4 Jeffreys, pp.69–70.
5 Ross, p.112.
6 HRA 3, 3, p.313.
7 Fawkner, p.22; Melville, p.110.
8 Widowson, pp.176, 192.
9 Knopwood, pp.53, 69, 120, 122.

[10] Hudspeth, 12/2/1823; Chapman, p.455.
[11] *HTG* 18/11/1820; Ross, p.110; Chapman, p.341.
[12] *HTG* 13/12/1823.
[13] Harrisson, pp.22–3; *HTG* 30/8/1817.
[14] *HTG* 16/8/1817, 15/11/1817, 4/5/1822.
[15] *VDLG* 21/5/1814; *HTG* 3/5/1817, 31/5/1817, 11/4/1818, 7/11/1818, 11/4/1818, 10/10/1818.
[16] *HTG* 17/2/1821; *HTC* 22/8/1829; *LA*, 14/9/1829.
[17] Knopwood, pp.79, 83, 105.
[18] *HTG* 4/1/1817, 16/6/1821.
[19] *HTG* 18/1/1823, 20/7/1822, 29/3/1823, 15/9/1821; *Tasmanian* 21/5/1830.
[20] HRA 3, 5, p.461.
[21] Humphrey, p.55.
[22] *HTG* 29/6/1816.
[23] *HTG* 19/10/1816.
[24] *LA* 20/12/1829; *CT* 4/2/1831; *Tasmanian* 17/12/1831.
[25] Walker, p.133.
[26] Andell, pp.4–6.
[27] *CT* 1/2/1831.
[28] West, vol.1, pp.34–5.
[29] Fawkner p.22.
[30] *HTG* 21/2/1818.
[31] *HTG* 9/6/1821.
[32] *HTG* 29/9/1821.
[33] Fenton, p.28.
[34] TA NS14/1/1, NS14/2/1; Harrisson, pp.22–3.
[35] *HTG*, 30/5/1818, 17/3/1821, 10/2/1821, 7/10/1826.
[36] Crawford, p.2.
[37] *Courier*, 23/9/1842.
[38] *HTC* 28/11/1829.
[39] *HTG* 26/10/1816, 16/11/1816, 4/1/1817, 1/2/1817.
[40] *HTG* 2/5/1818, 6/5/1820, 21/9/1822, 22/2/1823.
[41] Ross, pp.31, 222; Utas Special & Rare Collection, RS8-F8-5, Ann Weston to Jane Clark, 27/11/1826.

10. Jalop and tragacanth: healing illness

[1] Porter, p.39; medical information throughout from Dr Clare Smith.
[2] *Tasmanian* 26/11/1830; *HTC* 29/3/1828; *HTG* 30/11/1822.

3 *Tasmanian* 26/11/1830; *HTG* 30/11/1822; *CT* 4/5/1837.
4 *Tasmanian* 26/11/1830.
5 *HTC* 19/4/1828.
6 HRA 3, 3, pp.418–21, 501–3.
7 *HTG* 9/3/1822.
9 Knopwood, pp.391–2.
10 Hamilton-Arnold p.140.
11 Knopwood, p.268.
12 HRA 3, 3, pp.418–21, 501–3.
13 'Luttrell, Edward', *ADB*; HRA 3, 3, 502–3.
14 *CT* 9/6/1826.
15 *HTG* 16/11/1822.
16 Hudspeth diary 9/12/1822, 14/2/1823, 24/2/1823, 3/3/1823.
17 Grehan, pp.32–44.
18 Andell, pp.6, 10.
19 Hamilton-Arnold, p.58; Chapman, pp.339, 345, 351.
20 Chapman, pp.364.
21 Chapman, p.415.
22 Chapman, p.377.
23 Knopwood, pp.219, 509–11, 451, 241.
24 Knopwood, pp.241, 281, 246, 454.
25 Knopwood, pp.235, 547, 385, 530, 512, 558, 474.
26 Utas Special & Rare collection, RS8–F6–7, Ann Weston to Jane Clark, 27/11/1826.
27 Fenton, pp.43, 54–63.
28 *CT* 23/9/1825, 15/1/1830, 22/1/1830, 17/9/1830; *Tasmanian* 4/6/1830, 18/6/1831; TA RGD32/1/1 no 1604; *HTC* 10/5/1828, 19/7/1828, 16/8/1929, 30/8/1828, 20/9/1828, 5/6/1830; *HTG* 23/8/1830.
29 *CT* 15, 22/6/1831.
30 *Tasmanian* 18/6/1831; *Australasian Chronicle* 13/12/1839; *CT* 13/11/1832; TA RGD 43/1/1 no 3410; *Colonist*, 15/10/1833; TA RGD37/1/10 100; *Mercury* 16/9/1912.
31 TA RGD37/1/10/100, RGD33/1/33/361 et al; *Examiner* 16/9/1912.
32 *CT* 10, 24/3/1826; *HTG* 11/3/1826.
33 Journal of Joseph Arnold, quoted in https://www.freesettlerorfelon.com/jacob_ mountgarrett_surgeon.html viewed 3/11/2024.
34 *HTC* 1/8/1829; *CT* 16/4/1830.
35 *CT* 27/2/1829.
36 Ken Hose, 'Water Supply & Sewerage for Launceston', https://www.launcestonhistory.org. au/wp-content/uploads/2016/11/

Ken-Hose-Water-Sewerage.pdf viewed 20/7/2024; HRA 3, 1, 759–60.
37 Chapman, p.411-2.
38 Andell, p.12.
39 https://pubmed.ncbi.nlm.nih.gov/3511335/ viewed 10/7/2024.
40 *HTG* 30/10/1819, 9/3/1822; Grehan, p.41.
41 *HTG* 21/9/1822, 17/9/1824; *CT* 4/8/1826; Crawford, p.18.
42 Knopwood pp.564–5.
43 Hudspeth, 18, 21–27/12/1822.
44 TA Sutherland diary 46, 30/3/1825, 3/4/1825.
45 Chapman, p.456.
46 HRA 3, 3, p.418; Carole Bacon, *The legacy of John Headlam*, Hobart, 2021, p.49.
47 Melville, pp.30, 222.
48 Ross, pp.44–5.

11. Education and culture

1 HRA 3, 2, pp.256, 280, 311, 361–2; 3 3, p.367; *HTG* 9/1/1819, 6/11/1819; Tipping, pp.273–4.
2 *SG* 10/11/1810; HRA 3, 3, p.367; Burkhardt, 'Convict and emancipist teachers New South Wales, 1789–1830'.
3 HRA 3, 3, pp.316, 367, 444.
4 HRA 3, 3, 367; Bigge, 'Third report', pp.76–7.
5 L. L. Robson, 'Mulgrave, Peter Archer' *ADB*; HRA 3, 4, pp.39–40.
6 *HTC* 12/4/1828; *HTG* 2/1/1824; CSO1/1/3/42; Alexander Stone, 'The story of Thomas & Ann Stone'.
7 *HTC* 8/12/1827.
8 *CT* 18/5/1827; *HTC* 1/12/1827.
9 HRA 3, 5, 154–67, 470; Melville, p.222.
10 Russell Craig, 'Conjectures on accounting education in Tasmania, 1803 to 1833'.
11 *HTG* 5/5/1821, 25/5/1822, 19/11/1824, 20/5/1825; *Tasmanian* 28/5/1830.
12 *Tasmanian* 28/12/1827, 16/5/1828; *CT* 16/2/1827; *HTC* 19/12/1829
13 *HTG*, *HTC*, *CT* passim, advertisements 1816 to 1831.
14 *HTG* 3/11/1821, 11/1/1823, 27/1/1827; *Tasmanian* 2/7/1831.
15 *HTG* 2/3/1822, 13/1/1821.
16 *HTG* 13/1/1821, 12/10/1822, 21/5/1824.
17 Knopwood p.381.
18 *HTG* 20/4/1822.
19 *HTC* 3/1/1829; *CT* 13, 27/3/1829.

20 *CT* 3/9/1830, 17/11/1826; *HTG* 10/11/1821.
21 *HTG* 7/6/1823; *HTC* 11/1/1839.
22 Andell, pp.5–7 and passim.
23 *HTG* 19/7/1823; *HTC* 26/9/1829; G. T. Stilwell, 'Clark, George Carr', *ADB*.
24 *CT* 15/12/1826, 23/2/1827, 24/8/1827, 14/9/1827; *HTG* 23/9/182, 9/12/1826, 21/7/1827, 15/9/1827; *HTC* 18/1/1828; *LA* 7/8/1832.
25 *CT* 19/10/1827; Chapman, p.69.
26 Chapman, p.308.
27 Melville, p.229; Ross, p.101.
28 'Ross, James', *ADB*.
29 *CT* 10/2/1826, *Tasmanian* 31/12/1831.
30 Jeff Brownrigg, 'Music', in Alexander, *Companion*, pp.346–7.
31 *HTG* 11/7/1818, 10/2/1821.
32 *HTG* 23/12/1820; *Penny Magazine*, 12/5/1832, 'An Emigrant's Struggles'; Backhouse, p.151.
33 *HTG* 25/1/1817, 23/6/1821.
34 *HTG* 18/5/1822, 20/7/1822, 5/10/1822, 23/4/1824.
35 Brownrigg; *HTG* 1/7/1825.
36 *HTG*,11/2/1826, 29/4/1825, 7/10/1826; *CT* 31/3/1826, 5/10/1827.
37 *Tasmanian* 18, 25/1/1828.
38 *HTG* 7/10/1826; *CT* 29/9/1826.
39 Knopwood, p.550.
40 *HTG* 8/4/1826; *HTC* 26/1/1828.
41 *HTC* 31/1/1829, 25/4/1829.
42 *Tasmanian* 27/8/1830; *CT* 27/8/1830.
43 *CT* 14/1/1831, 25/3/1831; *HTC* 23/4/1831; *Tasmanian* 18/2/1831, 22/4/1831, 9/7/1831, 3/9/1831.
44 Hamilton-Arnold, p.73; *HTG* 31/1/1818, 14/2/1818.
45 *HTG* 17 June, 6/8/1825; Keith Atkins, 'Libraries, early community-based', in Alexander, *Companion* p.215.
46 *CT* 19/5/1826; *HTC* 24/11/1827; Melville, p.226.
47 *CT* 15/9/1826; Peter Pierce, 'Literature' in Alexander, *Companion*, p.217.
48 *CT* 30/11/1831.
49 Utas Special and Rare, RS8.B(4), 10/7/1829, (10) no date.
50 Stefan Petrow, 'Mechanics' Institutes', in Alexander, *Companion*, pp.231–2.
51 *LA* 11/1/1830, 1/2/1830; *HTC* 23/1/1830; *Tasmanian* 29/1/1830, 19/2/1830; *CT* 29/1/1830, 19/2/1830, 19/5/1830.
52 *CT* 26/11/1830.
53 David Hansen, 'Art', in Alexander, *Companion*, p.26.

54 Chapman, p.421–2.

55 HTG 9/3/1822, 22/6/1822, 4/10/1823, 30/4/1824, 10/12/1825; *Tasmanian* 19/9/1828.

12. Sport and recreation

1 UTAS, RS8.B12(1), Charles Arthur to John Clark 6/4/1827.

2 LA 8/6/1829; *CT* 17/3/1826, 6/7/1831; *HTG* 25/3/1826.

3 *HTG* 22/7/1826.

4 *HTG* 16/12/1820, 6/3/1819.

5 *HTG* 3/6/1825.

6 Crawford, p.48.

7 Knopwood, p.216; *HTG* 25/9/1819, 19/3/1824.

8 *HTC* 26/4/1828 12/3/1824.

9 Knopwood p.517; *Tasmanian* 25/4/1828, 2/5/1828; *Colonial Advocate* 1/5/1828.

10 *Tasmanian* 25/2/1831; *CT* 25/2/1831.

11 Knopwood, pp.193, 220; *HTG* 4/1/1817, 10/12/1824.

12 *HTG* 8, 15/4/1826.

13 *HTC* 10/1/1829; *Tasmanian* 10/9/1830; *LA*, 15/2/1830, 28/12/1831.

14 *HTG* 4/10/1817, 1/11/1817, 14/3/1818.

15 *CT* 16/6/1826; *LA* 30/3/1829; *Cornwall Press* 31/3/1829.

16 *LA* 11/1/1830, 1/2/1830; *HTC* 9/1/1830; *Tasmanian* 23/7/1831.

17 *Tasmanian* 27/7/1828; *Cornwall Press* 26/5/1829; FCRC database, entry for Mary Buckley ID4457.

18 TA NS395/1/1, p.137; *HTG* 16/9/1826; *CT* 28/4/1835.

19 *HTG* 9/12/1826; *HTC* 20/10/1827; *Tasmanian* 28/12/1827.

20 *HTG* 8/6/1816; Knopwood, p.233; *Tasmanian* 2/5/1828.

21 *CT* 19/1/1827; *Tasmanian* 8/4/1831.

22 *HTG* 2/11/1816; Tipping p.317; Bert Wicks, 'Horseracing' in Alexander, *Companion*, p.182; *VDLG* 20/8/1814; *HTG* 5, 12/10/1816.

23 Knopwood pp.175, 183–4, 186, 196, 208–9, 211, 214, 223.

24 *CT* 21/1/1831, 5/1/1827; *TPDA* 23/3/1825.

25 *CT* 5/1/1827.

26 *CT* 5/1/1827; *Tasmanian* 25/10/1827, 4/1/1828.

27 *CT* 21/1/1831; Lloyd, p.281.

28 *HTG* 15/7/1826; *CT* 13/4/1827.

29 *Independent* 28/3/1831, 11/4/1831; *CT* 6/4/1827, 15/3/1831; *HTC* 12/9/1829.

30 *LA* 14/3/1831; *CT* 10/12/1831; Melville *Almanac* 1831 p.226; *LA* 15/2/1832.

31 *CT* 10/12/1830; *HTG* 31/12/1825, 7/1/1825.

32 *CT* 3/7/1829; *Independent* 11/4/1831.

[33] Crawford, pp.29-30.
[34] Chapman, pp.435, 501, 454, 463, 448, 366, 302, 465, 319; Crawford, pp.15, 19.
[35] Andell, pp.4–5, 7–8.
[36] Utas RS8.B12 (1) 21/4/1828, (3) 10/7/1829, (5) 4/9/1829, (7) 11/12/1829, (12) no date.
[37] Utas RS8.B(4), 10/7/1829.
[38] *Penny Magazine*, 5/5/1832, 'An Emigrant's Struggles'.

13. Community life

[1] West, vol.1, p.80.
[2] Hudspeth, 6/10/1822.
[3] Prinsep, p.52.
[4] Jane Roberts, *Two years at sea*, London, 1834, p.15.
[5] *HTG* 22/6/1816; Knopwood passim.
[6] *HTG* 29/12/1821.
[7] Hamilton-Arnold p.73.
[9] Knopwood, pp.175–7, 188.
[10] *HTG* 25/9/1819, 13/1/1819, 20/11/1819, 11/12/1819; CON31/1/1 image 107.
[11] Fenton, pp.20, 25–6, 36.
[12] Fenton, pp.65–8, 74–5.
[13] Knopwood, p.490; *CT* 17/11/1826.
[14] Crawford, p.31.
[15] Chapman, p.491.
[16] Widowson, p.52–3.
[17] Eustace FitzSymonds, *A looking-glass for Tasmania*, Adelaide, 1980, pp.96–8.
[18] Chapman, pp.496–7.

14. A small minority: women

[1] Bigge 'Third Report', p.80; Australian Bureau of Statistics, 'Population, Tasmania, 1820 to 1910.xls' viewed 16/10/2024.
[2] *HTG* 8/7/1826; *Colonist* 16/7/1833; TA RGD35/1/18/7; *Courier* 28/1/1845.
[3] FCRC database, entry for Mary Lynch, ID 9488.
[4] FCRC database, entry for Mary Ann Ashton, ID 9461.
[5] FCRC database, entry for Sarah Webb, ID 9501; *Advertiser* 7/1/1840; *Daily Telegraph*, 11/3/1884
[6] *HTG* 13/5/1825.
[7] *HTC* 15/3/1828; *LA* 11/1/1832; RGD34/1/1/125,1847.

[8] *Tasmanian* 17/12/1831; HTG 6/5/1826, 21/10/1820.
[9] FCRC database, entry on Jane Quinn, ID 7171; *HTG* 28/2/1818, 26/12/1818; *HTC* 27/10/1827; RDG34/1/1 no 4074; RGD36/1/1 1010; *HTC* 20/2/1830.
[10] *HTG* 21/2/1818, 12/8/1820.
[11] *HTC* 6, 13/12/1828.
[12] *CT* 5/1/1827; *HTG* 13/1/1827.
[13] *HTG* 15/10/1825; *CT* 20/2/1829; *HTC* 4/10/1829.
[14] *HTG* 4/5/1822, 14/9/1822, 3/2/1827, 11/1/1823, 23/11/1822.
[15] TA RGD36/1/1 no.638; RGD32/1/1 nos1447, 1807; CON31/1/38 image 38; *Tasmanian* 18/10/1827, 14/11/1828, 21/12/1832, 2/8/1833; *HTC* 20/12/1833; TC 29/6/1838.
[16] *HTG* 19/10/1816, 1/3/1817.
[17] Holt, 4/12/1805.
[18] Fenton, pp.32-3, 48.
[19] *HTG* 28/9/1822; RGD 36/1/1 721.
[20] *SG* 3/3/1825; *HTC* 4/4/1829, 21/4/1819, 2/5/1829; TA CSO1/1/405/9144; SC32/1/1 image 383; CON31/1/27 image 110.
[21] TA CON19-1-9 image 235, CON40-1-5 165, CON40-1-9 image 237, CON40-1-5 22; FCRC database, entry for Catherine Burns ID1027.
[22] TA CSO1/1/170/4092.
[23] TA CSO1/1/552/12168.
[24] HRA 1, 12, p.348.
[25] TA CSO1/1/58/1223.
[26] TA CSO1/1/558/ 12296, CSO1/1/815/17413; *LA* 16/2/1837; Jill Hansen, 'Moriarty, William', *ADB*.
[27] *Tasmanian* 4/1/1828, 15/10/1830, 19/5/1832, 13/7/1832, 4/10/1833; *HTC* 17/1/1829, 3/8/1832, 23/5/1834; *LA* 9/2/1829; TA CSO1/1/569/12796; *CT* 3/4/1829, 25/11/1834, 9/6/1835; *Port Phillip Patriot* 24/7/1845.
[28] TA RGD34/1/1/2687; CSO1/1/229/5615; CSO1/1/307/7385; RGD32/1/1/1011; *HTG* 19/12/1818; 28/10/1820, 7/7/1821; Lachlan Macquarie diary 7, 8, 9, June 1821 https://www.mq.edu.au/macquarie-archive/lema/1821/1821june.html viewed 13/9/2024.
[29] Knopwood, pp.139-40; *HTG* 10/1/1818, 7/2/1818.
[31] TA LC247/1/1 pp.128-30; Tipping, p.108; *HTG* 25/11/1820
[32] *HTC* 22/12/1827; SC4/1/1 p.351; *Launceston Advertiser* 14, 21/6/1830; RGD34/1/1/2311, 2312.
[33] TA RGD37/1/3 no.110; RDG33/1/28 275, 369; RGD35/1/19 no43.
[34] *HTG* 1/8/1818.
[35] West, vol. 1, p.50.

271

[36] FCRC database, entry for Ann Frame, ID 520.
[37] FCRC database, entries for Jane Murray ID 7165, and Ann Smith ID 7177.
[38] *Tasmanian* 19/11/1892 (recollections of George Pullen).
[39] FCRC database, entry for Bridget Judge ID 7151; *Independent* 22/9/1832; Allison O'Sullivan, 'Bridget Judge: the highs and lows of convict motherhood', in Alexander and Escott (eds), *Convict lives: mothers' trials and triumphs*, Hobart, 2025.

Part 3 Towards a model colony
15. Free settlers arrive

[1] *HTG* 2/12/1820; West vol.1, p.59.
[2] *HTG* 2/12/1820.
[3] Wentworth, section entitled 'Soil, Etc', first paragraph.
[4] Jeffreys, passim; Evans, pp.v–ix, p.26, 25, 37, 60–1, 70, 74, 77, 85, 87–8, 90, 101.
[5] Evans, pp.25, 121.
[6] Evans pp.v–viii.
[7] *Westmoreland Gazette* 20/4/1822.
[8] Harrisson, pp.3, 5, 19.
[9] Harrisson, pp.14-5.
[10] *The Times* 18/1/1822.
[11] *HTG* 8/7/1825.
[12] *SG* 13/9/1826.
[13] Hudspeth, passim.
[14] Hudspeth, p.124.
[15] Hudspeth, p.124; *CT* 26/8/1825; https://rst.org.au/artstory-12-elizabeth-hudspeth/ viewed 14/10/2024.
[16] Curr, pp.vi, 12.
[17] *HTG* 12/4/1817, 29/4/1825; *CT* 22/6/1827; Hartwell, p.130.
[18] *CT* 12/6/1829.
[19] *HTG* 2/9/1826; *Independent* 16/7/1831.
[20] *CT* 3/2/1826; *Tasmanian* 25/10/1827; *HTG* 4/1/1823, 9/7/1824.
[21] Christine Walch, 'Hopkins, Henry', *ADB*; *Tasmanian* 18/2/1831; Hartwell pp.6–7, 20, 107–20.
[22] TA NS61/1/1–2, Sutherland diary passim; *Independent* 2/5/1831.
[23] HRA 3, 4, p.314; 3, 9, p.440.
[24] TA CSO1/1/468 10394; *CT* 2/7/1830, *HTG* 27/11/1830; *HTC* 25/2/1832.
[25] TA CSO1/1/529/11518; McKay, p.26.
[26] TA CSO1/1/461 10219; Bruce Wall, 'Lawrence, William Effingham', *ADB*.

27 Colonial Secretary NSW Index, entries Nathaniel Mockeridge. https://colsec.records.nsw.gov.au/; *CT* 18/11/1825.

28 https://historyofparliamentonline.org/volume/1820–1832/member/dixon-joseph-1802-1844 viewed 10/9/2024; *HTG* 9/7/1824, 13/8/1824; *Colonist* 23/11/1832; TA CSO3/13/067/D, SC32/1/1/14.

29 Colonial Secretary NSW Index, entries Matthew Keane; *SG* 18/4/1812, 14/6/1817; TA CSO1/1/220/3515.

30 *Tasmanian Morning Herald*, 20/7/1866; *HTG* 8/4/1825; TA CSO1/1/155/3735; A. Rand, 'Talbot, William', *ADB*.

31 TA CSO1/1/210/ 4999; *Launceston Examiner* 13/6/1874.

32 TA CSO1/1/156/1151.

33 *Cornwall Chronicle* 29/9/1871; *HTG* 2/3/1822, 12/10/1822, 22/2/1823, 1/3/1823, 15/4/1825; McKay p.42.

34 *HTG* 1/4/1820, 17/2/1821, 31/3/1821, 14/4/1821, 8/12/1821.

35 *HTG* 19/7/1823; CSO1/1/164/3938, CSO63/1/1p.87

36 Hull, pp.10, 12.

37 McKay pp.69, 60–1; *HTG* 8/11/1823, 9/4/1824.

38 TA CSO1/1/187/4494; CSO63/1/1 p.121; McKay p.26.

39 TA CSO1/1/263/627, 6274.

40 *Cornwall Press* 26/5/1829, 23/6/1829; *CT* 17/8/1831; *LA* 22/8/1831.

41 Lloyd, pp.12–14, 115.

42 TA CSO1/1/84/1885; *HTC* 22/12/1827.

43 TA CSO1/1/149/3651, SC195/1/2/102, RGD36/1/1/856; RGD32/1/1/1932; Bacon, p.58; *HTC* 30/10/1830.

44 TA NS61/1/1–2, Sutherland diary passim.

45 McKay, pp.8–9, 91–2, 18, 59, 71.

46 TA CSO1/1/288/6884, CSO1/1/291;6968; *Mercury* 10/10/1874.

47 TA CON31/1/34 image 240, CON23/1/1 no36; CSO1/1/361/8279, RGD34/1/1/5205, RGD37/1/2/877.

48 TA CON31/1/1 image 65, CON31/1/34 image 229, *CT* 24, 28/8/1832.

49 TA CSO1/1/373/8502, CSO1/1/82/1869; TA CSO1/1/71/1453.

50 McKay, pp.66, 26.

51 Savery, pp.77–8.

52 *Tasmanian Times*, 8/10/1870; *CC* 30/9/1870; *Mercury* 28/9/1870; TA NS477/1/1.

53 Rubinstein, *The All-Time Australian 200 Rich List*, Sydney, 2004, pp.37, 102; McKay, pp.65–6.

54 *HTG* 1, 8, 22/11/1823, 2/1/1824, 27/2/1824, 5/3/1824, 12/3/1824; *Colonial Advocate* 1/1/1828.

55 Hartwell, pp.85–6.

16. The Land Commissioners: farming in 1826–1827

[1] Alexander, *Connorville*, p.19.
[2] HRA 3, 5, p.121.
[3] McKay, p.17.
[4] McKay, p.45.
[5] McKay, p.22.
[6] McKay, p.38.
[7] McKay, pp.9. 11, 21, 56.
[8] McKay, pp.28, 59.
[9] McKay, p.91.
[10] McKay, p.64.
[11] McKay, pp.1, 2.
[12] McKay, pp.51–3.
[13] McKay, pp.57, 38.
[14] McKay, p.84.
[15] McKay, p.28; Beattie, p.30.
[16] TA CSO1/1/134/3227, CSO1/1/307/3999.
[17] TA PRO CO201/330 332, NS14/1/1, NS14/2/1.
[18] For example TA CSO1/1/43/759 Bisdee, CSO1/1/163/388 Ashburner, CSO1/1/147/3614 Allison, CSO1/1/164/3930 McNab.
[19] McKay, pp.56, 28–9, 88, 12, 22–3.
[20] McKay, p.10.
[21] McKay, p.20.
[22] McKay, p.51.
[23] McKay, pp.90, 23, 27.
[24] McKay, pp.91, 86.
[25] McKay, pp.86, 85.
[26] McKay, p.86.
[27] McKay, p.86.
[28] Alexander, *Connorville*, passim.

17. Churches bring new opportunities

[1] Robert Mather, 'Mather, Robert', *ADB*; Donald Colgrave, 'Carvosso, Benjamin', *ADB*.
[3] *HTG* 18/8/1821, 15/9/1921, 6/10/1821, 25/5/1822, 22/6/1822, 14/9/1822, 31/5/1823, 25/10/1823.
[4] Colgrave; Melville *Almanac 1831*, p.226–7; Alexander, *Companion*, p.234.
[5] Backhouse, *Narrative*, p.138.

[6] Alexander, *Companion* p.289; Ross *Almanac 1831* p.xi; *HTG* 11/1/1823.
[7] TA NS477/1/1.
[8] John West, *The Hope of Life eternal*, Hobart, 1847, pp.63–4; Bonwick, p.11.
[9] *Tasmanian* 15, 22/10/1830; West, *Hope*, p.68.
[10] Beattie, p.38; Linda Monks, 'Conolly, Philip', *ADB*.
[11] Beattie, p.39.
[12] *CT* 18/5/1827, 18/11/1825; 'Bedford, William', *ADB*.
[13] Beattie, pp.40–1.
[14] TA CON40/1/5 290, CON40/1/5 302; Beattie, p.41.
[15] Ross, p.xi; The Bible, Old Testament: Ezekiel 18: 27; Prinsep, p.63.
[16] HRA 3, 4, pp.233–5; 'The story of Fr Samuel Coote', https://www.carmelites.org.au/item/50-carmelite-in-van-diemens-land viewed 23/11/20224
[17] Crawford, p.2.

18. Governor Arthur

[1] Bigge Reports 1, 2, 3, passim.
[2] *Mercury*, 19/9/1879.
[3] HRA 3, 4, pp.134–54, 364.
[4] Prinsep, pp.55–6.
[5] HRA 3, 8, p.xxi.
[6] HRA 3, 8, p.305; 3, 9, p.444.
[7] HRA 3,8, p.xxvii.
[8] HRA, 3, 9, p.439; 3, 8, p.404; 3, 7, p.448; Prinsep, p.63.
[9] HRA 3, 5, pp.46–7; 3, 4, p.208
[10] HRA 3, 6, pp.43–4; 3, 5, p.46.
[11] HRA 3, 5, p.578.
[12] TA CSO1/1/185/4451.
[13] HRA 3, 8, p.65; 3, 9, p.161.
[14] HRA 3, 8, p.58; TA CSO1/1/ 167/3999; TA CSO1/1/462/10236.
[15] TA CSO1/1/518/11283, CSO1/1/537/11685.
[16] Connorville archives, Burgh to O'Connor, 20/8/1825, box 24/1, folder 'Correspondence'; Alexander, *Connorville*, pp.20.
[17] HRA, 3, 10, p.851.
[18] HRA 3, 9, p.558; TA CSO1/1/ 315/7539.
[19] HRA 3, 9, pp.443–4.
[20] Chapman, p.376.
[21] HRA 3, 26 p.192; 3, 6, p.152.
[22] HRA, 3, 6, pp.140–2, 186, 345.

[23] HRA 3, 10, pp.52, 389.

[24] HRA 3, 10, p.441; HRA 3, 9, pp.97, 99, 436–7, 660; J.R. Morris, 'Woods, Roger Henry', *ADB*.

[25] HRA 3, 4, pp.152, 204–5, 220, 230, 285, 358–9; 3, 5, pp.20, 49–51; P.R. Eldershaw, 'Bromley, Edward Foord', *ADB*.

[26] HRA 3, 4, p.222.

[27] A.K. Weatherburn, 'Evans, George William', *ADB*; HRA 3, 4, p.315; 3, 5, pp.46–7, 534; 3, p.130.

[28] TA CSO1/1/158/3790;

[29] E.g. TA CSO1/1/68/1414.

[30] HRA 3, 4, pp.367, 371–4; 3, 5, p.53–5, 129, 288, 296, 456.

[31] HRA 3, 6, p.44.

[32] HRA 3, 9, p.437; 3, 8, p.634.

[33] HRA, 3, 5, p.588.

[34] HRA 3, 5, pp.328, 586.

[35] HRA 3, 6, p.329.

[36] Utas eprints, Charles Arthur letters, 2/4/1829, 10/7/1829.

[37] Savery, p.175; F.C. Green, 'Gregson, Thomas George', *ADB*.

[38]. *Tasmanian* 21, 28/5/1831.

[39] *Tasmanian* 11, 18/10/1827; *CT* 15/5/1825; Chapman p.406.

[40] HRA 3, 10, p.1078; TA RGD32/1/1/4000.

[41] *Tasmanian* 1, 8/11/1827; Widowson, p.31.

[42] A.G.L. Shaw, 'Arthur, George', *ADB*.

[43] Prinsep, p.106.

[44] HRA 3, 10, pp.lxiii, 729, 731.

[45] HRA 3, 6, p.243.

19. The Black War with the Aboriginal people

[1] Clements, pp.xiv, 1.

[2] Clements, pp.15–17.

[3] Clements, p.24, *HTG* 16/7/1824.

[4] Clements, p.43.

[5] Clements, pp.44–5.

[6] *HTC* 23/1/1830.

[7] *Tasmanian* 19/2/1830.

[8] Clements, p.44; *Tasmanian*, 26/2/1830.

[9] Clements, pp.45–8.

[10] Clements, pp.50–3, 56–8; Henry Reynolds, email to the author, 17/10/2024.

[11] Clements, p.49.
[12] Clements, p.110.
[13] Clements, pp. 59–64.
[14] Clements, pp.80–90.
[15] Clements, pp.94–6.
[16] Clements, pp.101–2.
[17] Clements, pp.110–12.
[18] Clements, pp.114–18.
[19] Clements pp.118–24.
[20] HRA 3, 9, p.xl.
[21] HRA 3, 9, 573–4.
[22] Clements, pp.125–9.
[23] Clements, pp.130–6, 142–3.
[24] Clements, pp.137–9.
[25] Clements, pp.138–44.
[26] Clements, pp.144–56.
[27] Clements, p.207.
[28] Clements, p.168.
[29] HRA 3, 9, p.lxiii, 3, 10, p.lxiii.

MAJOR CHARACTERS

Edward Abbott (arrived 1815), deputy judge advocate
Charles Arthur (arrived 1824), free settler, nephew of Governor Arthur
Lt-Gov George Arthur (1824–36), army officer, excellent governor: sent to enforce law and order in the colony and did so, despite strident opposition
Lord Bathurst, secretary of state for war and the colonies 1812–27, based in London. In charge of Van Diemen's Land
Major Thomas Bell (1818–24), in command of the troops, convicts, and building roads and bridges
Commissioner John Bigge, sent by the British Government to look into the colony; in VDL 1820. His report influenced future development.
Alice Blackstone (arrived 1818), convict, punished by having to wear the iron collar
James Bonwick (arrived 1841), teacher, historian
George Boyes (arrived 1826), official, auditor of civil accounts, wrote diary and letters
Lt-Gov John Brabyn (1808–10 in the north), army officer, competent and honest
Edward Bromley (arrived 1820), naval doctor, treasurer, embezzler
William Broughton (1816–17), sent by Macquarie to organise the VDL commissary: defeated by Edward Lord
Commandant Gilbert Cimitiere (1818–22), army officer, competent commandant at Port Dalrymple
Lt-Gov David Collins (1804–10 in the south), marine officer, established the colony, honest but weak, allowing rampant corruption by others
Edward Curr (arrived 1820), settler, Van Diemen's Land Company manager, wrote description of the colony (1823)
Lt-Gov Thomas Davey (1813–17), army officer, abysmal governor: alcoholic and incompetent
John Philip Deane (arrived 1822), free settler, musician and teacher
John Drummond (arrived 1815), scandalous naval officer
Richard Dry (arrived 1807 in the north), convict, commissary and settler
George Evans (arrived 1812), surveyor, corrupt. Wrote a description of the colony (1822).

John Pascoe Fawkner (arrived 1804), son of convict, later helped found Melbourne. Wrote memoirs.

Elizabeth Fenton (arrived 1829), free settler, farmed at Gretna, wrote description of her time in the colony

Leonard Fosbrook (arrived 1804), official, commissary, corrupt, tried and dismissed 1814

Lt-Gov Andrew Geils (1812–13), army officer, poor governor: more interested in amassing wealth than governing

Joseph Gellibrand (arrived 1824) free settler, lawyer, briefly attorney-general, opponent of Arthur

James Gordon (arrived 1814), naval officer, magistrate, settler

Lt-Gov G.A. Gordon (1810–12), army officer, commandant at Port Dalrymple, gullible

Thomas Gregson (arrived 1821), free settler, farmed Jericho and Risdon, opponent of Arthur

George Harris (arrived 1804), official, surveyor, wrote letters describing the colony, died 1810

Peter Harrison (arrived 1822), free settler, wrote back to England describing the colony

Lord Harrowby, in Britain, powerful patron of Governor Davey

John Headlam (arrived 1820), free settler, teacher and innkeeper

Dr John Hudspeth (arrived 1822), free settler and doctor, farmed at Jericho

George Hull (arrived 1819), army officer, commissary. His son **Hugh** wrote memoirs.

Adolarius Humphrey (arrived 1804), official, mineralogist, settler and chief of police in Hobart

Patrick Hogan (arrived 1813), commissary, alcoholic and embezzler

Henry and Sarah Hopkins (arrived 1822), free settlers, merchant, established the Congregational Church

Michael Howe (arrived 1812), convict and bushranger, executed

Charles Jeffreys (arrived 1814), naval officer, smuggler, later settler. Author of a description of the colony.

Anthony Fenn Kemp (arrived 1804), army officer turned settler, agitator, opposed Arthur

Thomas Keston or Kenton (arrived 1808), free settler, servant, farmer, wrote memoirs

Rev. Robert Knopwood (arrived 1804), clergyman, kept diary.

George Lloyd (arrived 1819), free settler, nephew of Charles Jeffreys. Later moved to Victoria and wrote a description of both colonies

David Lord (arrived 1817), son of successful convict, gained a large amount of land by chicanery. No relation of Edward Lord

Edward Lord (arrived 1804), marines officer and settler. Became the richest man in the colony through corruption and skullduggery, and the acumen of his ex-convict wife Maria. Their story is told in my book *Corruption and Skullduggery: Edward Lord, Maria Riseley and Hobart's tempestuous beginnings.*

Joseph Lycett (arrived in Sydney in 1814), never in VDL but painted idealised scenes, published in 1825

Dr Edward Luttrell (arrived 1816), doctor, criticised as inept and negligent

Commandant John McKenzie (arrived 1814 in the north), army officer in charge of Port Dalrymple, abetted bushranger Mills

Governor Lachlan Macquarie (1810–22), VDL governors' superior in Sydney who tried, mostly in vain, to order them to rule responsibly. His wife **Elizabeth** was interested in women's activities.

Thomas Massey (arrived 1804 in the north), convict, chief constable

Robert Mather (arrived 1822), free settler and merchant, Methodist

Peter Murdoch (arrived 1825), government official, settler, Land Commissioner with O'Connor

William Maum (arrived 1808), convict, commissariat clerk, settler: corrupt

George Meredith, (arrived 1821), free settler, amassed a large property using skullduggery, opposed Arthur

Peter Mills (arrived 1807), commissary, turned bushranger

Dr Jacob Mountgarrett (arrived Risdon 1803), official, later settler, corrupt

Lt-Gov John Murray (1810–11 in the south), army officer, poor governor, drunkard

Roderic O'Connor (arrived 1824), free settler; as land commissioner wrote forthright report on colony's land use

Lt-Gov Paterson (1804–09 in the north), army officer: established the colony, honest but weak

Alexander Pearce (arrived 1820), convict and cannibal, executed

Thomas and Ann Peters (arrived 1804), convict and wife who prospered

James Pillinger (arrived 1808), ex-convict Norfolk Islander, subsistence farmer. His son **James** gained a grant and prospered

Hannah and Matthew Power (arrived 1804), convict and his wife. Hannah lived with Governor Collins until 1808 when the pair returned to England with their pickings

Augustus and Elizabeth Prinsep (arrived 1829), visitors. Elizabeth published letters by either Augustus or herself, describing the colony.

James Ross (arrived 1822), free settler, teacher, newspaper editor

Lt-Gov William Sorell (1817–24), army officer, reasonable governor: competent but implicated in corruption, living with Louisa Kent to whom he was not married

Commandant James Stewart (1815–18 in the north), army officer in charge of Port Dalrymple

James Sutherland (arrived 1823), free settler near Campbell Town, kept a diary

John Wade (arrived 1804), convict, settler, chief constable

John Wedge (arrived 1824), surveyor, kept a diary.

Rev. John West (arrived 1838), Congregational minister, historian

Henry Widowson (arrived 1826), failed settler, returned to England, wrote a book about the colony

William Williamson (arrived 1820), free settler, embezzled money in England, unsuccessful lawyer in the colony

Rev. John Youl (arrived 1818), clergyman in Launceston

SELECT BIBLIOGRAPHY

Books and articles

[Edward Abbott], *The Colonial Cookery Book for the many as well as for the 'upper ten thousand' by an Australian aristologist*, facsimile reprint Dee Why, 1974

Alison Alexander (ed.), *The Companion to Tasmanian history*, Hobart, 2004

Alison Alexander, *The O'Connors of Connorville*, Hobart, 2017

Lucille Andell, *Clerk of the House: the reminiscences of Hugh Munro Hull*, Melbourne, 1984

Colleen Arulappu, *I wood sent you my hart if I could*, Melbourne, 2006

James Backhouse, *Narrative of a visit to the Australian Colonies*, London, 1843

J.W. Beattie, *Glimpses of the lives and times of the early Tasmanian governors*, Hobart, 1905

John Bigge, *Third report [into Agriculture and Trade]* https://digital.sl.nsw.gov.au/delivery/DeliveryManagerServlet?embedded=true&toolbar=false&dps_pid=IE3732195

James Bonwick *The Bushrangers*, Hobart, 1856

Rutherford Browne, *From convict to chief constable: the story of Thomas Massey and the first 50 years of Launceston*, Sapphire Beach, 2018

Geoffrey Burkhardt, 'Convict and emancipist teachers New South Wales, 1789–1830', https://dehanz.net.au/entries/convict-emancipist-teachers/

Peter Chapman (ed.), *The diaries and letters of G.T.W.B. Boyes*, Melbourne, 1985

Nicholas Clements, *The Black War: fear, sex and resistance in Tasmania*, St Lucia, Queensland, 2019

Robert Cox, *A compulsion to Kill*, Carindale, 2014

Ewan Crawford (ed.) *The diaries of John Helder Wedge 18242–1835*, Hobart, 1962

Edward Curr *An account of the colony of Van Diemen's Land*, London, 1824

John Earnshaw (ed.), 'Select letters of James Grove', THRAPP 8/2, 1959

George William Evans, *A geographical, historical and topographical description of Van Diemen's Land*, London, 1822

John Pascoe Fawkner, 'Reminiscences of John Pascoe Fawkner', La Trobe Library, typescript copy in the possession of the author

Elizabeth Fenton, *Mrs Fenton's Journal*, Adelaide, 1986

Madonna Grehan, ''Midwifery paid': James Murdoch MD', THRAPP 71/3, 2024

Barbara Hamilton-Arnold (ed.), *Letters of G.P. Harris 1803–1812*, Sorrento, 1994

Max Hartwell, *The economic development of Van Diemen's Land*, Melbourne, 1854

Joseph Holt, *Memoirs of Joseph Holt*, volume II, London, 1838

Ken Hose, 'Water Supply & Sewerage for Launceston', https://www.launcestonhistory.org.au/wp-content/uploads/2016/11/Ken-Hose-Water-Sewerage.pdf viewed 20/7/2024

Adolarius Humphrey (ed. John Currey), *A voyage to Port Phillip and Van Diemen's Land*, Malvern, 2011

Charles Jeffreys, *Geographic and Descriptive Delineations of the Island of Van Diemen's Land*, London 1820

G.T. Lloyd *Thirty-three years in Tasmania and Victoria*, London, 1862

Lachlan Macquarie, *Journal of a Voyage ad Tour of Inspection to Van Diemen's Land 1821*, https://www.mq.edu.au/macquarie-archive/lema/1821/1821may.html viewed 4/7/2024

Anne McKay (ed.), *Journals of the Land Commissioners*, Hobart, 1962

Thelma Mackay, Index to early land grants

Henry Melville, *Van Diemen's Land Annual*, Hobart, 1831

Mary Nicholls, *The diaries of the Reverend Robert Knopwood*, Hobart, 1977

Shannon O'Keefe, Matthew Allen, Hamish Maxwell-Stewart, and Michael Quinlan, 'Alcohol, work and play in convict Australia', *Labour History* 127, 2024, pp.145–69.

Roy Porter, *Blood & Guts: a short history of medicine*, Melbourne, 2003

Augustus Prinsep, *Journal of a voyage from Calcutta to Van Diemen's Land*, London, 1833

Henry Reynolds and Nicholas Clements, *Tongerlongeter*, Sydney, 2022

Jack Richards, *Fifteen Tasmanian letters*, Christchurch New Zealand, 1955

J.D. Ritchie, *Punishment and profit: the reports of Commissioner John Bigge*, Melbourne, 1970

James Ross, *The Van Diemen's Land annual*, Hobart, 1830

Henry Savery, *The hermit in Van Diemen's Land*, St Lucia, 1964

Jane Sorell, *Governor, William and Julia Sorell*, Hobart, 1986

Dan Sprod, *Alexander Pearce of Macquarie Harbour*, Launceston, 1977

Karl von Stieglitz, *Longford past and present*, Launceston, 1947

Alexander Stone, 'The story of Thomas & Ann Stone', https://www.orphanschool.org.au/downloads/THE_STORY_OF_THOMAS_and_ANN_STONE_The_Ki.pdf

Marjorie Tipping *Convicts Unbound*, Melbourne, 1988

Peter Benson Walker *All that we inherit*, Hobart, 1968

W.C. Wentworth, *Statistical, historical, and political description of The Colony of New South Wales, and ... Van Diemen's Land*, London, 1819

John West, *History of Tasmania*, vols 1 and 2, Launceston, 1852

Henry Widowson, *Present state of van Diemen's Land*, London, 1829

Websites

Australian Dictionary of Biography: https://adb.anu.eseptedu.au/
Old Bailey Online: https://www.oldbaileyonline.org/
Female Convicts Research Centre database: https://femaleconvicts.org.au/
Historical Records of Australia: https://nla.gov.au/nla.obj-442186184
Hobart Town First Settlers: https://htfs.org.au/settlers1804.php
Colonial Secretary's Papers: Index (NSW): https://colsec.records.nsw.gov.au/

Newspapers

Australian: *Austral-Asiatic Review, Colonial Advocate, Colonial Times, Colonist, Cornwall Chronicle, Derwent Star, Hobart Town Gazette, Hobart Town Courier, Launceston Advertiser, Sydney Gazette, Tasmanian, Tasmanian and Port Dalrymple Advertiser, True Colonist, Van Diemen's Land Gazette*
British: *Caledonian Mercury, Morning Post, The Times*

Tasmanian Archives

NS14/1/1, 14/2/1 Williamson letters
NS381 Samuel Guy to his brother
NS395/1/1 diary of Thomas Keston
LSD354 land grants
NS61/1/1, NS 61/1/2 Diary of James Sutherland

University of Tasmania Special and Rare Collection

RS2/2(8), Journal of John Maule Hudspeth https://eprints.utas.edu.au/3243/1/RS_2_2%288%29.pdf
RS8-F8-5, Letters of Ann Weston
RS8.B12(1), Letters of Charles Arthur
RS47, Peter Harrisson, 'Memorandum of a voyage to Van Dieman's Land 1822', https://eprints.utas.edu.au/view/authors/Harrisson=3APeter=3A=3A.html

State Library of Victoria

Diary and notes of John Pascoe Fawkner F Box 4606/2
Papers of John Pascoe Fawkner, 1832-1871, MS Safe 3

INDEX

Abbott, Judge Edward 89, 92, 153, 278
Aboriginal Committee 248
Aboriginal people iv, 2–3, 6, 37, 40, 62, 73–8, 93–4, 96, 124, 131, 137, 140, 145, 165, 175, 185, 187, 189, 192–3, 212, 243–56
    Black War 246–54
Agriculture *see* Farming
Alcohol 33–4, 56, 103, 115, 120, 122, 128, 166, 187, 192, 205, 218 *and see* Drunkenness
Alcoholics 2, 33, 55–6, 126, 134, 164, 166, 181, 200, 238, 278–9
Allen, Steve 257
Allport, Mary Morton 47, 108–9, 142
America 6, 175
Amos family 202
Anglesea Barracks 46
Ankers, Fanny and Daniel 45, 47
Anstey, Thomas and family 173, 178
Anti-social personality disorder 28
Archer family 16, 60, 201–2, 215
Archer, John Lee 238
Army Museum of Tasmania 257
Arnold, Dr Joseph 122–3
Arthur, Charles 140–1, 144, 155–6, 241, 278
Arthur, Eliza 228, 244–5
Arthur, Lt-Gov. George 2, 128, 149, 155–6, 165, 168, 173–6, 184, 195, 197–8, 203, 209, 214, 218, 222–6, 228–45, 250–6, 277, 279–80
    children 136–7
    popularity 242
Arthur, Henry 241
Art 143

Ashburner family 172, 247
Ashton, Mary Anne 166
Athletic races 149–50
Atkins, William 203
Atkinson, Charles 146
Austen, Jane 9, 26, 62, 64, 67, 157, 160
Auxiliary Bible Society 96, 158
Ayers, Mr 115–16

Back River 132
Backhouse, James 137, 223
Badley, Eliza 175
Bagdad 76, 89, 96, 169, 197, 249
Baker family 126
Balfour, Colonel and family 126–7, 238
Ballance, James and Hannah 168–70
Balls (dancing) 53, 56, 137–9, 151, 154, 160, 163
Bamber, Miss 134
Bands (musical) 138–9, 147
Bank of Van Diemen's Land 143, 205
Banks 25, 91, 205, 214, 243
Baptists 224
Barclay, Captain Andrew and family 92, 164
Bass Strait islands 25, 77, 254
Bathurst, Lord 59, 66, 71–2, 81, 88–9, 92, 188, 235, 240, 278
Batt, John 26
Baudin expedition 75–6
Beamont, John 91–2
Beattie, John 214, 224–5
Bedford, Rev. William 224–6, 237
Beenac 76–7
Bell, John 202
Bell system of education 131

285

Bell, Major Thomas 67–8, 84–8, 189, 212
Bennett, Joseph 161
Bethune, Walter 236, 241
Bevan (bushranger) 198
Bigge, Commissioner John 24, 33, 71–2, 76, 79–96, 102, 128–30, 218, 226, 228, 235, 255, 278
Bignell, Mary 126
Binfield, Elinor 135–6
Bisdee family 16, 201, 234
Black Brush 108, 131
Black Line 251–3
Black Snake Inn 86
Black War 246–54
Blackstone, Alice 88, 180, 278
Blackwood, John 257
Boat racing 145–7, 149
Bock, Thomas 48, 69, 130, 143, 167, 179
Bonwick, James 38, 278
Boothman, John 44, 90
Boston, William 126
Bothwell 111, 128, 194, 200, 223, 248, 250
Bowden, Matthew 45
Bowen, Henrietta 115
Bowen, Lt-Gov. John 36, 174
Bowsden 191
Boxing 148–9
Boyes, George 102, 119, 125, 136, 143, 154–5, 163, 165, 237, 278
Brabyn, Captain John 48–50, 61, 278
Bradstreet, Richard 95–6
Brady, Matthew 237
Brighton 157, 165
Briscoe, Benjamin and family 161
British Empire 6–8, 41, 46, 62, 233, 255
British Government 3, 9, 12, 26, 41, 44, 48, 61–2, 67, 71, 73, 78, 131, 184, 188, 198, 202, 205, 209, 228, 231, 233, 235–7, 242, 251, 255–6 *and see* London
Broadmarsh 198, 202
Broadribb, William and Hannah 170
Bromley, Dr Edward 70, 239, 241, 278
Broughton, Bartholomew 239
Broughton, William 59–60, 278
Brown, John (bushranger) 36–7
Browne, Rev. W.H. 140
Brown's River *see* Kingston
Bruny Island 93, 189
Bryant, Dr 119–22
Bryant, James
Buckley, Mary 149
Buist, Arthur and Christian 199–201
Burbury family 201
Burnett, John 238, 242
Bushrangers 3, 11, 18–19, 22, 27, 34, 36–40, 49, 55–7, 61, 67, 69, 72, 77, 89, 92, 96, 110, 122, 124, 136, 140, 144, 168, 193, 198, 200, 228, 233, 238, 243, 255
Bushwalking 155

Campbell Town 127–8, 132, 166, 195, 200–1, 203, 223
Canada 160
Cannibalism 3, 39–40, 280
Carvosso, Rev. Benjamin 157, 161, 221–3
'Catherine, Fat' 145
Cato family 72
Cawthorne family 176–7
Chambers, William 197
Chaplin, Edward 202
Chapman, Andrew 257
Chapman, T.E. iv–v
Childbirth 117–18, 126–8
deaths in 126–8

Chorley, Mr and Mrs 134
Christmas celebrations 147, 149, 153
Churches 2, 9–10, 26, 54, 81, 94, 138,
    151, 153, 184, 221–9, 230, 237
    Anglican 9–10, 53, 71, 82, 90, 221, 223–6
    Baptist 224
    Catholic 136, 223–4, 226
    Congregational 223, 226, 279
    Quakers 50, 223, 224
    Presbyterian 133, 223, 226
    Wesleyan (Methodist) 132–3, 140, 157, 221–3
Church buildings
    St Andrew's, Hobart 223
    Sr David's, Hobart 87, 138
St John's Launceston 140
Cimitiere, Major Gilbert 61, 70–1, 88, 278
Civil (public) service 161, 228–9, 231, 238–9
Claiborne, Rev. Richard 136
Claremont 13, 18, 22
Clarence Plains 20, 110, 129, 163, 203
Clark, Hannah and George 135–6
Clark, Mary Ann 170
Clarke, Marcus 40, 158
Clements, Nicholas 78, 246, 248, 257
Climate 1, 92, 112, 115, 120, 159, 185, 217
Clothing 104–07, 154
Clyde River 188, 197
Coaching service 110
Cockfighting 149
Collins, Lt-Gov. David 8–9, 13–16, 19, 29, 35, 43–4, 50, 54, 56, 66, 75, 77, 89, 96, 115, 123, 137, 159–60, 165, 174, 178, 278
Con, Rum John 202
Congregational church 223, 226, 279

Conolly, Rev. Philip 224, 226
Contraception 128
Convict Department 239
Convicts and ex-convicts 2–3, 6–8, 27, 77–8, 83–4, 104, 140, 184–5, 212, 222–4, 228, 249, 256
    and crime 26–41, 49, 77, 81–2, 87, 149, 159, 177–8, 213, 230, 236–7, 243, 255
    as workers 12, 17–8, 29, 46, 87, 101, 122, 130–1, 158, 160, 173, 190–3, 199, 201, 239–41, 252
    children of convicts 2, 23, 88, 95, 129, 132, 165, 186–7, 239
    female 88, 92, 123, 149, 166–8, 178–81, 223–6, 232–3
    'gentlemen' 159
    in the community 11, 26, 32, 83–5, 89, 95–6, 102, 139–41, 149, 157, 159–60, 164–5, 212, 226, 236, 246
    individuals 2, 18, 26, 29, 43, 55, 59, 70, 89, 95–6, 103, 129, 140, 143, 150, 157, 161, 169–70, 196, 198, 202, 278–81
    land grants to 12–15, 19, 21–3, 94, 181, 186–203
    number 7, 9, 21, 78, 85, 158, 230
    reform of 82, 87–88, 90, 222, 233, 237
    stigma 3, 85, 125, 132, 139, 141, 158, 162–4, 256
    system 70, 85–9, 94, 229, 231–3, 243, 278
Cooking 101, 103–4, 154, 178
Coote, Rev. Samuel 226
Cornwall Collegiate Institute 136
Corruption 10, 43, 59, 81, 67–9, 71, 84, 86, 90, 93, 161, 190, 194, 203, 209, 215–8, 229, 231, 233, 278–81

Costantini, Charles 143
Court system 28-9, 31, 48, 60, 81, 90, 94, 169-70, 177, 181, 225, 230, 243
 cases heard in Sydney 28, 30-1, 36, 46-7, 49, 60, 70, 89
Cox, James 70, 136, 165
Cox, Mrs 127
Crahan family 31
Cricket 144, 147
Crime 3, 11, 17, 26-40, 95, 158-9, 161, 178, 198, 213, 228, 230, 233, 243, 255, 287 *and see* Convicts – crime, Theft
theory of 6, 256
Crowther, Dr William 117
Curr, Edward 21, 194, 278
Currency 25, 33, 91, 205

Dancing 133, 136-8, 147 *and see* Balls
Darling, Gov. Ralph 67
Davey, Lt-Gov. Thomas 22, 33, 37, 39, 51-62, 64, 84, 89-90, 93, 108, 150, 159, 228, 231, 237, 242, 278-9
 Margaret and Lucy 51-2, 53, 56, 160
Davice, Hannah 135 *and see* Clark George and Hannah
Dawes, Caroline 134, 164
De Burgh, Thomas 236-7
De Sainson, Louis 172
Deane, John Philip 138-40, 278
Deaths, causes of 124-8, 166, 215-6
Debating society 140-1
Dent, John 257
Derwent River 8, 22, 47, 58, 145-6, 186
Divorce 176
Dixon, Captain 35-6
Dixon, Joseph 196
Doctors' activities 59, 112-28, 177, 189

Domestic service 173, 178, 233
Domestic violence 168-71
Drowning 49, 124, 126, 144-5, 161, 216
Drummond family 69-70, 278
Drunkenness 17, 24, 28, 32-3, 41-2, 55-6, 59, 61, 72, 84, 87, 89, 91, 94-5, 117, 121, 126, 128-30, 132, 144, 149, 160, 166, 168-71, 178, 180, 198, 200, 211, 216-8, 231, 236, 243-4, 280
Dry, Richard (senior) and Ann 49, 122, 174, 278
Dry, William 137
Duels 141, 196, 241
Duffield, John and Lucy 170
Dumaresq, Edward 209

Earl, John 29
Easter celebrations 147, 153
Economy, colonial 91, 94, 185, 230, 242-3
Eddington, Eliza 165
Education 10, 94, 129-37
Elite 7, 9, 41-3, 48, 53-4, 56, 61-2, 95, 159, 163, 175, 189, 239, 255
Ellinthorpe Hall 135-6, 139
Engineers, lack of 238
Epping 38
Escapees, convict 35-6, 40, 49, 88-9
Escott, Ros 257
Evans, George 29, 59, 68-9, 83, 92-3, 143, 158, 176, 184-5, 190, 239-40, 278
Everett Jim 257
Executions 30-1, 37, 40, 70, 124-5, 178, 238, 279-80

Farming 2, 9, 12-25, 27, 31, 61, 82, 91-5, 173-4, 185-7, 189-95, 197-9, 201-4, 209-12, 215-8
 machinery 194

Fawkner, Elizabeth 18, 174
Fawkner, John and Hannah 13, 18, 20, 33, 106, 174
Fawkner, John Pascoe (son) 18–20, 30, 33–4, 37–9, 55, 102, 107, 140, 279
Female Convicts Research Centre 257
Female Factories 173, 233
    Cascades 123, 171, 225–6
Fenton, Elizabeth, Michael and Flora 109, 120–1, 161–2, 165, 172, 278
Fenton Forest 162
Feutrill, Captain 38
Field, William 213
Fishing 100, 106, 155, 165, 232
Fitzgerald, Thomas and Mary 129, 134
Fletcher, Thomas 210
Flinders Island 2, 253 *and see* Bass Strait islands
Foley, John 15–16
Food 100–04, 116, 128, 153–4
Foot races 149–50
For the term of his natural life 40, 158
Fosbrook, Leonard 8, 44–7, 60, 278
Foveaux, Joseph 54–5
Franklin, Jane 56
Frankland, George 230, 238, 240, 247
Free settlers 2, 6–7, 9–10, 12, 21, 83, 93, 157, 184–206, 230–2, 256
French, explorers 6, 73–5
Frogmore 32
Frost, Mrs James 21
Furniture 109–10, 214, 234

Gambling 34, 45, 85, 87, 89, 144, 146, 148–51, 153–5, 159, 165, 181, 242
Gardens 28–9, 102, 108–9, 120, 154–5, 157, 191, 211
Garrett, Rev. James 242
Gatehouse, George 89

Gatenby family 211–2
Geason, Susan 257
Geils, Andrew and family 45–7, 150, 160, 279
Gellibrand, Joseph 239–41, 279
George IV (Prince Regent) 64–7, 71–2, 235
George Town 70, 87–8
Germaine, Hugh 76
Gibson family 16, 201
Gleason, Susan 257
Glenorchy 107, 132
Glover, John 27, 142–3
Goitre 128
Gordon, James 35, 88, 279
Gordon, Major 48–9, 279
Gould, William Buelow 143
Goulder family 125
Governesses 137
Grant family (Ballochmyle) 122
Great Swanport 128
Grene, Kevin 257
Gregson, Thomas and Elizabeth 127, 191–2, 201, 222, 240–2, 279
Gretna 120, 279
Gribble, Nicholas 197
Grimstone, Mary 140
Grove, James 43
Guest, Edward 15
Guy, Samuel 21

Hammant, Thomas 236–7
Hammond, Eliza, John and family 121–2, 235–6, 241
Hammond, Mary 124
Hanigan, Catherine 170–1
Harris, George and Ann 8–11, 18–20, 28–9, 43, 50, 58, 115, 119, 140, 143, 160, 279

Harrisson, Peter 24, 103, 109, 185, 188, 190, 279
Harrowby, Lord (Ryder, Dudley) 53–4, 59, 93, 279
Harwood, Mary 257
Hayes, Henry and Thomas and families 9, 89, 96, 157, 159, 171, 174
Headlam, John and family 128, 132–4, 137, 200–1
Health 112–28
Henderson, Dr 141
Henderson, Lieut 43
Historical Records of Australia 76, 82
Hobart Rivulet 123
Hobart 1, 3, 6, 8, 13, 15, 29, 34–5, 46, 54, 58, 68, 75, 83, 109, 116–7, 123–4, 129–30, 132–4, 138–40, 143–5, 147–50, 153, 156, 158, 173, 189–90, 196, 205, 213, 217, 222, 224, 228, 243, 248, 254
Hobart Town Gazette 29–31, 33–4, 108, 115, 168, 246
Hobbs, Jane and family 9–10
Hobson, Mr 134
Hogan, Patrick 59–60, 90, 244, 279
Holdship, Captain William 199–200
Holsgrove, William 38
Holt, Joseph 19, 171
Hood, Dr Samuel 115, 233, 235
Hope and Anchor pub 63
Hopkins, Henry and Sarah 113, 161, 194–5, 203–5, 223, 226, 237, 242
Hopley, Lieutenant 29
Horse racing 144, 150–3, 159, 242
Horton, Rev. William 221
Hospitals 54, 116–18, 124, 128–9, 169
Housing 107–10
Howe, Michael 38, 56–7, 140, 279
Hudspeth, John and Mary 31, 68, 102, 117–18, 127–8, 158, 189–90, 192–3, 195, 237, 240, 279
Hull, Hugh 106, 118–19, 125, 134–5, 155, 197–8, 279
Hull, George 68, 70, 83, 86, 94, 106, 238–9, 279
Huon River 88
Humphrey, Adolarius and Harriet 27, 68, 73, 82, 84, 87–8, 93, 104, 124, 160, 211, 279
Hunting
for meat 73, 75–7, 100, 144, 192, 246
for sport 144, 155, 165

Infanticide 70
Ingle, John and Rebecca 10, 157
Immorality/morality 9–10, 26, 34, 45, 61, 64–72, 79, 81, 84, 88, 90, 92, 94, 129, 149, 160, 168–70, 178, 209–11, 224–5, 227–9, 236–7, 243
Ireland/Irish 19, 39, 169, 209
Iron collar 88, 180, 278

James, Mary 168
Jeffreys, Lieutenant Charles 32, 68, 76, 101, 105, 107, 173, 184–5, 193, 199, 221, 279–80
Jemott, William 30
Jericho 31, 38, 117, 128, 173, 189–91
Jews 148, 171, 224
Johns, Phillis 224–5
Johnson, John 203
Johnson, Joseph 202
Jones, David 33
Judge, Bridget 181
Justice system 60, 89–90, 241, 251 *and see* Court system

Kangaroo Point 29, 145–7
Keane, Matthew 196
Kearney, Catherine 102, 172
Keating, James 30
Kelly, Captain James 88, 93, 205
Kemp, Anthony and family 48, 71, 79, 84, 156, 240–2, 244, 279
Kempton 202
Kent, Louisa 64–7, 71–2, 79, 92, 281
Kent, William 64, 66, 71
Keston/Kenton, Thomas 15–19, 42–5, 49, 55, 66, 68, 71, 149, 237, 257, 279
Kimberley, Edward 87, 93
King, Gov. P.G. 78
Kingston 17–18, 196
'Kit, Carrotty' 145, 172
Knopwood, Rev. Robert 29, 50, 88–9, 92, 127–8, 134, 139, 146, 153, 159, 177, 280
    as clergyman 9, 76, 90, 115–6, 130, 157, 221–4
    diary 28, 35–6, 43–4, 53, 64, 82, 100, 102–3, 147, 150, 157, 160–1, 163
    health 119–20

Land Board 189, 202–3
Land Commissioners 17, 203, 209–18, 229, 231, 280
Land grants 2, 13–15, 21–3, 61, 69–70, 78, 94, 172–5, 177, 186–78, 196, 206–8, 216
    dishonesty in gaining 1, 63, 69, 92, 213–5, 228, 231, 233–6
    farming on 16–22, 93, 157, 195–201
    individual grantees 17, 20, 31–2, 69–71, 120, 175, 181, 196–7. 204
    system of granting 188–9, 235–6

Lansdell, Harriet and family 173–4
Launceston 8, 10, 34–5, 49, 60, 70, 87–8, 91–2, 109–11, 114, 116, 123, 129, 132–3, 136, 139–40, 143, 145, 147–51, 156, 164, 174, 194, 196, 198, 204, 222, 238 *and see* Port Dalrymple
Lawrence, Robert 252
Lawrence, William Effingham 196
Leake family 201, 203
Leintwardine 176
Leith, William 88
Lemon, Richard 36–7, 77
Lemon Springs 189–90, 214
Lempriere, Thomas 39, 225
Lewis, Richard and Isabella 69, 219–20
Lewis, William 7
Libraries 140, 222
Lister, Captain 195
Lloyd, George 32, 72, 76–7, 151, 199, 280
Lloyd, Henry Grant 135
Loane, Roland 82, 93
Locally born 11, 144, 165, 174
London 9, 18, 32, 85, 95, 141, 146, 178, 188, 195
    meaning 'British government' 7, 17, 42–4, 49, 58–9, 66–7, 71–2, 91, 175, 195–6, 222–3, 228, 231, 233–4, 238–42, 250
Longford 111
Lord, David 16, 213, 280
Lord, Edward and Maria 3, 8, 16, 20, 38, 43–5, 59–60, 84, 89, 107, 116, 150, 157, 159–60, 164, 172, 184, 196, 203, 213–4, 233, 239, 280
Luttrell, Alfred 235–6
Luttrell, Dr Edward 59, 96, 114, 116, 280

Lycett, Joseph 13, 22, 101, 143, 185, 190, 280
Lynch, Mary 166
Lyttleton, William 194, 215

McAllenan, Daniel 29
McAlpine, Colette 257
Macarthur, Rev. Archibald 223, 226
McAuley, Mrs 153–4
McCarty, Mary and Dennis 38, 96
McCleland, Thomas 238
McCra family 200
McDonald, Norman 214
McHugo, Jonathan 48–9
Mack, Elizabeth 127
McKellar family 69–70, 219–20
McKenzie, Alexander and Elizabeth 178
McKenzie, Captain John 60–1, 280
McLachlan, Mary 70
Macquarie, Gov. Lachlan 9–10, 21–2, 31, 36–7, 44–7, 49, 54, 56–61, 66–7, 70–1, 77, 82, 129, 138, 174, 176–7, 197, 255, 280
Macquarie Harbour penal station 39–40, 67, 143, 170, 173, 191, 229, 233, 237
Macquarie Plains 176
Macqueen, Thomas 129
McTavish, Mrs 126
Magistrates 28–9, 35, 53, 60, 71, 84, 86, 89, 157, 191, 198, 201, 203, 225, 236
  police magistrates 162, 175, 200, 232–3, 239
Malahide 198
Mansfield, Michael 37
Maria Island penal station 209, 232–3
Marines 3, 7, 14, 17, 33, 35, 43–4, 54, 74, 184
Martin, Joseph 169

Massey, Thomas 89, 91, 280
Mather family 106, 113, 221–3, 280
Maum, William 59, 90, 96, 280
Maxwell-Stewart, Hamish 257
May, Marian 257
Mechanics' Institutes 141–2
Medical care 112–28
Medicines 112–15, 117–19, 121
Melville, Henry 56, 128
Merchants 10, 24, 82, 91, 104, 109, 149, 161–2, 164, 203, 205–6, 214, 216
Meredith, Elizabeth 168
Meredith, George 213, 280
Methodist Church *see* Churches, Wesleyan
Midwives 109, 117–8, 126–7
Miller, Rev. Frederick, 223–4, 226–7
Milliken, William 197
Mills, Peter and Jennifer 49, 61, 280
Mockeridge, Nathaniel 196
Monaghan, Mary and family 174–5
Montagu, John 144
Morey, John 36–7
Moriarty, Ellen and family 175
Morrisby family 163
Mountgarrett, Dr Jacob 47–50, 60–1, 78, 114–6, 122–3, 128, 280
Mulgrave, Peter 131
Murdoch, Dr James 118, 126
Murdoch, Peter 209, 280
Murray, Capt John and Lucy 45, 89, 160, 196, 280
Murray, Robert Lathrop 159
Music 133, 137–9, 151, 154, 196

'Native born' *see* Locally born
Neil, Robert 197
New Norfolk 31, 38, 104, 110–11, 116, 118, 121–2, 126, 128–9, 132, 177, 210, 252

New South Wales 6, 8, 19, 21, 36, 71, 81–2, 84–5, 89, 94, 188, 212, 230, 240, 255 *and see* Sydney
New Town 35, 57, 108, 149–52, 155
New Zealand 35
Newspapers 56, 103–4, 106, 110, 115, 121, 131–2, 139–40, 144, 147–8, 158, 161, 231, 240–1, 247
Newton, John 212, 214
Norfolk Island/Islanders 7–8, 15, 19–20, 22, 31, 104, 174, 178, 281
Norfolk Plains 108, 128, 131–2, 194, 236, 252
Norfolk Plains Grammar School 136

Oakes, Mr 212
Oatlands 20, 133, 178
O'Brian, Sarah 177–8
O'Connor, Roderic 17, 68–9, 201–03, 209–18, 238, 240, 280
O'Ferrall, Rolla 238
Ommanney J.O. 98–99, 138, 210
Orphan Schools, King's and Queen's 132, 134, 173, 239
Ouse 175–6
Owen, Sir John 214
Oxley, John 77

Page, George 214
Panshanger 215
Pardelotes 8
Parramore family 203
Paterson, Alexander 235
Paterson, Lt-Gov. William 30, 47–8, 74, 78, 137, 174, 280
Paterson's Plains 181
Patronage 41, 53–4, 64–7, 71–2, 90, 93, 228, 235, 238, 244, 255–6, 279
Pearce, Alexander 39–40, 280

Penal stations *see* Macquarie Harbour, Maria Island, Port Arthur
Peters, Thomas, Ann and family 13, 20, 159, 174, 249, 281
Pillinger family 20, 24, 212, 280
Piper, Hugh 48, 50
Pitt, Miss 135
Pitt, Richard 107
Pittwater 20, 87–8, 91, 144, 185
Plenty (township) 120, 162–3
Polding, Archbishop 224
Police force 10, 26, 28–9, 34, 45, 68, 87, 157, 171, 175, 228–9, 233
    Field police 104, 233
Pollution 112, 123, 128
Population numbers 6–8, 85, 93, 243
Port Arthur 233
Port Dalrymple 6, 20, 30, 36, 38, 47–9, 60, 75, 129, 131, 177 *and see* Launceston
Postal service 110–11
Power, Hannah and Matthew 9, 13, 44, 281
Presbyterian Church 133, 222–3, 226
Priest, Dr Richard 122–3
Prince regent *see* George IV
Prinsep, Augustus and Elizabeth 158, 231, 233, 281
Private Secretary's cottage 107, 109
Prosser, Thomas and wives 168–9
Prostitution 156, 167, 173–4, 227
Prout, John Skinner 253
Public houses (pubs) 9, 34, 86–9, 91, 149, 153, 159, 200, 227
Public service *see* Civil service
Punishments 28–30, 33, 36–7, 39–41, 48, 60–1, 67, 77, 82, 88–9, 148–9, 157, 170, 173, 178, 180. 191–2, 196, 233, 252

Quakers 50, 223–4
Quinn, Jane 169

Racecourses 150–2, 165
Ramus, Henry and Maria 175–6
Rape 38–9, 57, 77, 170, 177–8, 246, 249
Ratcliffe, James and family 202
Reading 129–30, 140, 154–5, 192, 212, 221
Reago, Carmino 202–3
Records, lack of 93–4
Regatta, first 147
Reichenberg, Joseph 138–9, 196
Representative government 241
Reynolds, Henry 248
Richmond iv–v, 226
    bridge 238
Ricketts, Ann 257
Risdon 73
Riseley, Maria *see* Lord, Maria
Ritchie, Captain 49
Roberts, Joseph 236
Robertson family (merchants) 166, 204
Robinson, George Augustus 105, 137, 249–50, 253–4
Rochford, James 177
Roe, Michael 257
Roper family 162
Ross, James 100–01, 128, 137, 141, 156, 281
Ross (town) 136, 151, 197
Rous, Captain 146

Salt Pan Plains 189
Salter, George 94, 96
Sams, William 197
Sandy Bay 47, 147, 150–1
Savery, Henry 140, 204

Schools 10, 26, 84, 93, 129
    government 129–32
    private 106, 130, 133–7
Schouten Island 76
Science, interest in 141
Scott, Archdeacon T.H. 131–2
Scott, Dr James 114, 116, 225
Scurvy 102–3
Sealing 25, 88, 77, 91
Selma 200
Sexual activity 70, 156
Sherbud, Mary 172
Shipman, Francis 44
Ships
    Argo 35–6
    Calcutta 21
    Indefatigable 21
    Kangaroo 68, 179–81
    Minstrel 51
    Morley 166
    Myrtle 35
    Skelton 184, 223
Shipwrecks 36, 144–5
Shops 9, 12, 20, 30, 84, 87, 104, 140, 198, 203–4, 231
Sly grog selling 27, 31, 34–6, 91, 151, 198
Smith, Archibald 166
Smith, Dr Clare 257
Smith, Malcolm 236
Smuggling 34–5, 45, 56–9, 69, 84, 91–2, 184, 229, 238
Snakebite 125
Social class 161–5 *and see* Elite
Sockett, Captain and Mrs, 197
Solomon, 'Ikey' 140
Solomon, Mark 170–1
Sorell, Lt-Gov. William 9, 31, 43, 61, 64–72, 76, 79–80, 82, 84, 89–90, 92–4, 116, 129, 131, 159–60, 175,

189, 192, 196, 202, 225, 228–9, 231, 233, 235, 239–40, 242
Harriet 64, 66–7
Sorell (town) 32, 76, 111, 131, 199
Speed, Eliza 134
Spiers, John and Leigh 257
Sport 144–53
Spring Hill 199
Sprod, Michael 257
Stanfield, Daniel and family 16, 157, 212
Steenbergen, Eddy viii, 257
Stephen, George 154
Stephen, James 242
Stewart, Major James 61, 281
Stewart, William 77
Stirling, John 198
Stocker, William and Mary 157, 159
Stodart family 198, 205
Stone, Thomas and Anne 131
Stowaways 35
Straten, Sanders von 103
Suicide 126, 201, 216
Sunday schools 132–3, 221–3
Survey Department 69, 92, 203, 209, 233–4, 239–41 *and see* Evans, George
Sutherland, James and Lucy 127, 195, 201, 281
Sutton, Corporal John Jubal 49
Swimming 110, 135, 144–5, 155, 172, 200
Sydney 6, 9, 14, 20, 22, 28–9, 31, 35–6, 42–3, 45–6, 49, 60–1, 66–7, 70–1, 73, 82, 84, 89, 92–3, 103, 110, 122, 131, 176, 206, 221 *and see* New South Wales

Talbot, William 196, 198
Taroona 104
Tasman, Abel 73

Tasmania/Van Diemen's Land
    description 1, 139, 184–5, 231
    independence 94, 230, 241
    locally-born people 165–6
    name 3
    pride in 158, 165
    reputation 58, 115, 140, 185, 221, 231, 256
Tasmanian (newspaper) 240
Tasmanian Archives 177, 257, 284
Tasmanian devil 215
Tasmanian Historical Research Association 257
Tasmanian Museum and Art Gallery 107, 109
Tasmanian Turf Club 142, 151
Taylor family (Campbell Town) 200–1
Taylor, Jonathan 22, 63
Theft 3, 9, 27–32, 35–7, 61, 70, 84–7, 89, 159, 161, 239, 243
    convicts transported for 13, 26, 143, 159, 166,
    stealing stock 30–2, 35, 49, 84, 86, 93–4, 124, 159, 173, 197, 202, 212
Thomson, Philip 257
Thomson, James 134–6, 196
Thrupp, Henry 93
Thylacine 215
Tombs, Henry 150
Tomkins, Charles 86
Tongerlongeter 78
Trial by jury 241
Transvestite 178

Upward mobility 160–1
University of the Third Age 257

Van Diemen, George 131
Van Diemen's Land *see* Tasmania
Van Diemen's Land Society 141, 247
Van Straten, Sanders 103
Vegetables 101–03, 120, 154
Venereal disease 114–6, 168

Wade, John 44, 87, 89, 91, 281
Walford family 2
Walker, Thomas 92
Walters, Jeremiah 188–9
Ward, Malcolm 257
Water supply 93, 103, 123, 189, 197, 213
Waterson, William 203
Webb, Sarah 168
Wedge, John 110, 127, 145, 153–5, 163, 227, 281
Wegman, Sheelagh 257
Wells, Thomas 140
Wentworth, William 184, 221
Wesleyan Church 132–3, 140, 157, 221–3
Wesleyan groups 222
West, Rev. John 3, 51, 56, 60, 73, 76–8, 107, 179, 184, 206, 249, 281
Westbrook, Dr 120–2
Westbury 175
Weston, Anne 111, 120
Whaling 22, 25, 88, 91, 142, 145–6, 172, 243
Wheat 23–4, 45, 59–60, 91, 93, 172, 181, 189, 191, 194, 200–2, 215
White, Lachlan 198
Whitehead, Andrew 35–6, 157
Widowson, Henry 31, 102, 281
Williams, George 49
Williams, Thomas 15
Williamson, Agnes 1–2
Williamson, William 1–2, 6–7, 109, 164, 184, 196–7, 214, 231, 281

Wives, sale of 171
Women 82
    convicts 88, 92, 123, 149, 166–8, 178–81, 223–6, 232–3
    farming 174–5, 211
    employment 133, 173
    land grants 13–14, 22, 174–5, 181
    marriage and 43, 137, 159, 166–71, 178, 225, 237
    number of 7–9, 85, 95, 164, 166
    in the community 10, 16, 56, 144, 148, 157, 159. 166, 173, 212
    wife sale 171
Woods, Roger and family 238–41, 244
Wool industry 2, 21, 25, 91, 193–5, 199, 201, 204, 211, 218, 243

Yaldwin, Rev. Richard 121–2
York, Duke of 41–2
York Town 11
York Plains 38, 110, 125
Youl, Rev. John 10, 90, 116, 129, 281
Young, Thomas 196
Younge, Dr Henry 59, 70